INSIGHT GUIDES

Created and Directed by Hans Höfer

CURTNERS
425 FENTON STREET
SAN JOSE, CA   95727
(408) 929-5115
garycurt @ aol.com

MEXICO CITY

Edited by Jutta Schütz
Update Editor: John Wilcock
Managing Editor: Martha Ellen Zenfell

Editorial Director: Brian Bell

Dear Bill and
Sharon,
It has been an excellent
experience getting to meet you and
work with you both. We know our paths
will eventually cross again. We looks forward
to that time. We loved coffee breaks with
you. Love,
Gary & Carol

Houghton Mifflin

APA PUBLICATIONS

Höfer

Schütz

Wilcock

Zenfell

Cowrie

Gross

Haufe

Few people are blessed with as much natural affinity for a place as artist Diego Rivera and his partner, the equally talented painter Frida Kahlo. "Rivera was deeply Mexican in his love of color and soft shapes and in his strong identification with the Mexican Indian." wrote Kal Müller and Guillermo García-Oropeza in the campanion volume to this book, Apa Publications' *Insight Guide: Mexico*. Both books are part of the 190-strong series created in 1970 by **Hans Höfer**, found of Apa Publications and still the company's driving force, and are edited in the belief that, without insight into a country's character and culture, travel can narrow the mind instead of broadening it.

Mexico has played a leading role in the lives of both people primarily responsible for *Insight Guide: Mexico City*, the book's original editor **Jutta Schütz**, and its update editor, **John Wilcock**. Although situated in different parts of the world, both visited Mexico for the first time more than 25 years ago, and both have written other guides to the country – in Wilcock's case, one of the first travel guides to Mexico ever published. For this volume, Schütz found the writers and provided the framework, while Wilcock, aided by Apa Publications' editor-in-chief of North American titles **Martha Ellen Zenfell**, put a contemporary spin on things.

An important factor in all Schütz's visits to Mexico has been her Mexican friends, many of whom contributed to this book. One friend, **Christa Cowrie**, emigrated from her native Hamburg when she was 14, and worked in Mexico for several well-known newspapers. Cowrie provided many of the photographs for this guide, along with fellow lensman, **Marcus Wilson Smith**, who was brought in by Zenfell to freshen up the images.

Andreas M. Gross studied art, archaeology and languages in Munich, Mexico and Brazil. He lived in Los Angeles for five years and has worked as a tour guide for various educational travel organizers, making use of his rich knowledge of North and Latin America. In this book Gross, who as a boy had always wanted to be an Indian, wrote the detailed chapters on the Indian history of pre-Spanish Mexico City, the Revolution and its famous protagonists, Zapata and Villa.

Also completing part of his studies in art history, history and archaeology in Mexico was **Hans Haufe**. He devoted his dissertation to 20th-century Mexican painting and his doctorate to 19th-century Mexican art, and so is extremely well qualified to write about Mexico during the Colonial epoch, the post-Revolutionary murals and modern architecture.

Gabriele Gockel took on the task of describing Mexico's bumpy road from colony to Republic. She lives in Munich and works as an author, translator and language teacher. As a supporter of the Third World movement, she takes a keen interest in Mexico's historical and political development.

A native of Switzerland, **Ernesto Riedwyl** has adopted Mexico as his home ever since 1976. He studied the science of teaching and Latin American studies and has made many journeys throughout the country. For some years, his main objective has been to popularize Mexico as a tourist destination and to make it better known, not only in the Uniterd States, but also in Europe. He knows the best restaurants in the capital, and loves to cook.

The nightlife of Mexico City should always be described by an insider: **David Siller** was born in Mexico City. He has worked for several Mexican newspapers and one year received Mexico City's first prize for journalism. His city reportage was published in book form (*Uno de estos días*) and he is now involved in Mexican television.

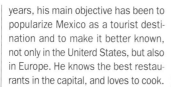

Gormsen

Erdmann Gormsen, geography professor at the University of Mainz in Germany, is a long-time Mexico specialist. Since 1964, the year of his first long stay in Mexico and his work with the major Mexico project of the German Research Society, he has visited Mexico repeatedly. In this book he writes about the urban development of the Mexican metropolis as well as the city of Puebla.

Elena Poniatowska was born in Paris and moved to Mexico while still a child. Today, as a journalist and author, she is one of the country's best-known writers. Her pen gives a voice to those who can no longer speak, the victims of the tragedy in Tlatelolco. In this book, she describes with biting humor her fellow residents of Mexico City, her artist colleagues and the sophisticated non-conformists in the Zona Rosa.

Poniatowska

Schumacher

Working for the Friedrich Ebert Foundation at the German embassy in Mexico City for over 15 years has been **Anne Schumacher de la Cuesta**. She has developed a strong affinity with the country and its people through her two Mexican children, and for a number of years worked for the Mexican State Tourism Office.

Switching from financial planning for multi-national firms to anthropology studies in Mexico was contributor **Sigrid Diechtl**. Along with her field research with monkeys in sub-tropical rain forests, she has spent years studying the attitudes of Mexican drivers in the capital. She describes Coyoacán, where she lives and survived the 1985 earthquake.

Diechtl

Roger Franz is a educational travel guide with a doctorate in journalism. He has studied ethnology, political economy, art history and archaeology. Since 1975, he has traveled throughout America. As his special interest is in the Indian roots of the country, he takes the reader through the Anthropological Museum in Tula.

Franz

The high volcanoes that surround Mexico City are presented by two mountain climbers and guides: **Wolfgang Koch** and **Till Gottbrath**, chief editor of the journal *Outdoor*. The widely traveled journalist **Imogen Seger** has a doctorate in sociology. Her chapters on the Guadalupe cult and Teotihuacan reveal her fascination with Mexico. Wilcock recruite **Wendy Luft** wrote the article on the Sonora Market, and will hopefully keep an eye on this book from her Mexico City base for any subsequent updates.

Seger

In the London editorial office of Apa Publications, **Christopher Catling** and **Pam Barrett** completed the proofreading and indexing and **Jill Anderson** guided the text through a variety of Macintosh computers.

CONTENTS

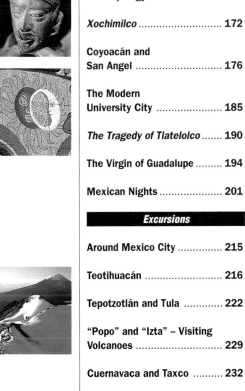

Excursions

Maps

TRAVEL TIPS

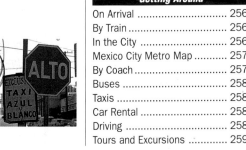

A MEGALOPOLIS OF EXTREMES

Mexico City is a city of miracles. The Indians who survived the Spanish conquest experienced their first miracle with the manifestation of the Virgin of Guadalupe, now the country's patron. Doubtless the population tolerates the discomforts of urban life with such stoic patience because the Virgin can be called upon in cases of need.

It is also a miracle that so much in this city – one of the largest in the world – functions at all: the public transportation system with its modern underground network, the telephone system and food distribution all continue to cope despite the pressures on them. Residents often organize themselves and overcome urban problems which the city fathers cannot, or will not, do anything about. It was through their resilience and strength of character that the people mastered the disastrous results of the earthquake of 1985.

The agglomeration of 19 million people living in a valley 2,200 meters (7,220 ft) high can best be appreciated when approaching from the air. Twenty percent of the population and 50 percent of Mexico's industry is concentrated in one percent of the country's area. The megalopolis not only manufactures most of the country's goods, but also produces air one can cut with a knife and 10,000 tonnes of rubbish per day. Fiery murals may cheer up Mexico City's public walls, but thick smog smothers the sky like grey flannel, often obscuring the volcano Popocatépetl, 75 km (46 miles) to the southeast. No longer is Mexico City a place *Where The Air Is Clear,* as Mexican novelist Carlos Fuentes titled his most popular novel.

At the same time as it pollutes its air, the monster is quickly depleting its water resources. Moreover, the city still continues to draw people from the provinces like a magnet. Experts paint a nightmare picture of 25 million permanent residents of Mexico City within the next few years.

"Nevertheless" is the key word for Mexico City. Despite the disadvantages, many Mexicans would not choose to live anywhere else, and for the millions of visitors – seven or eight million each year from the US alone – there are many beautiful and interesting aspects of the city worth exploring: excavated Aztec temples, the old city's baroque churches and palaces from the colonial period, the still-sleepy districts of Coyoacán and San Angel, gloriously spacious Chapultepec Park with its colorful weekend life, the canals of Xochimilco and many incomparable museums.

"This city is so great and so beautiful that I can hardly say half of what I could say about it. And this bit alone is practically unbelievable. It is even more beautiful than Granada." With these words, the Spanish conquistador Hernán Cortéz graciously described Mexico-Tenochtitlán, the capital of the Aztecs, in a letter to Charles V.

On that November 8, 1519, the resplendent city lay before the amazed Europeans as they crossed the pass between the two high volcanoes, Popocatépetl and Iztaccíhuatl. The Spaniards looked out over the expanse of Lake Texcoco, which partly covered the high plateau of Anáhuac.

The lake was full of barges and canoes. Located in the middle of a subsidiary lagoon, with paths across dikes joining the city to the banks, Tenochtitlán must have seemed to the European soldiers like an Indian Venice – a magical mirage after all their fighting and deprivation on the march. In the middle of the canal-riddled city, they could make out an imposing central plaza with pyramids crowned by temples.

One and a half years after this first glimpse of the city, Cortéz had achieved his military objective and the empire of the mighty Aztecs was under his control. Tenochtitlán, the economic, political and cultural center of the empire was robbed of all its treasures. The European Renaissance's lust for gold and conquest had put to the sword the heart of Mexico, indeed the heart of all that was ancient America.

Bernal Díaz del Castillo, an ordinary soldier in the service of Cortéz, is considered by many to be the most reliable eye witness and vivid chronicler of the conquest. He described the end of the Tenochtitláns in this way: "The streets, plazas, houses and courtyards were so filled with corpses that it was nearly impossible to get through. Cortéz himself was nauseous from the stench."

Preceding pages: model of the ancient Aztec metropolis of Tenochtitlán. **Left,** fountain depicting the founding of the city.

Less than 200 years had passed between the founding of the city and its conquest by the Spanish, in the year of 1521. With unparalleled speed, Mexico-Tenochtitlán had developed from a shabby hamlet into an Indian metropolis of breathtaking beauty and almost Prussian sense of order. When Cortéz and Montezuma met for the first time on the dam path to Tenochtitlán in 1519, the Aztecs were at the absolute pinnacle of their power (the Aztecs, in fact, called themselves Mexica, a name derived from that of their patron god or possibly a corruption of *metzli* (moon) and *xictli* (center), meaning the town in the middle of the lake of the moon; the term Aztec came later and is derived from Aztlan island, the tribe's legendary ancestral home).

The Aztec emperor, who bore the title *tlatoani* (he who speaks), ruled over an enormous territory that extended from Guatemala to the steppes of northern Mexico and from the Atlantic to the Pacific. Between 6 and 7 million people were his subjects and Tenochtitlán lived off their tribute.

Nevertheless, a few enemies, such as the Tarascas in the northwest or the powerful Tlaxcaltecs in the east, frustrated the Aztecs' imperialist appetite. Nor could it be called a tightly controlled empire since other peoples within the Aztec sphere of influence resisted central subjugation. It was more like a patchwork of tribute-paying vassal states which could be torn apart at any moment. Cortéz was an adept politician and he knew how to exploit this by playing the different Indian peoples, not only off against each other, but also the Aztec state.

The Indians, Cortéz recorded, "live almost as we do in Spain and with quite as much orderliness. It is wonderful to see how much sense they bring to the doing of everything."

A migratory people: According to the widely propagated official state history, the Aztecs believed themselves to have embarked on a mass migration in the year AD 1111. In the course of 200 years, these fighting people wandered from the mythical island of Aztlan, in the high north, to the banks of Lake

Texcoco, all the while bringing with them their god Huitzilopochtli for whom they built a temple wherever they settled for any period of time. The god, they believed, spoke to seven priests through this simple temple, his sacred pronouncements then being transmitted to the seven groups which constituted the whole tribe.

In AD 1300, the Aztecs, numbering only a few hundred, came to the hill of Chapultepec, which lies in today's park of the same name in Mexico City. There they stayed for 20 years until they were expelled by their neighbors, whom they had been trying to wear down with constant surprise attacks

these peoples, like the Aztecs, spoke *náhuatl*, which soon became the lingua franca of the highlands.

Although still an insignificant group, the Aztecs seemed even then to be convinced of their future glory. They believed themselves to be the chosen people of Huitzilopochtli, a god of war who had destined his people for greatness, and who had proclaimed that one day they would no longer be anyone's subjects. This all-pervading sense of mission among the Aztecs was seen by other tribes as incredible arrogance.

The eagle on the cactus: At the time of the founding of Tenochtitlán, there was little

and raids. The Aztecs were treated as barbarians, so-called Chichimecs; no one wanted them as neighbors, and at least according to the Aztecs themselves, they were always being pushed around. At that time the high valley around the Anáhuac lake was controlled by many small and mutually antagonistic states. (The Aztec term *anáhuac*, meaning "on the edge of the water," came to refer to the whole Valley of Mexico.)

After the collapse of the Toltec empire in the 12th century, which preceded that of the Aztecs, these states had formed from Toltecan and Chichimec (barbarian) peoples. Many of

reason for such self-confidence. In 1325, the Aztecs passed through an internal crisis having just lost a battle against their rulers, the Colhua. They sought refuge on some reed-covered, swampy, uninhabited islands in Lake Texcoco, and from here they maneuvered themselves into the no-man's land that lay between the two powerful states bordering the lake.

On the western side, the Chichimecan Tepanecs lived in their capital, Azcapotzalco. On the eastern side, in Texcoco, the Toltecan Acolhua ruled. The choice was ingenious from a strategic point of view. Huitzilopochtli also had a hand in the choice: the god commanded the Aztec high priest, Tenoch, to establish the city on a very special point: on a rock (*tetl*) where a pear cactus (*nochtli*) grows on which sits an eagle with a rattlesnake in his beak. From this highly debatable legend the place supposedly derives its name, Tenochtitlán.

The Mexica duly sighted their eagle and erected a shrine to Huitzilopochtli on the spot. By digging canals and leveling pasture using the earth they had dug out, the initially very poor Aztecs created small plots of arable land, the so-called *chinampas*. Today visitors to the somewhat seedy "floating gardens" of Xochimilco can view this skillful system of land reclamation.

Shortly after Tenochtitlán, a second independent city named Tlatelolco was established on a neighboring island.

Acamapichtli is the first recorded Mexica ruler during this period, governing from 1376–96 and allegedly descended from old Toltecan (Tula) nobility. The Aztecs regarded everything Toltecan as the pinnacle of cultural superiority. The *tlatoani*, or ruler, had to be a descendant of the kings of Tula, thereby legitimizing his sovereign authority. Many elements of Aztec architecture are, in fact, copied directly from the Tula. Socially as well as artistically, the Toltecs were admired as the predecessors and the forefathers of the Mexica.

The Triple Alliance: For the first 90 years of Tenochtitlán's existence, the children of Huitzilopochtli served the nearby tribe of Tepanec Azcapotzalcos, primarily as soldiers, helping to create the Tepanecan empire, which finally dominated the whole region around the lake.

In 1426, the powerful Tepanecan lord Tezozómoc died. For many years thereafter, the empire lay in chaos and finally, in 1430, the Aztecs of Tenochtitlán took their chance to free themselves from the Tepanecan yoke. Together with Tlacopán and Texcoco, they conquered Azcapotzalco and destroyed the

Tepanec empire. From then on, the *tlatoani* gave the orders, together with the princes from the other two cities. Thus the so-called Triple Alliance (Tlacopán, Texloco and Tenochtitlán) came into existence and ruled the Aztec empire from then on.

After the *tlatoanis* Huitzilihuitl (1397–1417) and Chimalpopoca (1417–28) came the energetic Itzcoatl (1428–40). His successor was Montezuma I Ilhuicamina, who ruled from 1440–69. His real name in *náhuatl* was *Motecuhzoma* (the irascible prince), originally a title of the fire god. The surname Ilhuicamina means "heavenly fire." He was the grandfather of the second ruler of the

same name, Montezuma Xocoyotzin, the "Younger," – who would later suffer at the hands of the Spanish.

Montezuma I led the imperial expansion, especially after a famine in Tenochtitlán, in order to acquire the fertile area of the Gulf region (now the Gulf of Mexico). During his rule, Tenochtitlán was fundamentally renovated. An aqueduct was laid to provide drinking water from the Chapultepec hill to supply the growing metropolis and a dam was built across the lake. This project was directed by the ingenious prince, master builder and poet Nezahualcoyotl of Texcoco. The dam was

Left, model of the Aztec temple district. **Right**, maize planting on the *chinampas* and the preparation of tortillas as depicted by Mexican artist Diego Rivera.

intended not only to stop the floods which had regularly afflicted and laid waste to the city, but also to separate the salt water that filled the main lake from the freshwater lagoon in the capital.

During the reigns of the Aztec emperor Montezuma, in the 15th century, and that of his neighbor Tlacaetel in the Valley of Puebla the need for human sacrifices to appease the gods was so great that the two emperors forged a macabre pact. At designated intervals at a particular place and time battles would be fought between the two armies to provide prisoners that each side could sacrifice on its altars.

These ritual contests (wrote Nigel Davies in *The Aztecs*) came to be known as the Wars of Flowers. The seventh Tlatoani Axayácatl (1469–81) as well as his successors Tizoc (1481–86) and Ahuitzotl (1486–1502) expanded the Aztec empire, with the changing fortunes of war, to its final size. In 1473, the neighboring city of Tlatelolco was annexed with its important market and, in 1502, the 34-year-old Montezuma Xocoyotzin (Montezuma II) was elected supreme chief of the empire.

The largest city in the New World: The population of Mexico-Tenochtitlán with all its suburbs, and of Tlatelolco, is generally accepted by historians to have reached 400,000 during the reign of Montezuma. That would have made it the largest city in the New World with an area of between 12 and 15 sq. km (5 and 6 sq. miles). When the population of all the rest of the valley was added, the total probably exceeded one million. The inhabitants were primarily *nahuátl*-speaking, but Mixtec, Otomí, Zapotec and other Indian languages of the empire were also spoken. The Aztecs forced many craftsmen from throughout the conquered territories to resettle in the capital.

Tenochtitlán was organized into four *barrios* or districts which were then subdivided into 80 wards. Each administrative unit, the smallest being the clan-sized *calpulli*, was headed by a council leader and had its own assembly rooms. The life of the average citizen was tightly regulated by strict customs and laws and everyday life was determined by trade, war, and religious practices.

The influence of the state was ubiquitous. The Aztecs took for granted compulsory education, cleanliness regulations, taxes, military service and many other sophistications in their urban society.

Physically the city was like a checkerboard, intersected by canals, which carried all the freight traffic. The causeway, with a width of up to 5 meters (16 ft), that connected Tenochtitlán with the mainland could be raised by a system of drawbridges to allow the passage of ships or to defend the city.

The accommodations of the residents were flat roofed, single-storied and built from stone or clay bricks. The *chinampas*, or areas

of arable land, belonged to everyone although at best they yielded only enough crops for bare subsistence.

An aggressive empire: In this highly stratified society, the *tlatoani* was practically a god-like figure at the pinnacle. He was like an emperor, pope and commander-in-chief all rolled into one. Montezuma's court was extremely luxurious and he was naturally polygamous. In many ways the Aztec imperial household resembled that of an ancient Japanese emperor or oriental potentate, and it has many counterparts in history. The ruling elite came almost exclusively from the Aztec upper nobility. The sacerdotal class of priests exercised special powers, and the "orders" of eagle and jaguar warriors enjoyed special prestige and possessed great personal influence.

The broad mass of the people consisted of free craftsmen and peasants. The lowest class in this society were the slaves who, in contrast to those of the old world, possessed well-established rights.

The Aztec empire based its power on war and intimidation through the use of its highly efficient and splendidly organized army. The Aztecs considered their battles a divine service or holy act. Subjugated vassals regularly imperial borders and served the state as spies. They brought back the most astonishing imports to Tlatelolco.

The respected Spanish historian Bernal Díaz del Castillo wrote of this flourishing trade: "Every sort of commodity had its place. There were gold and silver wares, jewels, cloth of all kinds, feathers, cotton and slaves… Then came the stands with simpler products, such as twine and cocoa… There was sisal cloth, rope, and knitted shoes… There were raw and tanned hides from… wild cats and other beasts of prey. We also found stands where beans, sage, and many other vegetables and spices were sold. There

had to supply the capital with luxury goods, clothing, labor and, most importantly, food. Without this tribute, the enormous population of Tenochtitlán was practically incapable of proper survival.

The central market: The majority of these goods were traded at the central market in the second city of Tlatelolco, which formed the commercial heart of the empire. There the trading castes predominated, highly privileged people who journeyed far beyond the

Left, Montezuma II by an unknown artist. Above, Rivera's mural *Tenochtitlán*.

was a special poultry and game market; one for the cake bakers and one for the sausage dealers. In the pottery stands we found everything from the largest vase to the smallest nightpots.

"We passed sellers of honey, honey cakes, and other delicacies; past furniture, wood and coal dealers… And I nearly forgot the craftsmen that make flint knives, the salt, the fish market and the breads which are made from dried silt fished from the lakes. It tastes like cheese. Finally there were instruments made of brass, copper, and tin, hand-painted cups and pitchers made out of wood. In short, there were so many goods that I would run out of paper to list them all."

Human sacrifices: Along with the high taxes, those tribes subject to the Aztecs were angered by Tenochtitlán's constantly growing demand for human sacrifices. Not only were prisoners of war sacrificed, but the Aztecs expected regular supplies of "high value," that is to say, younger, stronger men and women, for their rituals. Bodies, blood, and human hearts were the sustenance of the gods. According to Aztec beliefs, without these the world would come to an end, and with the expansion of their domain, the Aztecs intensified their sacrificial activities. Although the Spanish chroniclers greatly exaggerated the numbers of victims, the sacrificial cult bordered on decadent excess by the time of the conquest.

Tenochtitlán's sacred precinct, Teocalli, was the site of these rituals (Tlatelolco had its own place adjacent to the market). The Teocalli was a monumental plaza of anything up to 440 meters (1,440 ft) wide, depending on the source cited. A battlement ornamented with carvings of snakes surrounded the quadrangle. Four gates led into the plaza, which was oriented toward the west. Through three of these gates ran causeways to Ixtapalapa, Tacuba, and Tepeyac respectively.

Out of a total of 78 shrines in Tenochtitlán, the most important temples, pyramids, and platforms were to be found on the Teocalli. Among these were included shrines to non-Aztec gods which had been integrated into the state religion after the conquest of their followers. Montezuma's palace complex (which covered around 2.5 hectares/6 acres) adjoined the Teocalli where today the National Palace, on the Zócalo, is situated. The two-story residence, with its pleasure gardens, game preserve, fountains, and grand rooms from which Montezuma managed his affairs of state, greatly impressed the conquering Spaniards.

Surrounding the plaza were the school for the nobility (*Calmecac*), assembly halls, and various manor houses as well as the palace of Montezuma's father, Axayacatl. It was here, in the year 1519, that the conquering Cortéz was billeted.

The Templo Mayor, the double pyramid of the main temple, was unearthed not too many years ago; the ruins lie northeast of the cathedral. This temple was by far the most important building of the Aztec empire, almost its sacred heart.

For more than 200 years, the Templo Mayor was under continuous construction, being constantly enlarged and encased in new constructions. Such over-building of sacred places had a 1,000-year tradition in Central America, and it involved the preservation and at the same time the enlargement of the decayed walls. The expansion of the Aztec empire was expressed in ever more gigantic building projects around the Aztecs' main temple, where the pyramids and the temple itself not only honored the gods but also served to promote the self-image of a powerful kingdom, reflecting it in all its glory.

The Templo Mayor was, like all other sacred and government buildings, built with stucco-covered walls, ornamented and, presumably, colorfully painted. It must have been an awe-inspiring sight: a ramp with double staircases, oriented westward, led up the approximately 30-meter (100-ft) high pyramid, which was crowned with two imposing, high-roofed temples.

Sun god: On the northern side of the platform stood the temple dedicated to the rain god Tlaloc while next to it, on the southern side, was the temple to the tribal god, Huitzilopochtli, who was not only the lord of war but also the god of the morning sun. When victims were about to be sacrificed they were first painted, and then covered with feathers and led up the great staircase before being forced to dance in front of the god's image.

Looking to the west from atop the pyramid, the Huitzilopochtli temple stood on the southern half of the pyramid facing the midday sun. When an Aztec warrior fell in battle, he was thought to accompany his war god, the young sun, as a hummingbird (called *náhuatl* in *huitzizl*). *Pochtli* means "to the left," hence "hummingbird to the left." In this way the whole building symbolized a religious concept and represented for the Aztecs a piece of petrified heaven on earth.

Also in the Teocalli was the round temple

to Ehecatl (a variant of Quetzalcoatl), the shrine of the dark god, Tezcatlipoca, as well as the spring and fertility god Xipe Totec. In March, the latter's priests wore a costume made from the skin removed from a sacrificial victim in order to celebrate spring, nature's rejuvenation.

To the northwest of the holy court the sun god Tonatiuh had his temple. It was there that the famous calendar stone, with its Sun God face surrounded by reliefs representing prior world history and glyphs depicting the 21 days of the ceremonial calendar, was found in 1790. The stone is now the pride of the Anthropological Museum to which it

quently dismembered her. She stands as a symbol for all the human sacrifices which were to be offered to the gods in the Teocalli.

The skulls of sacrificial victims were arranged in ranks on the *tzompantli*, a skull scaffold, whose base was also adorned with skulls made of stone. Cutting out the victim's heart with a stone knife, a form of death to which many Spaniards fell victim during the conquest, was a deeply religious act, like every other offering of life. This might seem both perverse and savage to modern civilizations, but it should not be forgotten how many deaths have been ordered in the history of European nations for similarly spurious

was moved in 1984 from the National Museum which is situated on Calle Moneda.

In front of the Templo Mayor lay the sacrificial stone of the Coyolxauhqui, discovered accidentally by construction workers in 1978 and today adorning the Museum of the Templo Mayor. On it, the moon goddess and sister of Huitzilopochtli is depicted as a naked woman with disjointed limbs after the god had killed her in a battle and subse-

The eagle was the emblem of the founders of the city and later symbol of the "eagle warriors." <u>Above</u>, an example from the Templo Mayor.

reasons. The Aztecs remain, through their art and culture, a people animated by mysticism, magic, and divine service. These Indian lords of the ancient American world ruled at the time of Leonardo da Vinci, Albrecht Dürer and Martin Luther. To them, our idea of enlightenment would have seemed just as alien as theirs is to us.

Montezuma taken by surprise: It was into this strange world ruled by magic, unearthly idols and bloody rites, that Cortéz and his men ventured. Coming from Cuba, they landed on the Gulf Coast in the Holy Week of 1519 and founded Veracruz.

The army of Cortéz consisted of more than 110 seamen, 553 soldiers, 45 crossbow and longbow marksmen, 200 Cuban Indians, 12 horses and 12 artillery pieces. Initially, the Totonac Indians received him warmly. They sensed the long-awaited possibility of finally casting off – with help from the Spaniards – the hated repression of Aztec supremacy. Cortéz was fortunate that one of the chiefs presented him with a woman who was both well-educated and a fluent linguist. Doña Marina, or the "Malinche" was to become his interpreter and advisor during the entire conquest and proved to be invaluable to him.

With Indian auxiliary troops, Cortéz marched up into the highlands to inflict an annihilating defeat on the Tlaxcaltecs, the Aztecs' arch-enemies. By doing so he not only gained thousands of battle-tried prisoners who turned into warriors, but the Tlaxcaltecs also provided him with the strategic expertise for his campaign against Montezuma's empire. Montezuma was certainly taken aback when he heard that these neighbors, who were considered invincible, had been beaten in a head-on confrontation by the "White Gods."

Montezuma's final moment: Montezuma's best efforts to keep the Spaniards out of Tenochtitlán failed. As a result, he had no choice but to receive the mysterious foreigners as hospitably as possible and to quarter them in his capital.

From then on he was obviously overwhelmed by the rapid pace of events. Imagine that the France of 450 years ago had been wiped out by General Eisenhower and several brigades of modern soldiers with tanks and machine guns and that Eisenhower had then marched down through Spain into Seville. Emperor Charles V would certainly have been stunned by the seemingly limitless power of such an invader.

Montezuma was similarly impressed. He was considered unusually pious, which in those days meant inspired with magic, so it should not be surprising that he saw Cortéz as the Toltec culture hero and legendary god-king, Ce Acatl Topiltzin, alias the "feathered serpent" Quetzalcoatl, who had sacrificed himself after his flight from Tula and prophesied that he would return one day from the east. At first this seemed to Montezuma to be the most likely explanation for the phenomenon of Cortéz, an interpretation that subsequently proved to have fatal implications for the Aztec leader.

In the Indian tradition Quetzalcoatl is usually depicted neither as white nor as blond, and the year of his return is nowhere to be found in the ancient sources. To suit their purposes Spanish historians conveniently redefined the god after the conquest. But in some ways the legend matched: Quetzalcoatl is said to have had a beard and to come from the east, as did Cortéz.

Shortly after his arrival, Cortéz found an excuse to imprison Montezuma and seemed to have gained the initiative. But when the conqueror left the city to deal with an urgent problem on the coast, catastrophe struck. On May 23, his deputy, Alvarado, caused a dreadful bloodbath among the Aztec nobility during a celebration in the holy district. As a result, the Spaniards were besieged in their billets by the furious Aztecs.

When Cortéz came back to Tenochtitlán, he found the city in a state of chaos and his fellow Spaniards in acute danger. He asked Montezuma to speak to the masses in order to calm them down, but as the ruler did so he was stoned to death by the angry mob.

The situation grew even more threatening, and Cortéz decided to retreat on the night of July 30. The Spaniards tried to take with them their stolen gold treasures and escape over the causeway to Tlacopán (Tacuba), but the Aztecs fell upon them mercilessly and Cortéz could only barely save himself. He lost more than half his troops, all of his artillery and horses and most of his booty in the fray, which went down in history as the "Noche Triste," the night of sorrow.

The decline of Tenochtitlán: The defeated Spanish soldiers retreated to Tlaxcala and

was captured while trying to escape over the lake. Cortéz had him executed in 1525. The last decisive battle between the Spanish and the Aztecs was in Tlatelolco, the trading city. In the afternoon of August 13, 1521, the Aztec empire and the power of the capital were broken forever. In the end the sword and the cross of the Spaniards triumphed over the magical world of the Aztecs.

Tenochtitlán lay on the lake, totally devastated. The *chinampas* had been ransacked during the siege by the city's starving inhabitants in their desperate search for anything edible. The Spaniards had torn down the houses to make the canals passable for horses

the safety of their allies. With fresh soldiers and new artillery, that had arrived in the meantime from the coast, Cortéz spent months preparing for a great attack on Tenochtitlán. Using newly built boats and crossing the causeways, the Spaniards and their Indian auxiliaries managed to take the city after a 90-day siege.

The *tlatoani* Cuauhtémoc (1520–25), who had taken command of the Aztec resistance,

Left, the stone "tzompantli" or skull scaffold from the days of human sacrifices. **Above**, snakes' heads on the Templo Mayor.

and artillery and the streets and waterways were filled with corpses. The stench was atrocious. After the evacuation of all survivors, Cortéz had the city torched and the once gleaming metropolis ended as a smoking pile of debris.

One year later, in 1522, Cortéz began to build what he called New Spain, the new capital of the future viceroyalty, on the ruins of the Aztec capital. New Spain had a population of only 30,000 people, and not until the year 1900 would it again have as many inhabitants as Greater Tenochtitlán at the time of *tlatoani* Montezuma.

The decision to establish the new Spanish capital on the ruins of the Aztec Tenochtitlán was a political as well as a symbolic act. Strategic, climatic and practical considerations played a decisive role in the siting of the city, as well as the availability of the necessary labor force and materials.

The Spanish Court received reports of the progress of colonization with great interest, particularly the sketch by Cortéz of the city as it was when conquered in 1520. It was made for Charles V and published in Nuremberg as a woodcut; in it Cortéz emphasized the square-sided structure of the temple precinct in the center, the residential quarters artfully divided by numerous canals and the bridges which joined dams to the mainland. This infrastructure of islands and bridges became the most important factor in the plan for the new city and it inspired the utopian fantasies of the Spanish.

Colonial chessboard: Work began in 1521 when Cortéz appointed Alonso Garcia Bravo to draw up the ground plan. The first city architect and the conqueror faced a difficult problem. They could draw on their experience in redesigning the Moorish cities of Spain, but the topographical characteristics of Mexico were infinitely more complicated. Neither Renaissance concepts of city planning, nor the styles developed by the conquistadors for their magnificent Caribbean cities could be applied except with difficulty. Accordingly, Mexico became the most important Spanish experiment in urban planning on the continent.

The Spanish liked the geometric layout of the Aztec ceremonial center and Garcia Bravo retained the ground plan of the main temple plaza for the new center as well as the north–south and east–west axes. In the resulting chessboard form, more space was earmarked for plazas. The streets mainly followed the pre-Spanish waterways, thereby preventing absolute regularity.

Left, Cortéz enters Tenochtitlán (detail of a painted screen from the colonial period).

The services of the conquistadors were rewarded with land and the interests of Church and Crown were taken into account when the city was divided. Since the new capital was to serve as a base for the consolidation of Spanish power in the New World, it had to be built as quickly as possible, or else the Spanish would miss the best opportunities. The ambitious plan for the new city, however, could only succeed if the subjugated Aztecs were made to work as laborers for the Spanish elite.

This was accomplished with massive force. The Franciscan Motolinia, who came to Mexico in 1524, compared the sight that greeted him to the construction of Solomon's temple. A "seventh plague" broke out among the subjugated Indians. In order to protect themselves and the Indians, the Crown ordered the separation of the Spanish city from the Indian districts. But this plan only worked for a short while, and then the Indian settlements and the Spanish areas were reintegrated again.

The new city rapidly grew to 100 blocks and it had to be broadened as early as 1527. Some useful elements of the pre-Spanish infrastructure were taken over by the Spaniards. For example, Cortéz had the water lines from Chaputepec repaired, and the city continued to be connected with its surrounding areas by canals and dams, based around four great canals from which dozens of others flowed in a coordinated system. The Canal de la Viga, paved over long ago, led past the west side of the National Palace to the city hall. It was used by the Indians to transport their goods to market and by the Spanish to ship building materials.

Center of power: The colonial Plaza Mayor (Zócalo) is the result of a long process of development. Cortéz, anxious to secure lasting influence, acquired two large plots of land. He had his residence, the Casas Viejas, built over the ruins of the Axayácatl palace on the south side of the Plaza. (The Monte de Piedad (Mount of Mercy), a pawnshop, was built on this site in the 18th century.) On the north side, the former site of Montezuma's palace, the Casas Nuevas was erected.

Riches and power: Cortéz' desire for riches and power soon led to conflict with a Crown that wanted to assure its decision-making power in all important questions, and Cortéz lost the governor's title in 1527. A five-man Audiencia assumed power until 1535 when Antonio de Mendoza was made the first viceroy. This made efficient administration and city planning possible.

To the chronicler Francesco Cervantes de Salazar the magnificent houses built by the Spanish in the city center seemed like fortresses, an impression which was created by the battlements on the towers and upper storys which were reminiscent of the buildings of Extremadura, the homeland of many of the conquistadors. The arcaded buildings also resembled those found in Cáceres on mainland Spain. There were, in addition, some noticeable topographical innovations. De Salazar pointed out that the broad streets provided room for two coaches, a feature uncommon in Spanish urban planning.

The first cathedral, built in 1525, was a very small church. In 1552 Philip II ordered a new cathedral to be built that would express the significance and wealth of New Spain. It took the Spanish many many years just to build a solid foundation on the swampy ground. Claudio Arciniega of Burgos designed the layout for the five-naved basilican structure, and work commenced in 1616.

The overall concept meets the requirements of a processional church with the outer naves housing numerous chapels, but during the cathedral's long process of construction there were many changes to the aesthetic detailing of the building. While some chapels have Gothic vaults, the vaults in the naves are in Renaissance style and the entrances to the transept have columns in the classical style of the 17th century. The main facade (1681) with its dominating twin spires (1788) is baroque in style and the dome over the transept was not completed until 1813.

The city administration was one of the metropolis' most important new institutions. The mayor held wide-ranging authority in disputes while the city councillors enjoyed a form of diplomatic immunity. The viceroy was not allowed to interfere in the internal affairs of the city. The permanent city hall was built in 1532, fundamentally renovated between 1692 and 1724 and rebuilt in 1948 in neo-colonial style.

The *portales*, arcades and colonnades, which provided protection from the sun and rain, were an important architectural element of the Plaza Mayor and beneath their shelter silk merchants conducted their trade. At the same time, the *portales* gave the plaza a uniform character.

Only a representative seat of government was missing. In 1562, the Spanish king acquired the palace on the north side of the plaza from the Cortéz family and had it reconstructed at great expense in 1693. Its three portals served different functions. The law courts, prison, mint, revenue office, chapel and audience hall could be reached from the main courtyard. The apartments of the viceroy were in the courtyard to the left and opened into the garden. The palace was also planned with enough room to accommodate a complete garrison of soldiers. Here was the center of power, the focus of the political rituals by which the viceroy and president, after mass in the cathedral, demonstrated their supremacy in processions through the capital.

Belly of the city: The plaza served as a festival stage for these occasions as well as for religious holidays. Along with its structural features, it was furnished with mock facades of wood and cloth and decorated with carpets, flags, flowers and artful triumphal arches especially for the *fiestas reales*. Although it is empty today, during the colonial epoch the plaza was the belly of the city. In it was a permanent market hall for the sale of precious commodities, the *parián*. Next to it were the countless stands of the *tianguis*, the Indian market for fruit, vegetables and handicrafts.

The plaza was New Spain's most important commercial center. Here goods from Spain or from the Far East and the Philippines were traded. The abundance of products, many of them new to the Europeans, were constantly augmented by the cargo boats traveling between New Spain and Manila in the Philippines. As a result of their control of this international trade the Mexican merchants became a respected and influential class in the 17th century.

City of cloisters: The new dioceses formed by the Spanish in the conquered territories further propagated the Catholic faith. In 1527, Mexico was designated an episcopal see. All the major religious orders established missionary activities in the metropolis and in the regions which were specifically allocated to each order. There were 41 cloisters in the capital as the colonial epoch came to an end. They each consisted of a church, an atrium, the cloister itself with its several courtyards, living quarters, study rooms, offices, work-

King Philip IV to forbid the founding of further cloisters.

Whoever makes the effort to follow the cloisters' history is sure to discover some fascinating gems. The Franciscan cloister (1525) was among the largest of its day and covered an entire ward. A part of the two-story court, dating from 1649, is still intact and has served as a Methodist church since 1873. The Church of San Francisco (1716) has also survived.

The San Jerónimo cloister was founded in 1585 and its church was consecrated in 1623. It was here that the religious poetess Sor Juana Inés de la Cruz worked. The Claustro

shops, schools, dispensaries and gardens.

Together these formed complex islands of spiritual life, because each cloister exerted a tremendous influence on its surrounding neighborhood. The wealth of the Church was based on its earnings from tithes and charitable foundations and was invested in real estate; in addition the clergy had a thriving banking business. This enormous influence led to conflict with the secular powers, until in 1644, the city council petitioned

Above, at the beginning of the 18th century, Mexico City was still surrounded by a lake.

La Merced, whose court is ornamented with simple pillars, makes an elegant picture. The rich botanical ornamentation creates a vivid three-dimensional effect – a vibrant play of light and shadow.

Mexican cloister architecture produced a number of innovations such as the twin portals that were developed for the Church of La Concepción in 1655, designed to cope with enormous crowds of the faithful during processions. The church was built as part of the oldest nunnery in Mexico, which was founded by the first archbishop Juan de Zumárraga (1540), a student of Erasmus.

Soon the twin portal motif was further developed in more elaborate versions at the Church of Santa Teresa la Antigua (1678–84) and at San Agustín (1691). Here, we find the twisted "Solomon" columns, made famous by the Italian architect Bernini in the first part of the 17th century.

Building fever of the baroque: In the course of the 16th century, Mexico became the capital of an enormous land area and by the middle of the 17th century, a real building boom took hold of the city. Trade, the prosperous mining industry, and successful agriculture and livestock farming formed the basis of an economic and cultural golden age. This

verted pyramid, creates an impressive spacial effect. One finds similar *estípites* on other churches and palaces. The Churrigueresco-style facades at La Santissima (1783), for example, add a dramatic touch to the urban landscape.

The facade of the three-nave Jesuit church of San Felipe Neri (1751) is very impressive even though a mere fragment of its former glory. After the order's expulsion, the church served as a theater, and today it is a library. The church of Regina Coeli also conveys the range of expression achieved by the Churrigueresco. New spacial conceptions emerged, such as those exemplified in the

wealth was reflected in the overwhelming demand for decorative ornaments with which to display the owner's prosperity. The metropolis played a key role in the propagation of the Churrigueresco style, a variation of Spanish high baroque.

With its tendency toward luxurious, ostentatious decoration, Churrigueresco became the preferred style for stately buildings. One pioneering work is architect Lorenzo Rodríguez's sacramental church, the Sagrario, next to the cathedral (1749–60). The staggering of the *estípites*, pilasters tapering toward the base to resemble an in-

churches of El Pocito and Nuestra Señora de la Enseñanza. Regina Coeli's narrow facade (1772–78), flanked by two former religious seminaries (1754), conceals a treasure: the bright, dome-ceilinged space has an octagonal, practically an oval, layout. Despite its small dimensions, the architecture, sculpture, painting, light, and color combine to produce a baroque masterpiece of the highest order.

Life in the palaces: The viceregal elite was concentrated in the metropolis. The nobility of the 18th century formed a plutocracy and much-desired titles were expensive. Access to the select circle of the oligarchy, as well as the pleasure of a title, cost a fortune. The Crown earned extra money from this system, but it led to a sharpening of social contradictions. Nonetheless, it also favored the arts.

The aristocracy also had to pay high taxes. Charitable foundations and the support of church construction were *de rigueur*. Building a palace was one way of securing a part of one's personal wealth for the family's long-term benefit; its furnishings and size were matters of prestige and a testimony to the social rank and business success of the owner. Such houses were naturally very expensive to maintain and an aristocratic house-

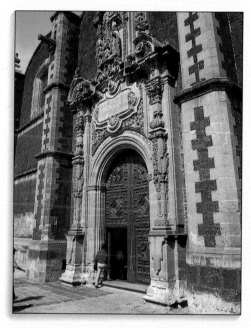

hold usually employed a minimum of 10 to 20 servants.

Sites along the route which the viceroy used for his procession into the city were favored by the aristocrats. For this reason, a whole series of elegant palaces were built on the Calle de San Francisco (today Madero). For example the Palacio de Iturbide, an 18th-century masterpiece designed by Francisco Guerrero y Torres, was the residence of the

Left, architectural evidence of colonial rule can still be seen today. **Above**, Mexican baroque in the facade of the church of Santa Veracruz.

family of Juan de la Moncada, Count of Jaral de Berrio. The facade is covered with medallions with pastoral iconography and furnished with rich ornaments and figures of Hercules. Balconies and an arcaded upper story flanked by two turrets emphasize the owner's importance. The courtyard itself, following an Italian motif, is framed by elegant columns.

The Casa de los Azulejos, built as a residence for the Count of Tales de Orizaba at Ares Madero and Lázaro Cárdenas is decorated in the Puebla tradition with *azulejos* or colored tiles on the outer walls. The courtyard with its stone pillars has survived and is now Sanborn's Restaurant.

Buildings of more modest dimensions were by no means less extravagantly designed. The house of Don Hernando de Avila and Doña Gerónima de Sandoval, dating from the second half of the 18th century, is remarkable for its harmonious proportions. The interior is embellished with *azulejo* ornaments depicting a cycle of popular characters of the period, preserving a picture of everyday life in the colony. The baroque buildings of religious, public, and private institutions were also characterized by palace-like edifices. For example the complex of the Colegio de las Vizcaínas in Coyoacán, a girls' school founded in 1734, filled a whole block and features more than seven courtyards.

Patios, streets, and plazas: In the 19th century, the Englishman Latrobe raved over the "city of palaces," an impression which was based on the uniformity of the colonial ensemble. The basic elements of the palace are still to be found in miniature in the bourgeois patio house which has proven its suitability to the climate of the Mexico valley. The patio house, in turn, served as the model for the aristocratic versions. Through the use of similar materials, lattices, ornaments and proportions, a townscape developed in which each element corresponded with the others surrounding it.

Many streets do not intersect at right angles. Slight bends and curves, according to the terrain, lead to amazing views. Entrances, windows, cornices and recesses on the facades echo each other down the streets. These architectural characteristics, developed over centuries, were never abandoned, only modified in the 19th century. It was progress-obsessed modernism which finally posed the first real threat, but today Mexico's colonial heritage and architecture is recognized as a part of the country's important modern cultural identity.

In the old city there are still charming colonial streets such as the Calle Moneda. In the enclaves of Coyoacán and San Angel, complete ensembles have survived – reminiscent of an epoch of amazing beauty, now long gone. The Irishman Thomas Gage summed up the impressions of his contem-

poraries when, in 1625, he called Mexico the "Venice of the Americas."

The waterways which divide so many streets, the effect of their reflections, the changing perspectives offered from the boats, all shaped the way the city presented itself to those early visitors. As in Venice, for a long time the canals formed the most important transportation arteries, but they were gradually displaced as the city grew larger. Land reclamation has altered the natural environment with enormous ecological consequences, destroying the island character as well as the lake landscape.

In the colonial city the road network was interconnected through 78 plazas, most of which had some commemorative purpose. With their various functions, these plazas were a mirror of urban life. Among them were smaller plazas, such as the Plaza de Santa Catalina with its church of the same name (1740) which was originally a hospital founded in 1537.

The impressive Plaza de Santo Domingo, two blocks north of the cathedral, was built on the site of the Dominican cloister (founded in 1537) and assumed its present form in 1628. The baroque facade and bell tower of the Church of Santo Domingo (1716–36) dominates the plaza.

The former Palace of the Inquisition (1736), now the School of Medicine, on the same square is reminiscent of the character of this influential colonial institution. The Inquisition was formally introduced in 1571 in order to defend the faith and morals of the Spanish, but the Indians were exempted from its jurisdiction. The Alameda Park and a small plaza near the cathedral served as execution sites.

Alameda Park, one of the most important urban projects of the baroque era, was laid out when it became clear that the city was going to outgrow its old boundaries. Expanded in 1717 and completed with diagonal paths, it has been complemented with monuments and sculptures right up to the present. The Alameda, with its fountains and *portales*, was an important crystallization point for city life, a favorite place for meeting and relaxation.

The Alameda also marked a counterpoint to the Zócalo and became a new axis of expansion. Soon new neighborhoods sprang up around the park, as did the Plaza de la Santa Veracruz. This small space, opening onto the Alameda, grew out of a simple but effectively realized idea, namely the combination of the forecourts between the churches of Santa Veracruz and San Juan de Dios.

From the steps of the church of San Juan de Díos (1764), whose niche facade with triumphant images resembles an altar piece moved outdoors, the double-towered facade of the church of Santa Veracruz (1765–76) fills the view.

From baroque to classicism: The last phase of colonial culture was shaped by the Bourbon reforms, which were intended to reorganize the administration and economy to the Crown's advantage. New institutions were founded in the spirit of the Enlightenment, among them the Academy of San Carlos, started in 1785, whose master craftsmen were oriented toward classical ideals. The Academy's royal charter practically guaranteed a monopoly role in controlling building activity in the colony.

As director of the architecture division, the Valencian Manuel Tolsá was responsible for setting the tone for the first generation of

the viceroyalty which had yielded silver and gold worth more than US$650 million in the previous two and a half centuries.

Another great project, the tobacco factory Real Fábrica de Tabacos, a textbook example of early industrial architecture erected between 1792 and 1807, was in line with Bourbon financial policies. Its significance lay in its functional character, generous lighting and ventilation and new stylistic expression together with a clear division of the interior spaces. These new constructions, as well as the growing destruction of the baroque buildings, were symptomatic of a shift in the dominant taste.

young artists. The Palacio de Minería (1797–1813) on Calle Tacuba, the first mining school in the Americas, was built under his supervision. It was a palace-like building with a monumental courtyard lined with pairs of classical pillars, a chapel, staircase, lecture hall and adjoining courtyards. When Alexander von Humboldt, renowned Prussian scientist and explorer, visited in 1803 he estimated there were about 3,000 mines in

Left, royal fiesta in Chapultepec (18th century). **Above**, *San Rafael and Tobias* by Miguel Cabrera; painted tile from the Casa Sandoval.

While in 1803 Alexander von Humboldt compared Mexico City with Berlin and St Petersburg, the signs of decadence in some precincts were unmistakable. It was mainly the city center which benefitted from improved infrastructure with lighting, road-paving and urban planning measures. In 1803, the Plaza Mayor acquired a new focal point with the erection of Manuel Tolsá's equestrian statue of Charles IV. Although it praised the new enlightened monarch depicted in classical garb, the Bourbon reforms could not stop the crisis which would lead to Mexico's political independence.

In the 18th century Mexico made enormous economic progress, a development which above all benefitted the *gachupines*, members of the colonial administration sent from Spain, and the increasingly wealthy *creollos*. The latter, the Mexican descendants of Spaniards, saw themselves as being more and more restricted by Spain. Through economic and political restrictions, Madrid held the country on a tight rein. The higher posts in the administration, the military, and the Church were reserved for the *gachupines*, while the *creollos* were represented only in the city councils. Needless to say, the Indians and landless peasants had no political voice whatsoever.

Exports and imports were subject to state monopolies and industrial goods had to be imported from Spain. The development of a national industry was almost completely obstructed and only in the large cities were there wool and cotton industries.

Insurrection and reform: It was under these conditions that events in mainland Spain provoked the revolt of 1810 which brought with it an 11-year war of independence and 600,000 dead. After Spain's defeat by the British at the Battle of Trafalgar, Charles IV of Spain was unable to bring his heavily indebted country out of a recession.

His wife's favorite, Manuel Godoy, opened Spain to Napoleon, who marched in and occupied the country, interned the king's son Ferdinand and put his brother Joseph on the Spanish throne. In the eyes of the astonished *creollos* in Mexico, this usurpation threw the Crown's legitimacy as their colonial ruler into serious question.

The *creollo*-dominated city councils of Mexico City forced the viceroy Iturrigaray to summon a municipal assembly which was to obey only the orders of the imprisoned Ferdinand. Naturally the Audiencia (the highest Spanish authority in the colony) felt its power threatened. The viceroy was quickly dismissed, but this only served to infuriate a small group of *mestizos* and whites who were followers of the ideals of the French Revolution and the American War of Independence.

Captain Ignacio Allende from San Miguel planned the first conspiracy against colonial government and won the support of Father Miguel Hidalgo, the parish priest of the poor village of Dolores. Since his transfer to this primarily Indian parish, Hidalgo had developed a rather unusual understanding of his pastoral duties: he dedicated himself almost exclusively to the practical instruction of his flock and taught them nearly everything which was forbidden under Spanish law – wine and olive farming, leather-tanning and weaving. He had nothing but contempt, bordering on hatred, for the *gachupines* who drained the land of everything it possessed and for whom the fate of the Indians and peasants was totally irrelevant.

On the evening of September 16, 1810, Hidalgo stirred up the peasants and Indians assembled in his church with the words "Viva Mexico! Long live Our Lady of Guadalupe! Down with the terrible government! Death to the *gachupines*!" and bid them to follow him. Even today on Independence Day, it is possible to hear the "Cry of Dolores" from the balcony of the government palace in the capital, and from numerous city halls in the provinces – although today's version does not include an incitement to bring down the government.

March on the capital: The army of the *insurgentes*, which was made up of peasants and barefooted Indians, scored amazing victories. In rapid succession, they seized San Miguel, Celaya and Valladolid (Morélia). Hidalgo proclaimed a new constitution that provided for the redistribution of land and the abolition of castes and privileges. As he began his march on Mexico City, he already had 80,000 men following him.

However, the viceroy gathered his troops north of the city and forced Hidalgo to retreat. The priest retaliated, took Spanish pris-

Preceding pages: the Independence, from a mural by Juan O'Gorman. Left, the Palacio de Iturbide (engraving by C. Castro, 1874).

oners and put them to death, but then was captured and executed himself. The revolt was suppressed, but in 1813, one of Hidalgo's students, Father Morelos, summoned a national assembly which proclaimed Mexico's independence. The new constitution called for the expropriation of the *latifundia* (aristocratic estates), the abolition of Church tithes, universal equality, and the dissolution of the state monopolies.

The Spanish were to leave the country for good. The *creollos*, the descendants of Spaniards, however, refused to support this plan since the aim of the revolutionaries – a fundamental agrarian reform – far exceeded

this plan failed, they decided their only hope lay in separation from the motherland.

In order to achieve independence they needed a strong leader, which they found in the man who was supposed to lead the southern army against the last remaining guerrilla troops – the creole General Augustín Iturbide. He was able to win the rebels over.

On February 24, 1821, the Iguala Plan was announced: Mexico was declared independent; Spaniards and *creollos* were granted the same rights; Roman Catholicism was made the state religion and the new state was to be a constitutional monarchy. The proclamation was nowhere near what Hidalgo and

their own wishes and their own interests.

Independence: Morelos was shot dead in 1815, but things were changing in Spain. Upon Ferdinand's release from prison and restoration to the Spanish throne, the central junta in Cadiz, which had agreed a new revolutionary liberal constitution, threatened a military revolt if the king did not accede to their wishes.

In Mexico, the *creollos* now feared they would lose their privileges over the *mestizos*. They allied themselves with the Spanish upper classes and encouraged the viceroy to ignore the new liberal constitution; when

Morelos had advocated. A conservative alliance, which included the Catholic Church, had pushed itself into the forefront of the independence movement.

But when one province after another, as well as the majority of the Spanish officers, announced their support for the plan, the new viceroy O'Donojú saw no way out. On his way to Mexico City from Veracruz, he met Iturbide. The upshot of their meeting was that he was given a seat in the ruling junta and in turn ordered the Spanish troops to leave the capital. Shortly afterwards the treaty of Córdoba/Mexico was signed, but mainland

Spain did not officially recognize Mexico as independent until as late as 1836.

Soon the flags of the *Trigarantes*, the symbol of independence, religion, and equality, were flying everywhere. On September 27, 1821, Iturbide rode into the capital at the head of his army. O'Donojú received him in the viceroy's palace and the archbishop honored him with a *Te Deum* celebrated in the cathedral. The next day a regency council was formed and the colony of New Spain had ceased to exist.

The young nation: Immediately conflict broke out within the coalition over whether the new state should be central or federal in only to enjoy being emperor for 10 months before falling victim to a revolt.

Many of the former rebels, disenchanted with Iturbide, joined the republican captain Santa Anna. Eventually the latter had so many followers that Iturbide voluntarily relinquished the throne and retired to exile in Europe with a fat pension, allowing Santa Anna's rebel army to march into the capital without meeting any resistance.

This time the deputies did not compromise, but adopted a constitution along the lines of their North American neighbor in which every prerogative of birth and property was abolished and all citizens were

form. The Congress itself could not agree on a head of state until a cry from the ranks of the Iturbide supporters broke out "Long live Augustín I, Emperor of Mexico!" The capital was suddenly full of frantic activity. A throne was erected; flags were hung from the church steeples, and peasants filled the streets. A spectacle was prepared the likes of which the inhabitants had never seen, to celebrate the new monarch. In the event Iturbide was declared fundamentally equal. The remains of Hidalgo and Morelos were brought to the capital and were honored as the founders of the independence movement. Guadalupe Victoria was declared the first president of the new republic. The last Spaniard embarked at Veracruz for Spain in 1825.

Proud city: At the time when the republic was proclaimed, the city was the center of culture and administration, and whoever approached it for the first time saw it as if it were surrounded by a mystical aura. The city boasted 60 churches. From the Chapultepec hill one could see the surrounding villages

Left, Emperor Augustín (artist unknown) and Emperor Maximilian (bronze by Felipe Sojo). **Above**, by the Salto del Agua fountain (C. Castro).

which supplied the city with fruit, vegetables, laborers and domestic servants. Five *calzadas* (avenues) led across the lakes into the city center. Next to the Paseo de las Vigas ran a canal along which Indian canoes brought goods from throughout the vicinity directly to the Zócalo.

Here, next to offices and vendors' stands, were the presidential residence, the Senate and the House of Representatives. In the cathedral, Mass was celebrated every half hour. The city hall stood on the south side of the Zócalo and the great trading houses on the west side. The finest homes were to be found in the Traza, the Spaniards' enclave to

the south and southwest of the central Zócalo.

Water was brought to the city's residents in huge clay containers. Twenty-nine public and 505 private fountains were fed through a conduit system. On feast days and holidays, municipal employees and water sellers worked together to obstruct the water supply in order to push the price up.

Waste water drained into sewers which led through the middle of the city into Lake Texcoco. There was no escape from these overflowing sewers when the heavy rains came. The overflow was the result of years of neglect, since no money had been invested in the sewer system since the beginning of the century and, in the eastern quarters of the city, the water often rose knee-high. Wherever the streets were too narrow for wagons, porters had to carry the heavy loads out to the merchants. In these streets robbery and assault were a daily affair and whoever went out at night did so armed – not only against men but against the many stray dogs.

The dictator Santa Anna: But despite its supposed integrity the new constitution was for the most part a mere facade. The colonial political and economic structures remained essentially intact, along with the domestic difficulties which had preceded independence. The Indians were again the victims and were often forced to leave their communal lands on account of enormous accumulated debt. The central government in Mexico City was too weak, and numerous conflicts and power struggles continued among the people of the provinces. The few laws which had been passed in the capital to protect the Indians were also as a rule ignored. Mexico came under more and more pressure from foreign creditors who, on account of the country's enormous debts, attempted to interfere in its internal affairs.

In the first 30 years of the young republic, 50 different governments occupied the Palacio Nacional, of which 11 were led by Santa Anna. Despite his dictatorial manner, the Congress elected him time and again as the head of state. Many construction projects in the capital had their roots in Santa Anna's vanity: the Gran Teatro de Santa Anna, a new market, and the paving of the streets. The year 1842 marked the pinnacle of his dictatorship – the capital was wrapped in constant celebrations: Santa Anna's birthday, Independence Day, parades, pomp-filled mass in the cathedral. His Majesty had to be entertained. All of this cost money which the dictator raised with a 20 percent import duty and "voluntary" contributions from the capital's residents. Understandably this extravagance made him increasingly hated among the population, until finally his short-sighted policies in the conflict over Texas led to his downfall.

The Anglo-Saxon settlers of Texas, until then a part of Mexico, were in no way prepared to pay the taxes demanded by Santa Anna. Instead, they declared their state a free republic. In response, Santa Anna personally led a 6,000-man army against the rebels in Texas. His soldiers brutally slaughtered hundreds of settlers at the mission station of El Alamo, providing the US with the opportunity and justification for attacking and defeating Santa Anna's forces. To save his life, the dictator was forced to recognize Texan independence. He returned humiliated to Veracruz, where he abdicated.

The North American Congress subsequently annexed Texas, provoking the Mexican generals to declare war once again. The lives resisting the invading Yankees. For a mere 15 million dollars, the Mexican government was forced to cede the territories of Texas, California, Arizona and New Mexico to the US. The whole nation had been humiliated, producing a "Yankeephobia" or hatred of the Americans, traces of which remain in the Mexican outlook to this day.

Meanwhile intolerable economic and political conditions led to a sharpening of the conflicts between the liberals (the leaders of the middle class with their preference for a North American constitutional system) and the conservatives, who represented the *latifundia* (estate owners) and who were

Americans were only too happy as it gave them the chance to seize other northern provinces from Mexico, which they did with ease. In February 1847, General Winfield Scott grouped his troops ready to storm the Mexican capital. By September of the same year, the American flag flew over the National Palace. At the foot of the Chapultepec hill stands a monument to the Niños Héros, the young military cadets who gave their

Left, artist Lizard's realistic portrait of Benito Juárez. **Above**, the puppet regime of the longtime dictator General Porfirio Díaz.

supported by the Roman Catholic and military hierarchies, who wanted a European-supported dictatorship. Again the command was given over to Santa Anna who proceeded to suppress the liberals. The result was a revolt in 1855 which finally forced Santa Anna out of power permanently.

The Juárez reforms: Comonfort became president and an Indian attorney from Oaxaca, Benito Juárez, became vice president. In 1861, Juárez became president and soon after he enacted the so-called Reform Laws, the main effect of which was to neutralize the clergy. All the property of the Church was expropriated and the legal and education systems were secularized.

However, the years of war and internal turmoil had left the country so deeply in debt that Juárez had no choice but to suspend payments to Mexico's creditors. Using this as a good excuse, Spain, France, and Great Britain seized the chance to come to the aid of the conservatives. They landed at Veracruz on the pretense of forcibly collecting the money from the Mexican government and with grandiose designs of helping the "regeneration of Mexico."

After friction developed between the trio of invaders, Britain and Spain quickly with-

drew, but Napoleon III took advantage of the invasion to extend his dominion in the New World. The French army was eventually defeated near Puebla on May 5, 1862. Nonetheless, they were able to occupy the capital for a short time through the massive support of the conservatives.

Imperial intermezzo: The National Assembly set up by the French offered the Mexican crown to Maximilian von Habsburg, the brother of the Austrian emperor. Shortly afterward he and his wife, Archduchess Charlotte, arrived in Mexico and took up residence in the Chapultepec Palace where they

were to live most of the time. Maximilian and "Carlota" were very much impressed by Mexico, spoke Spanish whenever possible and frequently traveled through the provinces. They were also great patrons of literature, the arts and the sciences. The emperor, however, followed a liberal line in politics and since he refused to restore the Church's property, he lost the support of most of the conservatives.

In the meantime, the North American Civil War had come to an end, enabling the United States' federal government to return its attention to Latin America. In pursuance of the Monroe Doctrine, the US placed its backing behind the liberals in order to force the French to withdraw.

It wasn't hard to get rid of them. Napoleon had not only lost interest in the devastated country, he also needed his valuable troops more urgently for the war against Prussia. Maximilian, whose intentions were apparently honorable, but he had been misinformed that the Mexican people approved of him taking the crown, and so decided to abdicate. But, according to legend, hesitated at the insistence of his mother who declared "We Habsburgs never abdicate!" On June 19, 1867, the unfortunate emperor was set before a firing squad. It was Benito Juárez, having resumed the presidency, who actually gave the execution order.

For a further decade calm prevailed in the republic although continuing economic problems left the government too weak to exercise much power outside the capital. Juárez reformed the education system and had the railway line to Veracruz completed. Surprisingly he also privatized the Indian communal lands, with the result that they fell into the hands of the *latifundia*, the former estate owners. The Indians were again forced to sell themselves into semi-slavery.

Juárez defeated his opponent Porfirio Díaz a second time in the 1871 national elections, only to die just one year later of a massive heart attack. He was succeeded by Sebastian Lerdo de Tejada.

Left. Don Porfirio, portrait by G. Morales. Right, the elegance of the turn-of-the-century Palacio de Comunicaciones, built as a ministry.

Don Porfirio had every reason to be proud as he solemnly dedicated the "Angel," the monument on the Paseo de la Reforma, to the memory of liberty. It was exactly 100 years since Father Hidalgo had called on his compatriots to take up the struggle against the Spanish on September 16, 1810. The dictator Porfirio Díaz had invited the whole world to Mexico City as guests for the grandiose centenary celebrations which were being held in honor of Mexican independence.

There was reason enough to celebrate. Díaz had himself just been elected head of state for the seventh time and he had just reached his 80th birthday. For more than 30 years, all but for one brief break in 1880–84, he had held Mexico in his iron grip. Since coming to power in 1876, he had fought relentlessly for the maintenance of order after decades of chaos. Through the centenary celebrations of 1910 he managed to present his epoch, the Porfiriat, as a series of economic successes to the world at large.

Decline of the Porfiriat: Díaz had expanded the railway network to over 20,000 km

(12,500 miles). He had brought foreign capital into the country. The oil and mining industries were flourishing. The enormous *haciendas* were producing fabulous surpluses. The export balance looked splendid. Eighty percent of the exports went to the US, to which the regime was so closely tied that Diaz was said to have uttered the classic sigh "Poor Mexico, so far from God and so near to the USA." None of the foreign guests for the celebrations of 1910 could imagine that within a few months, Mexico, the "paradise of progress" would mourn nearly a million victims in the first great social revolution of the 20th century.

Certainly the Porfiriat was heading for trouble. The price which had been paid by Mexico's 15 million people for the ambitious policies of the career president was too high. After the turn of the century, inflation rose, prices increased rapidly, illegal strikes paralyzed mines and industry. Riots resulting from the social tensions were bloodily suppressed by the dictator. Even the bourgeoisie began to grumble.

Díaz had surrounded himself with a geriatric clique of advisors, the *Cientificos*. "Much administration, little politics" had been their motto. Foreign capital and a few Mexican career bureaucrats were the real beneficiaries of the ossified and corrupt administration. In 1910, one percent of the Mexican population owned 90 percent of the land while 97 percent of the peasants owned no land whatever. Their communal lands, the *ejidos*, had been lost to the *latifundia* which had swollen to take over the traditional village commons. The peasants were reduced to serfs, slaving on plantations for subsistence wages.

The Madero revolt: By 1908, the stubborn potentate Díaz had accelerated his own end. In a famous interview with an American journalist, John Creelmann, he declared that he would welcome an opposition candidate in the coming elections. Francisco Madero, a landowner from Coahuila state, took him at his word with the motto "No re-election."

His quickly organized Partido Anti-Reeleccionista enjoyed astounding success in 1910. Díaz showed that he had not been so earnest about having serious opposition. Shortly before the election he had Madero arrested, and the ballot was rigged.

Madero escaped from prison and sought exile in Texas. There he proclaimed the Plan de San Luis Potosi, in which he called for armed struggle against the dictator. After initial failures, in February 1911 the Madero revolt gained ground. The peasant leader, Emiliano Zapata, joined the revolution along with the charismatic bandit leader from Chihuahua, "Pancho" Francisco Villa. By April,

tal, accompanied by his victorious revolutionaries. On the same morning the city was shaken by an intense, billowing earthquake – a very bad omen.

Out of the frying pan: Now it was Madero's turn. He discharged his revolutionaries. For him, the struggle was won with his election to the presidency. He planned to build a new Mexico through the implementation of far-reaching reforms. But Zapata refused to cease fighting as long as the estates of the *latifundia* were not radically redistributed. In his opinion Madero was too hesitant, an enemy of the revolution. Zapata proposed in his Plan de Ayala the partial breakup of the *haciendas*

18 Mexican states had rebelled against the decaying Porfiriat. The army leaders, Orozco, Villa and Obregón defeated the government troops (federales) in the north. Zapata advanced on the capital from the south. The border city of Juárez and the railway junction at Torreon were captured. In May 1911, Díaz gave up. In the ensuing confusion he resigned and fled to Paris. On June 7, 1911, Madero marched triumphantly into the capi-

Left, Francisco Madero started the Revolution. **Above**, revolution is the subject of many murals, including this one in the castle of Chapultepec.

and the return of all communal lands to the villages. Madero rejected such ideas; as the "apostle of democracy" he shied away from dictatorship and radicalism. He hoped that the "Mexicans would use their newly won liberty within a responsible democracy." He hoped in vain.

The big landowners and conservatives in his cabinet felt threatened by the liberal reforms and it was only with great effort that Madero was able to quash the revolt led by Orozco, Villa and Obregón in Chihuahua. Mexico was seething with dissatisfaction.

The US began to fear for its enormous

investments in Mexico. The US ambassador, Henry Lane Wilson, openly declared the idealistic Madero a dangerous dreamer. Uncertainty grew. The threatening clouds of an imminent civil war gathered over Mexico City. Then, in February, 1913, came what was to be called the "ten days of tragedy."

On February 9, Don Porfirio's nephew, the arch-conservative Félix Díaz, staged a coup. Madero and his cabinet entrenched themselves in the National Palace, surrounded by intense fighting. Madero gave the responsibility for the defense of his government to his Interior Minister, General Victoriano ("the Jackal") Huerta. The rebels had meanwhile occupied the Citadel (Ciudadela), and were well equipped for a long battle. The struggle in the streets of Mexico City lasted for days, during which hundreds were killed.

Treacherous pact: The US Ambassador Henry Lane Wilson supported Díaz and his fellow plotters but also made contact with General Huerta. On February 18, the National Palace fell into the hands of the rebels as a result of Huerta's betrayal. Madero and his vice president, Pino Suárez, were arrested. That same evening, Félix Díaz and Huerta concluded their treacherous pact in the residence of Ambassador Wilson, who had orchestrated the collaboration – Huerta was to take over. On February 22, 1913, Madero and Pino Suárez were clandestinely led out of the palace, and were later found shot dead against a prison wall.

To the relief of the conservatives, Victoriano Huerta now took over the presidency. His dictatorship proved to be one of unprecedented horror. Terror reigned in the cities and the country as a whole. All reforms were made null and void and the status quo of an earlier era was restored.

In the north, a follower of the murdered Madero, the Governor of Coahuilas, Venustiano Carranza, rose up against the new dictator and tyrant. As commander-in-chief of the newly mobilized revolutionary troops, Carranza challenged Huerta's claim to the presidency. On March 26, 1913 his Plan of Guadalupe proclaimed a national uprising and demanded re-establishment of the 1857 Constitution. At the same time, US President Woodrow Wilson occupied

Veracruz under a flimsy pretense and refused to recognize the Huerta regime. In the south, Zapata led a guerrilla war while in the north Generals Villa and Obregón again took up the fight – this time against Huerta. In fierce battles with tens of thousands of soldiers, cavalry and heavy artillery, Torreón, Chihuahua, Ciudad Juárez and other cities were captured.

For Pancho Villa, it proved to be his most successful year. However, the obstinate leader fell out with his *jefe* (chief) Carranza on account of insubordination during his glorious conquest of Zacatecas. The defeated "Jackal" Huerta resigned on June 17, 1914 and fled to Texas. The victorious leader of the revolution, Carranza, marched into Mexico City. Despite not being officially president, he managed to persuade the US to make a discreet withdrawal from Veracruz.

Revolutionary chaos: At this point Pancho Villa began to cause problems. The eccentric and unpredictable popular hero resisted Carranza. With the support of Zapata and other generals who were disappointed in Carranza, he began to take revolutionary matters into his own hands. A conference in the town of Aguacalientes was intended to reconcile the quarreling revolutionary leaders, but the result was further strife. The radicals around Zapata and Villa opposed the more moderate generals grouped around Carranza, and the revolutionary movement was split, with the various factions fighting against each other. Ultimately Mexico sank into anarchy.

As the advancing armies of the Villa-Zapata alliance approached Mexico City, Carranza evacuated the presidential palace and moved the government to Veracruz. The alliance quickly appointed their own president, the bland Gutiérrez and, at the beginning of December 1914, marched with thousands of troops into the devastated capital. The inhabitants of Mexico City, then around half a million, trembled before the hordes of revolutionaries.

Initially, it was possible to keep the wild boys in line. In the capital's famous "House of Tiles," which by then was already Sanborn's Restaurant, it was possible to photograph the Zapatistas displaying impeccable table manners, but Villa was less predictable. A hero of the masses due to his charisma and military prowess his deeds were already almost mythical.

It was at that point that Zapata and Villa met for the first time. They concluded a mutual assistance pact which had no practical results. After the withdrawal of the alliance in January 1915, Obregón marched into the city with his army. Mexico City was terrorized by plundering, raping, murderous soldiers. On top of this, food became scarce and epidemics broke out.

Fight for the north: After some months, Obregón finally left the shaken capital. He

rists, at the head of his *División del Norte.*

It is no coincidence that most of the leading revolutionary figures except Zapata – Calles, Orozco, Madero, Carranza, Obregón and Pancho Villa – came from the north. Zapata respected the interests of the US, which was, after all, his neighbor, but beyond that the "Centaur of the North" feared nothing and no one.

Obregón was to teach him fear. He knew that he who controlled the north, controlled the country. Clandestinely, the US channelled weapons across the border. Only with the railways could the convoys of men, material and horses get through. Torreón, Ciudad

set out for the north after Pancho Villa with fresh troops and reinforcements from the "Red Workers Battalions." In the north, Pancho Villa, the Governor of Chihuahua, was at the height of his popularity, ruling like a feudal prince.

Even today he is regarded as the prototype of the North Mexican, the *Norteño*, without old Indian traditions; a daredevil and adventurer, who cared little for the ideological delicacies of quibbling revolutionary theo-

<u>Above</u>, the Revolution brought rough guys into the posh city and made the bourgeois tremble.

Juárez and Chihuahua were cities of decisive strategic importance.

Obregón commanded 11,000 soldiers. Villa, with his *División del Norte* and his *Dorados* had 20,000, but numerical superiority didn't help him. Obregón was the better strategist and Villa was repeatedly routed. In the Battle of Celaya, the famous Villista cavalry was mowned down by Carranzista machine gun fire. In the end, General Villa was left with only 3,000 *Dorados.*

Carranza exulted in his triumph and re-established his government in Mexico City. However, Washington, which had shortly before honored Pancho Villa as the "greatest Mexican of the century," abandoned him perfunctorily and immediately recognized the Carranza regime. The fallen hero, embittered over his betrayal by the treacherous *gringos*, sought revenge.

Carranza government: No sooner was Villa defeated in 1916 than the Carranzistas marched with 30,000 soldiers against Zapata's revolutionaries who had been enjoying a certain period of peace because Obregón needed all his strength to combat Villa. After the *hacienda* owners had been executed or driven away, Zapata had actually implemented his land redistribution pro-

"Black Jack" Pershing to seek out Villa who cunningly managed to elude them for 10 months, all the while stirring up anti-American feeling. The outbreak of World War I forced the Americans to withdraw Pershing's expeditionary force, which had basically accomplished nothing.

Carranza, the moderate reformer, now had the country more or less under his control. On February 5, 1917, his government adopted the new Mexican Constitution. It improved the situation of the workers, reformed the education system and introduced a truly revolutionary land reform. Officially, this constitution re-established order in Mexico. But

gram. But that was over now. Carranza's troops brought Cuernavaca and a large part of the state under their control, forcing Zapata's armed peasants to go underground. Then, in March 1916, the avenging Villa struck again. He and his *Dorados* torched the US border town of Columbus, causing hundreds of casualties.

By burning Columbus Villa had hoped to provoke the Americans into invading Mexico and overthrowing Carranza, but the invasion did not materialize. Instead Washington, with the consent of the Mexican government, sent a punitive expedition under General John

Zapata was not satisfied that the reforms had gone far enough and continued to fight. In Chihuahua, the eccentric Pancho Villa also continued the war against the legal government of Carranza.

In 1917, Mexico found itself in a desperate state. Foreign investors, occupied with the war, hesitated to invest in Europe, but were put off by Mexico's socialist constitution. Carranza, who had in the meantime been elected president, rapidly lost popularity because of the economic crisis. Strikes and workers' uprisings increased the enormous pressure on him.

Carranzista officers assassinated Zapata in April 1919. But Carranza's time was also running out. When it became clear that he had no intention of retiring at the end of his term in 1920, his former supporter, General Obregón, reacted immediately. In Sonora, to which he had retired, Obregón organized a fighting force with the support of the labor movement and marched against Carranza. The president fled from Mexico City by railroad carriage, heading toward Veracruz. Because the convoy was blocked, the party continued on horseback. On May 21, 1920, during a fatal night attack in the mountains, Venustiano Carranza was shot dead. Alvaro

weapons. In 1923, he fell victim to an assassination which was believed to have been instigated by Obregón. In 1928, Alvaro Obregón was himself murdered in Mexico City's "La Bombilla" restaurant.

No event in this century has so influenced the identity of Mexico as has the revolution, which still prompts plenty of argument. Some still dispute whether the end of the revolution was marked by the 1917 Constitution, the presidency of Obregón or whether, in fact, it has continued right up to today.

The great deeds of the heroes and the evils of the traitors survive in the *corridos*, the ballads of the revolutionary troubadours

Obregón took charge as the new president.

Obregón himself had to contend with numerous coup attempts and unrest as did his successor, Calles, but the era of the guerrilla and of great battles was finally over. The constitution was no longer threatened. Under Obregón, a moneyed elite emerged, consisting of all-powerful, highly unrevolutionary politicians – the so-called *politicos*. In 1920, Pancho Villa also surrendered his

Left, **Villa and Zapata in the President's Palace.**
Above, **locomotive near the Revolution Museum, a reminder of troops transported by rail.**

(Zapata had several of these extemporizers among his followers). The anthem of Pancho Villa's powerful *División del Norte* was *La Cucaracha*. *La Valentina* praised the brave *soldaderas*, the women in the train of the revolutionaries who cooked, made love, bandaged, buried and not infrequently died with them.

Nearly every tenth Mexican lost his life in the revolution. Nearly all of the *caudillos* or leaders of the revolution died through betrayal, fundamentally as losers. The only winners have been the Mexican people. It is they who have survived.

VIVA ZAPATA!
VIVA PANCHO VILLA!

There is a vintage photograph of Pancho Villa in the presidential chair, grinning for the camera. Next to him sits the restrained and wary Emiliano Zapata. In Zapata's left hand is the inevitable cigar, and, right next to it, his legendary sombrero. These are two revolutionaries at the pinnacle of their collective successes.

Villa and Zapata had met for the first time some days before in Xochimilco, from where they had marched into the anxious capital city and then on to the National Palace with their combined armies of 50,000 Zapatistas and Villistas. It was here, on November 6, 1914, that the photographer of the Revolution, Casasola, took the classic photo of the two famous *caudillos*.

While Zapata stayed in a modest hotel on the edge of the city, Villa made himself conspicuous by his raucousness downtown. According to legend, Villa stormed the distinguished Café Tacuba with his horse. He seized the opportunity to settle a few old debts, shed tears of mourning at the grave of his murdered idol Madero, and then personally changed the name of the Calle de Plateros to the Calle de Madero.

Making brazen appearances – that was Pancho Villa's style. In 1914, aged 36, he weighed over 90 kg (200 lb). He spoke loudly, with a distinctive northern accent. He could be charming, but was frightful when he lost his temper. Shrewdness and cunning shone from his eyes. His skin was white, his face flushed. He was the Centaur of the North.

The smaller, dark-skinned Zapata was very different. He avoided calling attention to himself, was acutely sensitive to danger and spoke with a soft voice. He valued fine food and savored French cognac. There are hardly any pictures of him smiling, but he used to relax during a cock fight or village fiesta. Emiliano Zapata was undoubtedly the best-dressed *guerrillero* of his day. He was called, admiringly, *Charro entre Charros* (horseman among horsemen). He loved equestrian sports and, like Villa, was fanatical about horses.

There were other ways in which he was just like Villa. He competed in riding, shooting and bullfighting competitions. Each hated bureaucrats and loved dozens of women. Both left a widow when they died. Both feared betrayal and were shot by traitors. Their popularity makes all other Mexican revolutionary heroes seem like mere stand-ins. Zapata and Villa were born leaders with legendary charisma and their soldiers followed them unconditionally.

Despite all their similarities, they came from opposing worlds. Villa, a Norteño, came from a part of Mexico where cattle ranches were the size of an average European duchy, a region of outlaws and the landless. It was a breeding ground of tough guys, all-powerful cattle barons, and leaders of marauding bandits. In the Revolution, Villa intermittently controled up to half of Mexico.

Zapata's army of the south, peasant *guerrilleros* in sandals and straw hats, operated almost entirely in the state of Morelos. It was there, in the village of Anenecuilco, that Emiliano Zapata was born. Before too long, this small entrepreneur was elected head of his village. In 1911, he took up the armed struggle and with his peasants occupied the Hacienda Chinameca, where he had worked as a stable master. The owner was killed in the fighting.

It was on April 10, 1919, that his Carranzista political opponents lured him back to this farm and shot him. To the end of his life, Zapata neither served in a government nor did he recognize any president. He was an anarchist with fundamentalist, peasant ideals.

For generations, the powerful sugar haciendas (estates) of Morelos had been ruthlessly annexing the so-called *ejidos*, the village common lands. They made the peasants into peons. Like all Mexican peasants, Zapata had a religious bond with the sacred Mother Earth from the fruit of which their Indian forebears had lived for millennia. The *latifundia* (landed aristocrats) were his natural enemies. The Zapatistas carried the Virgin of Guadalupe as their battle standard. She and Zapata stood for Land and Freedom – "*Tierra y Libertad*!" When a journalist asked him what he fought for, Zapata pointed to a dusty tin box containing the ancient title deeds of his village. "That's what I fight for," was his reply. His manifesto from November 25, 1911, the Plan of Ayala, declared that all communal lands must be returned and a third of the remaining land divided among the peasants.

In contrast, Pancho Villa was a warrior who fought for the sake of fighting. Doroteo Arango (his real name) was born into bitter poverty on July 5, 1878, in the state of Durango. After the death of his father he assumed responsibility for the care of the family. As an adolescent, he shot his landlord after the latter had tried to rape his sister. He then fled to the mountains and led an adventurous life as a cattle thief and killer, taking the name Pancho (a Spanish diminutive

form of Francisco) Villa. As a gang leader, he terrorized the state of Chihuahua. With cattle rustlers organizing the meat supply, he became a prosperous butcher in Chihuahua. In 1910, Villa joined the Madero revolution against the despised Díaz regime.

Villa's charisma drew to him thousands of adventurers, landless people and *pistoleros* (gunfighters). From these he formed his elite troops, the *Dorados* – the Golden Ones. As *caudillo* of the Revolution, he took revenge against the rich and powerful in the name of

Left, the legendary Emiliano Zapata and, above, cardboard cut-out of Pancho Villa in the Museo Nacional de la Revolución.

those deprived of their rights, and he was imprisoned many times. Under Huerta he was forced into exile in the US – he had always been popular with the *Norteamericanos*. Initially he fought with Obregón in support of Madero. Then he fought with Carranza against Huerta and finally against both Carranza and Obregón.

In 1920, Villa and the last 759 *Dorados* surrendered. In Canutillo, Durango, he and his veterans built up a model farm. But in 1923 he entered politics once again, this time in opposition to President Obregón. On July 20, 1923, while driving his Dodge through Parral, Chihuahua, his body was riddled with bullets.

In his book *Insurgent Mexico*, John Reed described a Robin Hood of the poor and disinherited, reporting Villa's vision of a new Mexico. "In all parts of the Republic we will establish military colonies composed of the veterans of the Revolution... Three days a week they will work and work hard, because honest work is more important than fighting, and only honest work makes good citizens. And the other three days they will receive military instruction and go out and teach the people how to fight."

Pancho Villa's life was littered with corpses. He was dictatorial as governor of Chihuahua. As general of the renowned *División del Norte* (Northern Division), he was feared. After defeating the "Jackal," Huerta, he was celebrated as a strategic genius and the "Liberator of Mexico." A born showman, Villa granted Mutual Film exclusive film rights of his military actions.

His fellow revolutionary Zapata dreamed only of land reform. Pointing to the presidential seat, Villa said, "for this we are busily killing each other." Laughing, he offered the chair to Zapata, who turned it down. Villa threw himself gleefully into the symbol-laden throne, while Zapata sat next to him briefly for a photograph. Later Zapata, the peasant *guerrillero* from Morelos, hissed: "We ought to burn the thing and put an end to that false ambition." ∎

People still ask whether Mexico's revolution was successful or is still going on. All agree, however, that the revolution shook the entire country, bringing traditional political and economic structures to the point of collapse.

But just as the debris from the pyramids was used to build palaces and churches after the Spanish conquest, modern Mexico stands on pre-revolutionary foundations. Despite the facade of a democratic republic, underneath lies the ancient pyramid of authoritarian centralism. Mexico is sometimes mockingly referred to as a "democratorship."

Mexico City is the center of power, until recently exercised by a seemingly omnipotent president. The rules of the power game, set by the regime in the 1920s and 1930s, have ensured that no post-revolutionary president can become a despot, though they may well come close. This centralized power, however, has also helped to establish a certain amount of political stability.

Heir to the revolution: It was President Plutarco Elias Calles (1924–28) who first managed to tame and channel the political powers unleashed by the revolution. During his presidency, however, a policy of uncompromising persecution of the Church led to a great public uproar, largely because the president sought out and radically curtailed every means of public influence which had been embedded in the 1917 Constitution inspired by the revolutionary cleric, Hidalgo. The clergy were forbidden to wear their cassocks outside the church and to vote or carry on political agitation. They were also forbidden to own property or to interfere in primary or secondary education.

The Roman Catholic church finally admitted defeat and withdrew from the political stage as the revolutionary leadership and its centralized bureaucracy gained ground. Calles' founding of the National Revolution

Party (PNR) was an ingenious strategic decision. In the years that followed 1929, the party succeeded in absorbing all the significant social groupsw. It took as its own the national colors – green, white and red – and became synonymous with the state. Even the increasingly grandiose names which the party successively adopted show how the energy of the national revolution was gradually molded into a bureaucratic apparatus: Partido Nacional Revolucionario, Partido de la

Revolución Mexicana, Partido Revolucionario Institucional (PRI).

The PRI structure of today consists of three overlapping membership divisions: the *sector obrero* (workers' section) which includes the labor unions; the *sector campesino* (peasant section) recruited in large part from those working in agriculture; and the *sector popular* which absorbs practically everyone who doesn't belong to the other groups.

The latter division brings together such diverse people as civil servants, businessmen, intellectuals and slum dwellers. Some are not even aware of their party membership, since personal membership is not the norm. In return for absolute loyalty, party activists are rewarded with political as well as social advancement.

Over several decades, the PRI swallowed up all the other parties and over the same period supplied all the state presidents, most governors, nearly all the senators, the vast majority in the House of Representatives and virtually all the mayors. In contrast to previous practice in socialist countries, the party in Mexico is more or less the long arm of the government, functioning like a civil service.

The six-year cycle: Despite the enormous energy devoted to the election campaign the

privilege in return for favors from petitioners. The size of the morsel which a partaker gets from the cake (a bribe is called *una mordida*, "a bite") depends very much on his status. Corruption is inbuilt and apparently ineradicable. The American journalist Alan Riding (*Eighteen Times Mexico*) wrote that corruption "makes the system function, providing the 'oil' which keeps the wheels of the bureaucratic apparatus turning and the 'glue' which holds political alliances together."

In many respects the 1910 revolution ushered Mexico into the modern era, but above all in the business sector. President Calles began to modernize the economy. A decade

election itself had been little more than a charade until very recently. Every six years the elections bring the ossified system back to life. With the change in presidents comes a substantial shuffling of personnel in the government services. Although government positions only become well paid toward the end of the six-year cycle, many hope for an administrative position that offers at least some material security through the spoils of corruption.

It is not so much the individuals as the corporate structure of Mexico's political life that is to blame for this abuse of power and

and a half later, President Lázaro Cárdenas (1934–40) displayed a strongly reformist zeal in the spirit of the Revolution. He will be remembered by many Mexicans as the man who undertook great land reform in favor of poor peasants and, most importantly, nationalized the petroleum companies, most of which had been foreign-owned. Under his successor, Avila Camacho, the agrarian revolution was completed and the industrial revolution gained momentum.

During World War II, the warring countries wanted Mexican oil and agricultural products but exported next to no finished goods. This lack of overseas competition enabled the local industry to expand and produce goods for domestic consumption. Mexico's movie industry enjoyed an astonishing boom period during which the country became the major producer of Spanish-language films.

Under President Miguel Alemán annual economic growth passed six percent and Mexico became integrated into the world economy as a "boom country," albeit with a tendency to slide into crises. Economic growth accelerated from the top down but it couldn't broaden its base – the rich simply grew richer and there were no adequate struc-

former agricultural workers moved to the city just in order to hang on to the tail of this prosperity. But without the necessary professional qualifications the rural migrants who came to Mexico City more often than not joined the masses of underemployed slum dwellers.

Countrywide tension also increased because of the high rate of population growth (3.5 percent), but the situation did not become explosive until shortly before the 1968 Olympic Games. When the eyes of the world were on Mexico, spontaneous protests began among students in Mexico City. Unwisely, the Díaz Ordáz government sent in the police

tures for distributing the wealth through the lower classes.

Crisis of confidence: Industry was concentrated in the greater Mexico City area, while the peasant population received hardly any benefit from the headlong development. The income of city dwellers grew substantially and a broader middle class demonstrated how to spend the extra wealth.

By contrast, living conditions in the rural areas continued to deteriorate, so that many

Left, politics on the street. Above, politics in the parliament (Palacio Legislativo).

and the military as the students marched toward the Palacio Nacional. The outrage over the clash only served to spread the rebellion.

Ten days before the lighting of the Olympic flame, the government, afraid of losing international prestige, used armed force to suppress a protest meeting in Tlatelolco's Plaza de Tres Culturas. The massacre of many students coupled with more than 1,000 arrests resulted in the required effect: a Mexico as quiet as a graveyard for the period when it was in the world spotlight. But the Mexicans' own faith in their post-revolutionary state had been shattered. The ever-deepening economic crisis of the 1980s brought the Mexican "institutionalized revolution" further into chaos.

Enormous oil discoveries started an oil rush and the state greedily took out huge foreign loans in anticipation of even greater riches. In 1981, the drastic decline in oil demand and the resulting fall in price led to an economic collapse which only exacerbated prevailing social injustices. The price of basic foodstuffs soared while wage levels fell to those of the 1960s.

During the administration of Miguel de la Madrid (1982–88) the *peso* dropped drasti-

cally in value against the US dollar. A dollar had bought about 12 pesos in the 1960s; now it could buy more than 2,000. In 1985, Mexico City suffered a devastating earthquake which measured 8.1 on the Richter scale, the worst in recent memory.

Political collapse: The general loss of confidence in the PRI system became painfully obvious in the 1988 elections, when the party's Carlos Salinas de Gortari won with the closest majority since independence. The 40-year-old president assumed office despite protests in the streets and in parliament reforms. Salinas' major accomplishment was

to engineer, with considerable US support, Mexico's membership in the North America Free Trade Association (NAFTA) – the benefits of which are still being debated – but his triumph was marred on the day of its inception by fierce revolt in the southeastern state of Chiapas where landless Indians, banded together as "Zapatistas," took over the town of San Cristobal de las Casas.

Folktales and romantic heroes: With a charismatic masked spokesman who called himself "Sub-Commandante Marcos," the rebels pulled off a public relations coup, telling their story to the world through delighted reporters who descended on the area in droves. Marcos, a hero to the underclass, quickly became the subject of romantic songs and folktales eagerly passed on by his admirers throughout the country. Although the Mexican army quickly regained control, forcing the rebels back into the forests, the revolt simmered on for more than a year.

Meanwhile, President Carlos Salinas and the ruling PRI party encountered a series of setbacks. First came the murder of a church cardinal at Guadalajara airport: the official explanation regarded with cynical disbelief. Then, more significantly came successively the assassinations of Guadalajara's police chief and of Donald Luis Colosio, Salinas' hand-picked PR candidate for the next presidency. Although a nondescript Tijuana layabout was convicted and jailed for the murder it is hard to find a Mexican who thinks that justice has been done or that there is not some much deeper and more far-reaching plot yet to be uncovered.

Salinas picked another candidate – Ernesto Zedillo, who won the presidential election by the slimmest ever margin. After his accession the ex-president moved north of the border, leaving behind accusations that he had hidden the extent of Mexico's economic problems. In the closing months of his presidency, these problems resulted in a massive devaluation of the *peso*, which caused severe hardship for business as well as the middle and lower classes.

Left, ex-president Carlos Salinas engineered Mexico's membership in NAFTA. **Right**, the ancient symbol of the nation lives on.

tenochtitlan

colhuacan. pueblo.   tenayucan. puo

From the window of an airplane, Mexico City looks like an endless, amorphous sea of houses. Despite numerous attempts to plan the city, the growth of this gigantic metropolis has left its indelible mark on a previously harmonious landscape.

The landscape: The Aztecs reached the central Mexican basin in the 13th century, traveling south from the dry plains of the north. Five lakes glittered between huge, snow-capped volcanoes, mountain ridges densely covered with firs and pine-trees, petrified streams of lava and the cones of innumerable small volcanoes. The lake in the middle, Texcoco, was stagnant and filled with salty water, the result of a meagre inflow during the dry period combined with a high rate of evaporation. On the shores several Nashua peoples had created a blossoming paradise of gardens and fields. The *chinampas* – arable lands – were artfully extended by maize and beanfields (*milpas*) while the "floating gardens" were nothing but beds of mud, layered between wattle and poplars in Lake Xochimilco.

A system of canals, partly visible even today, connected the lakes. Pyramids, temples and ballfields were devoted to the worship of the gods. The principal places of worship, Teotihuacán and Tula, had however already been abandoned and fallen into decay. The famous ball game, *hachtli* had been played since ancient times and had both mythological and religious significance, although it was also the pretext for heavy gambling. Splendid ball courts still exist in the Mayan temples of Tula and Chichen Itza. It was a game reserved for upper-class players who were heavily padded and were only allowed to manipulate the ball with their knees or hips.

According to legend the Aztecs founded the city of Tenochtitlán around 1370 on a flat island in Lake Texcoco, on the very place

Left, view into a *vecindad* or neighborhood, showing cramped living conditions. Here everyone shares everything, even water taps.

where an eagle sat on an cactus devouring a snake – an image that was later to become the national emblem of Mexico. From this base they proceeded to subjugate major parts of the present Mexico. The tributes from these vassal peoples alone enabled them to expand their capital into the gleaming metropolis that so impressed the Spanish conqueror Hernán Cortéz within 150 years.

The Aztecs achieved miracles of hydraulic engineering to prevent the shallow lake from rising and flooding the city during the summer rainy season. A protective dam, 16 km (10 miles) long, was built to separate the city and the western part of the lake from the larger eastern part. Further dams, as well as aqueducts to supply water, connected Tenochtitlán with the older cities on the shore (Azcapotzalco, Tacubaya, Coyoacán), which have since become incorporated into Mexico City. Urban planning, therefore, played a significant role long before the conquistadors set foot on Mexican soil.

Tenochtitlán, which is said to have had between 60,000 and 400,000 inhabitants at the time of the Spanish conquest, was covered by a network of streets and canals. When the Spanish built their new capital Ciudad de Mexico (Mexico City), after the destruction in 1521, they based their design on the existing Aztec patterns.

As a symbol of their power, the Spanish erected churches on the sites of destroyed pyramids; the Franciscan cloister on the pyramid of Tlatelolco, for example, and the cathedral next to the former main pyramid of the Templo Mayor. Cortéz had his own palace built on the ruins of Montezuma's palace, also the site of the present seat of government. In the course of the conquest Cortéz destroyed the city, toppling most of its buildings and filling the canals with rubble. In a regretful dispatch to Spain he expressed regret for destroying what he termed "the most beautiful city in the world."

The colonial period: Starting from the central square, today called the Zócalo, the Spanish plan featured a right-angled street-grid with blocks measuring 80 by 160 meters (260 by 525 ft). The wealth culled from the nation's silver mines enabled the bourgeoisie of the capital to build patio houses with artfully designed facades decorated either with reddish *tezontle* stone or *azulejo* colored tiles. The many churches and cloisters bear witness to the important position which the Catholic Church then enjoyed.

Due to the massive growth of the city and to several floods the Spanish tried to drain the basin by connecting a 25-km (15-mile) canal to the Río Panuco river system in the north. But the first tunnel collapsed in 1627. In 1767, therefore, the Tajo de Nochistengo, the tunnel which today carries the railway line, was dug.

The drainage of the lake: The problem of draining the basins was not finally solved until this century when the large canal (Gran Canal de Desagüe), with its two tunnels, was dug. On the northern end of what remained of Lake Texcoco an evaporation spiral was built to produce salt; from the air this looks like a shell and therefore it is commonly called the *caracol* (snail). The negative consequences of draining the land, however, were not really considered even though, as early as 1807, Alexander von Humboldt had accurately predicted that such treatment would result in disastrous erosion, deforestation and dried out soil.

What actually happened, following the drainage of the substantial sediments and the increased use of ground water, was that the houses sunk up to 7 meters (23 ft) and cracks appeared in the walls. This is not only evident today in the massive marble building of the Palacio de Bellas Artes, whose front steps are buckled, but also in the Franciscan church in the Calle Madero, whose entrance is now several meters below street level. The 18th-century Capuchin church, right next to the Basilica de Guadalupe, had been leaning ominously eastward until it was recently given solid concrete foundations and straightened hydraulically. But this kind of sophisticated procedure is too costly to be used except in the most exceptional cases. The cathedral, still sinking to different levels, is an even more complicated problem.

The unstable subsoil is also partly respon-

sible for the extensive damage caused by the earthquake of 1985. Due to the geological structure, earthquakes are a common phenomenon in Mexico, as they are all along the Pacific. The upheavals of September 19, 1985 however, produced oscillations of different frequencies in the sand and clay layers and this led to the destruction of over 400 city buildings.

An important factor in the destruction was the quality of the housing stock. Solidly built colonial palaces stood firm as did the technically flawless steel constructions with deep foundations, such as the 181-meter (594-ft) 42-story Torre Latinoamerica which, when built in the 1950s, had been embedded 30 meters (98 ft) into the ground. Under the pressure of the earthquake it was the clay tile houses and the shoddily and densely built skyscrapers that collapsed.

Climatic changes: The drainage of the lake influenced the local climate, particularly in the dry season. The large water surfaces, which had previously balanced out the rise and fall of the temperatures, disappeared and the dry, salty clay was blown into superfine dust-clouds. Together with the smog produced by car exhausts and industrial emissions the clouds contributed to the unbearable air pollution prevalent during the long periods of fine weather in spring.

Under these specific and very distinct circumstances, the basin location of Mexico City has proved a further disadvantage. Stable inversion layers get stuck between the mountain ranges and dissolve into rain only on the rare occasions when they meet cold fronts. Then the air is clear and the volcanoes again zigzag across the horizon, just as they do on old paintings.

In general, the climate is influenced by the trade winds prevalent in the northern areas of the tropics. The dry season lasts from November to April and the summer brings rain which occurs mainly in the late afternoon. Substantial showers tend to cause terrible floods in Mexico City, which is notoriously subject to drainage problems.

Unfortunately, the annual precipitation – at 700 millimeters (28 inches) about the same as Northern Europe – is far too little to ensure the capital's water supply. This is mainly due to the unfavorable distribution of rain between summer and winter months – there is no regular intermittent supply – but also to the increasing expansion of the city into the drained areas and rising private and industrial water consumption.

The first mechanical pumps to produce ground water were introduced toward the end of the last century. In the 1930s more distant resources were tapped, at first via a pipeline from Xochimilco, then by a connection to the springs of the Río Lerma near Toluca. Recently, plans have been drafted to get water from the rainy Sierra Madre Oriental. Apart from the difficulty of providing

In the past 100 years: Mexico City grew beyond the boundaries of the old colonial city in the 19th century. Emperor Maximilian created an avenue, modelled after the Champs Elysées, called the Paseo de la Reforma, which led to his castle, the Castillo de Chapultepec. French influence on the capital's architecture, though short lived, brought happy diversity. Villas in the French style were built along the wide Paseo de la Reforma; some of them are still there in the Zona Rosa, while others had to yield ground to office towers and big hotels.

Since the turn of the century residential areas for the middle and upper classes have

sufficient amounts of water, there are also serious flaws in the distribution system, particularly in the growing suburban regions. Water quality, too, is not adequately monitored. Rapid urbanization, water shortage, canalization – and the far-reaching consequences of all these for the environment – are closely intertwined; the lack of water naturally affects the city's sewerage system and the health of its people.

<u>Above</u>, early morning activity in Chalco, a huge *ciudad perdida* (lost city) in the extreme outskirts of the metropolis.

been developed in the south and west, leaving the vast Bosque de Chapultepec as a public park. Today the classy Lomas suburb, rising in the west, is an exclusive area with stylish country houses. At the same time the old village of Tacubaya was devoured by urbanization. The distant colonial cities of San Angel, Coyoacán and Tlalpan were discovered only later as preferred residential areas. Artists such as Diego Rivera, who belonged to the avant garde movement, relocated to these romantic towns that today are part of Mexico City.

A significant factor in the city's extension

southward along the Avenida Insurgentes in the 1950s was the generously laid out university complex, the Olympic Stadium and the state-of-the-art residential development Pedregal (which means lava) on the site of an ancient and long extinct volcano. Further colleges, government offices and American-style shopping malls (such as Perisur) were also added to the complex.

In the north, the situation is entirely different. Under Porfirio Díaz the first factories were established along with the railway line. They formed the initial stage of an industrial area which has since grown to extend well beyond the northern city limits.

trous. On the dry bed of Lake Texcoco slums appeared, covered by mud in the summer and by dust in the winter. In addition to the planned suburbs, such as the monotonous Nezahualcóyotl, with more than three million inhabitants, new spontaneous settlements with access to the public infrastructure mushroomed seemingly overnight.

Even in the inner city there are now many slum-like neighborhoods, *ciudades perdidas* (the lost cities), which differ hardly at all from the cardboard and tin shacks that cover the hillsides of so many third world capitals. Innumerable patio-houses in the eastern part of the old town are deteriorating into over-

The people attracted to the capital by industrial development initially lived in neighborhoods of one-room apartments with cooking facilities along open hallways with one water tap for 10 to 20 families. In 1930 the city had one million inhabitants, but by 1950 this had increased to three million. This was only the beginning of a veritable population explosion. Today the metropolitan area, with its 20 million people, is one of the largest in the world, ranking alongside the world capitals of New York and Tokyo.

The consequences for urban development of such a population explosion were disas-

populated quarters in need of renovation.

Traffic problems: The infrastructure has not been able to keep up with the pace of change in the city, although the post-war economic boom has permitted some improvements. In the 1960s, for example, a number of urban highways were built, such as the Viaducto crossing the city along the east–west axis, or the Periférico. But they were not able to cope with ever-increasing traffic and had to be complemented by a network of four- and six-lane one-way highways, the *ejes viales*, covering the entire inner city. Even these are regularly congested during rush-hour.

Use of vehicles has been restricted to certain days of the week and tough exhaust emission control laws have been passed. Under such circumstances the opening of the subway, the Metro, in 1969, was extremely important. Since then the system has been extended to eight lines totalling more than 100 km (60 miles) and ferrying five million passengers every day. The subway is the best evidence that, even in a metropolis with seemingly unsurmountable problems, it is possible to organize a reliable service for the masses. It was not even disrupted during the earthquake in 1985.

However immense the losses caused by

met the needs of the population but were also aesthetically pleasing. Programs providing for the transfer of ownership to the tenants after a 10-year occupation have met with enormous success.

A master plan to stabilize traffic and to redevelop the colonial center has long been overdue. It has materialized at last and even made progress in spite of all the obstructions (the restriction on using your car on alternate days has been thwarted by those rich enough to own two cars).

Hope for the future: There is hope, then, that this city, which seems to be growing uncontrollably, can be saved. Regular visitors ex-

the catastrophic earthquake might have been, it also released enormous energies for renewal and solidarity. During the rebuilding of the poorer neighborhoods in the northern part of the inner city, local initiatives were instrumental in guaranteeing the proper completion of a public program to build 48,000 housing units. With the financial assistance of the World Bank and other organizations, small complexes were designed that not only

press surprise each time they return that the city has not yet been completely given over to chaos. It remains to be seen whether a program transferring government offices and industries to other parts of the country will bring the expected and hoped for relief on overstretched road, housing, infrastructure and population growth. But the present government is trying to set a positive example: the National Bureau of Statistics, Cartography and Computer Science has already been moved to Aguascalientes, 500 km (300 miles) west of Mexico City, and there are plans for other similar bodies to relocate.

<u>Left</u>, The *Casa Grande*, as described by Oscar Lewis in *The Children of Sanchez*, before and, <u>above</u>, after the earthquake of 1985.

Of Mexico's 85 million inhabitants, almost one-quarter are *capitalinos* living in the capital, and the other 65 million would like to be. The majority of Mexicans strive to live in the capital or one of the other major cities: no one likes living in the poor countryside. By 1976, a thousand Mexicans were arriving in the capital every day. Since then, this number has quadrupled. Many returned to their own provinces after the tragic earthquake of 1985, but they came back again. Others, who only came to look for their relatives, ended up staying for good. As a result, Mexico City has the dubious honor of being one of the world's biggest cities.

Creative citizens: The writers Octavio Paz and Carlos Fuentes are *capitalinos*, as are actress María Felix and artists Rufino Tamayo from Oaxaca and Francisco Toledo from the Tehuantepec isthmus. No one wants to be a provincial. Intellectuals need the Librería Francesa (a French bookshop) on Paseo de la Reforma, just as in the 1950s and 1960s they needed the bookstores that sold French editions of Henry Miller, whose works were banned in the US and had to be smuggled across the border. Similarly, artists need the Palacio de Bellas Artes, the white marble, cake-like construction endowed by the dictator Porfirio Díaz which is slowly sinking into the ground. For – as everyone recognizes, and visitors most of all – the city of Tenochtitlán-Mexico was built on a lake and the earth is pulling its buildings downwards and sucking them under.

At weekends, rich writers and painters (almost all of them are rich) drive out to their villas in Cuernavaca or Tepoztlán, but all of them continue to live in the incredibly ugly city, in spite of the traffic, the jams, the water shortages and a future which looks increasingly gloomy. The *capitalinos* can't live without their great city; they feel a need for the culture, the art galleries, the festivals and gatherings, the gossip and the problems to make them feel they're alive.

In the last 50 years, villages which once lay outside the city – Tacubaya, Tacuba, Azcapotzalco, Mixcoac, San Angel, Coyoacán, Tlalpan – have been integrated into it, along with several other villages belonging to the adjoining federal state of Mexico like Naucalpan, Tlalnepantla and Ecatepec. Once

upon a time, those who lived in the center, around the Zócalo, used to say they were going for a walk in the market gardens of Coyoacán, Tlalpan and San Jerónimo. These days the popular Sunday afternoon resorts are part of the city. It's sad but true that even places which are still weekend retreats, like Cuernavaca, Tepoztlán or Cuautla, will soon become *barrios* (districts) of one of the most heavily populated cities of all time, a city the like of which has never before been seen on this earth.

Marías of the streets: The *capitalinos* are very sharp; they know all the tricks a person

Preceding pages: Xochimilco, the "Venice of the New World;" silver jewelry in Tepotzotlán market; bright Sunday bargains from an urban street trader. Left, San Angel's Saturday crowd. Above, "Carnation for your buttonhole, Señor?"

needs to eke out a life in this city. They get around by Metro, Pesero, Combi, Minibus and Ruta 100, a magic bus that gradually extends or can blow itself up rapidly like a balloon, according to the number of passengers on the route.

Drivers never seem to mind that passengers are hanging out of the windows and doors, and Mexicans, whether they're working or not, travel like this from one end of the city to the other. In the mornings they leave their homes, regardless of whether they have jobs. If they're not working, they wander the streets and squares, buying whatever's for sale: the latest craze in toys, like models of

"*Andele* (come on!) Señor, buy a ticket, *ándele* (okay, don't then), look at this cute little number, *ándele*, you could travel, you could fly to Europe, you don't even have to take me with you."

Sometimes it seems there is hardly an inch of space anywhere that some enterprising vendor hasn't set up his little stall. The entrances to the subway stations are often so full of salesmen that the police have to crack down to make room for travelers to get in. But within hours the vendors are back again on their lucrative patches.

The streets of Mexico City are unusually rich in images. You'll see the *golondrinos*

Garfield the cat or Topo Grigio, a talking mouse, or Mickey Mouse and girlfriend Minnie, and all kinds of chewing gum. (The gum tree, incidentally, was "discovered" in Yucatán and chewing gum, like chocolate, is one of Mexico's cultural gifts to the world. The chicle workers used to chew little balls of gum while they drew off the white sap from the trees, a thankless task in the enervating subtropical heat.)

There are many more bargains on offer in the streets – Kleenex tissues, for example, and lottery tickets, which the sellers wave enticingly in front of your windscreen.

(street musicians) and the *marías*, the Otomí and Mazahua Indian women with their embroidered blouses and plaits braided with brightly colored ribbons. Their tradition as traders is inextricably bound up with their history as the oldest race in the land. In the past they used to sell fruit; now they approach the slow-moving traffic with trays of plastic toys. In short broken sentences (for they barely speak Spanish) they offer their meager wares to the captive audience of immobilized drivers.

And all the while they tend their children, embroidering them little caps and vests in bright colors to ward off the spirits and protect them from the evil eye of the elders.

Although the Mazahua and Otomí women are outstanding needlewomen, they have no desire to work in factories, preferring the streets. They find it more sociable to be outdoors, more exciting and infinitely more varied than sitting indoors sewing on a chair by the window. For sitting in the house wouldn't be the same as being in the big city with all its cars and attendant dangers, nor would they earn the 50 – on a good day even 500 – pesos that they can make during an eight-hour day out on the streets.

Behind high walls: Their men arrive con-

goods on the streets. All, or almost all, are unemployed or without full-time work, according to the economists. Many of them are farmers, who work on the land for one or two months of the year and have nothing to do the rest of the time.

They come to the city because they think they will have a better standard of living here than in the country. Here they can see electric light, walk on tarmac pavements, sit in the shade under the trees in the city's parks and, when they look up, there are skyscrapers to marvel at. There's no shortage of distractions to take their minds off their hunger. Even if these refugees from the country have

tinually in the DF (Distrito Federal), husbands and others who aren't their husbands, the fathers of their sons and the friends of their childhood, seducers of the moment and silver-tongued promisers of the future. They come from the country, their *sarapes* (woollen capes) slung over their shoulders, their faces shiny and clean-shaven. They jump down from the bus and stumble into the best job they can find, usually hawking cheap

Left, children form the majority of the city's population. **Above**, a few residents of the capital escape at weekends to old converted haciendas.

to live in miserable hovels, they still don't give up hope of one day winning the lottery or attracting the favor of some magical benefactor who will somehow help them to make their fortune in the city. As a rule, though, they remain the poorest of the *capitalinos*.

The richest have their own residential districts, entertainment and travel, mostly to Las Vegas. The upper classes live in Tecamachalco and Lomas de Chapultepec (which used to be known as Chapultepec Heights, Bosques, Herradura and Valle Escondido). They dress in US fashions and build themselves modern houses, which they surround with high walls to deter casual onlookers – for no one should be privileged with a glimpse of what lies beyond.

When the rich *capitalinos* aren't flying to Las Vegas to lose some money, they jet off to Houston "for some shopping" or for a medical check-up. The Mexicans are renowned for squandering their money. They maintain houses that they have built on the international border – "Taco Towers," as they've become known – and they keep their fortunes in North American banks because they're worried about the inevitable devaluation of the Mexican peso. Their children

attend universities in San Diego or San Antonio. Many of the major chain stores in the United States would go out of business if their Mexican clientele stayed at home.

Divided world: The Mexicans who count themselves among the upper echelons live in the south of the city, in Coyoacán, San Angel, Chimalistac, San Angel Inn, Tlacopac, El Pedregal and San Jéronimo. They prefer traditional Hispanic-Mexican architecture, and their taste tends towards the colonial style, visible in their choice of furnishings and pictures, although they also like Tamayo, Soriano and other modern artists.

They organize festivals in the historic city center (the *Centro Histórico*), charity bazaars full of knicknacks and "ladies' garlands," posies of flowers bound together in classical style. They distance themselves from the rest of the population and from the overcrowded, noisy streets full of traders, clowns, beggars, car washers, balloon sellers and gum sellers, fire eaters – all those we collectively call *mil usos* (of a thousand uses) because between them they practice all the professions in the world. Except of course banking – the province of the upper classes.

The affluent members of society meet in the San Angel Inn, go to art exhibitions, frequent art galleries, visit each other's homes, lunch and dine together, and go for weekends to their houses in the country.

The miserable plight in which the vast majority of the remaining *capitalinos* find themselves has led to an increase in violence, in the number of muggings and the number of people in prison. The rich will readily give a stream of advice to visitors: ay, ay, ay, only keep the bare minimum of money on you if you're walking around the streets, ay, ay, ay, and leave your passport and any valuables at hotel reception. Ay, ay, ay, it's better to go out in groups, rather than wander on your own, ay, ay, ay…

For the spirit of solidarity that was so much in evidence and appeared so strong in times of crisis like the 1985 earthquake has petered out again in everyday life. Only a very few have time to care about anyone other than themselves. Sadly, Mexico has too many politicians and too few true public servants.

The dizzy pace of city life slows down on Sundays. Public life takes a rest. The smoke from the factory chimneys stops; television – the so-called "idiot box" – starts up, and in the sports stadia the atmosphere is high. No one is left standing on street corners waiting for something to happen, for this is a day for getting together, for the family, for walking. This is the day to visit your mother in law – for after all, what we are talking about here is a matriarchy.

Left, as an industrial worker, he is one of the better off. **Right**, "My range of goods is my best advertisement."

Post-Revolutionary Mexico became the classic land of asylum for Latin America, which accepted revolutionaries of every color and creed imaginable. Indeed, many others who were persecuted have reason to be grateful to the Mexicans.

Spanish Republicans forced into exile by Franco as well as Jews and anti-fascists expelled from Hitler's Germany found refuge in Mexico. After Pinochet's overthrow of Salvador Allende, Chileans sought safety here and during the torture-junta in Buenos Aires, Argentinians fled to Mexico. Mexico has since

communist Ramón Mercader, acting on the orders of the Soviet secret service, succeeded in assassinating Trotsky after having insinuated himself as a friend of the household. The exiled Soviet leader's ashes are preserved in an urn in the garden of his house in Coyoacán, now a museum.

In 1939, after Mexico and the Soviet Union were the only countries to recognize the Republic during the Spanish civil war, President Cárdenas announced that Mexico was ready to accept Republicans fleeing from Franco. Among these were a high percentage of art-

accepted many political and economic refugees from El Salvador and Guatemala.

One of the first to take advantage of the generosity of the Mexican government under Lázaro Cárdenas was Leon Trotsky. The founder of the Red Army and his wife Natalia Sedova found refuge from Stalin's persecution in Mexico City – at first with the painters Diego Rivera and Frida Kahlo who were husband and wife. Later Trotsky moved into a house in the suburb of Coyoacán which he had fortified. But in spite of all his security measures, he was nearly killed in an attack by an armed commando of communists under the direction of muralist David Alfaro Siqueiros. Three months later, the Catalan

ists, scientists, and intellectuals who have enriched the country's cultural life. Fritz Pohle, in his book *The Mexican Exile*, notes that not only humanitarian reasons lay behind Mexico's immigration policies. One of the demographic objectives of the Mexican state has been the increase of the number of *mestizos* among the population through the assimilation of foreigners, an objective the Spanish seemed most likely to guarantee. Indeed, they became integrated relatively quickly. Even before the Spanish Civil War, refugees with skills and qualifications had been privileged for economic reasons, since they were needed to further the country's development.

In view of the desperate refugee situation created by the outbreak of World War II in Europe, many European émigrés arrived in Mexico after hazardous journeys of many kinds. Among them were several prominent German writers and journalists who, with the administration's consent, made Mexico the center of anti-Nazi resistance in Latin America. The journal *Freies Deutschland*, which began in November 1941, published the texts of authors living in Mexico: Anna Seghers, Ludwig Renn, Paul Westheim, Egon Erwin Kisch, and others.

Most of the refugees lived in Mexico City, since the climate of the high-lying metropolis was pleasant for the Europeans. As the country's political and cultural center, the city had more possibilities open to him than an illiterate native moving from the countryside to the city. Bruno Frei wrote the following recollection in his autobiography (*Der Papiersäbel*): "From our windows in newly built apartments on the city's edge, we could see the viscera of the city. The real Mexico consisted of barrack settlements where the Indio woman wrapped her newborn children in rags, held it up to the Mexican sun to ensure survival. Hardly a single day went by that a man with saddened eyes didn't leave the barracks with a roughly constructed child's coffin. Although our stone house was a slum, it seemed like a palace to the Indio children."

Other authors have also written about their exile in Mexico. Egon Erwin Kisch's book

was also the communications link to the outside world. Finally, the exiled found better living and working conditions here than they could have found in the Mexican provinces.

Most of them lived in what, by their standards, were modest conditions, but compared to the poverty around them, conditions which were quite privileged. Many European immigrants found cheap lodgings in former maids' rooms under the roofs of the city, but none of them had to work as servants. The penniless European refugee in exile in Mexico

**Left, President Cárdenas with Spanish refugees.
Above, Leon Trotsky and Natalia Sedova in their refuge in Coyoacán.**

Entdeckungen in Mexiko (Discoveries in Mexico) appeared in 1945 from El Libro Libre (The Free Book) Publishers, and remains very instructive even today. Twenty years after his return, he published two poetic stories about Mexico: *Chrisanta* and *Das Wirkliche Blau* (The Genuine Blue). Of those exiled who stayed in Mexico, some have devoted their efforts to the service of the country. The art historian Paul Westheim produced an inimitable description of ancient Mexican art in his *The Sculpture of Ancient Mexico* (Doubleday 1963). Gertrude de Duby, originally from Switzerland and now in Chiapas, has dedicated her energies to the Lacandon Indians and the protection of the tropical rainforest. ∎

Muralismo – the art of political and public wall-painting – is a child of the 1910 Mexican Revolution. Following the spontaneous uprising of the masses, a fundamental renewal of Mexican culture was to fill the ideological vacuum. Art was afforded a particular function: to communicate to the people an awareness of their own history. Artists were encouraged into the public domain, to address themselves directly to the people, in much the same way as they had been by the Italian Renaissance and colonial art movement. The Minister for Education, José Vasconcelos, took on the role of concerned patron and made available a series of centrally located buildings for artists' murals.

Testing ground: In 1922 the Escuela Nacional Preparatoria became the testing ground for the first phase of Muralismo. Formerly the Jesuit College of San Ildefonso, this magnificent churrigueresque construction dates from the 18th century. The themes that would later become hallmarks of Muralismo – the clashes with the conquistadors, Mexico's social and cultural problems – are already discernible in the murals here.

Diego Rivera's *The Creation* in the main hall reveals hints of Gauguin and Renoir, but also Renaissance influences. Inspired by the philosophy of Vasconcelos, it takes the form of an allegory of a cosmic race born from a symbiosis of American peoples and cultures.

If the rapt mood of *The Creation* brings to mind elements of Magic Realism, the murals in the stairwell and courtyard pertain more directly to Mexico. They arise out of a process of internal debate, whereby differing contextual and stylistic positions make themselves felt.

Jean Charlot has taken as his theme a Spanish atrocity, the *Massacre of Templo Mayor*. Just as traces of Uccello are perceptible in this mural, then Fernando Leal's

Feast of the Lord of Chalma opposite it suggests the proximity of both Impressionism and Realism.

Finally we come to José Clemente Orozco, who leans more toward the Expressionists. For Orozco, the Spanish conquest was essential to the birth of a new nation. Mexico grew out of the synthesis of two traditions, a condition that finds expression in a scene in which Cortéz and his Indian wife Malinche stand triumphant beside a defeated Indian.

For Orozco, Mexico's history is one of high tragedy and conflict. But he is also given to underlying symbolism: a comforting embrace from a corpulent monk for a half-starved Indian remains the ambivalent gesture of a victor.

Orozco's cycle of murals in the courtyard (1923–27) depicts the several stations of proletarian life in contrast to other sectors of society: the drudgery of work, the extravagances of the rich, the frantic activity of political agitators, fraternal feuding and the futility of struggle. Scenes like *The Trenches* and *Revolutionary Trinity* are, in his hands, unmistakably symbols of defeat.

Placard art: Grief and protest tend to dominate Orozco's work whereas Diego Rivera, in the nearby Ministry of Education (Secretaría de Educación Pública, SEP), celebrates the people's victory. His giant cycle of murals (1923–28) divided over two courtyards is an encyclopedic view of Mexican life. It devotes itself to conditions in pre-revolutionary Mexico, and the fate of the farmers and miners whose freedom was won in the revolution. As a reaction to Orozco's pessimism, it can be seen as representing the beginning of an era of happiness and justice, with the victorious revolutionary trinity of worker, farmer and soldier showing the people the way forward.

With this work Rivera is reinterpreting the Mexican Revolution from a Marxist perspective, a standpoint which simultaneously indulges a Utopian impulse and is used to correct history. His work is didactic and confrontational. Fat capitalists and larger-

Preceding pages: Orozco's mural *Catharsis* in the Supreme Court. Left, the dynamic metaphorical and visual language used by artist Siqueiros in the Polyforum.

than-life heroes of the revolution are set up as stereotypical opposites. Good and evil are immediately apparent to the viewer. There are clear stylistic parallels with the true-to-life tendencies of the New Realists. At the same time, Rivera makes references to Courbet and Rousseau and draws on his own experiences in Paris. That becomes particularly clear in his treatment of Indian rituals and festivals, the Mexican tradition of honoring the dead, the unmistakable atmosphere of the Mexican landscape.

History in paint: Among Rivera's most well-known works is the cycle on the staircase of the National Palace (1929–35), a deliber-

ately wide panorama of Mexican history from its earliest beginnings to the present day. Here, too, good and evil take the shape of unambiguous social forces and symbolic figures. The Spanish conquest is portrayed as a violent offensive against a peaceful land, in which even Indians fought on the side of the conquerors (Tlaxcalteken, who hoped by allying himself with the Spanish to free himself from the Aztec yoke).

The Spanish are caricatured as being motivated by greed, with the exception of those who defended the Indians, like the bishop Bartolomé de las Las Casas and Vasco de Quiroga. Scenes from the struggle for independence, the war against the United States and the French invasion, episodes from the revolution and contemporary life blend into one massive history lesson.

Rivera strives for an identification between the viewer and his heroes: national heroes like Morelos the priest, and liberal president Benito Juárez are immediately recognizable to the Mexican public – Rivera based his figures on famous portraits. As clearly as Rivera states his sympathy for the Aztec resistance, his standing toward the modern predicament of the Indians remains unclear. Tribal culture may have formed the roots of national tradition, but it has to bow to industrial progress. How far Rivera's ambivalent view of history contributes towards creating its own myth is evident in a series of smaller murals in the main hall of the National Palace. The Aztec capital Tenochtitlán, a kind of pre-Columbian Atlantis, here appears as the Garden of Eden.

These works are based on what was for Rivera another important source of creativity – his archaeological studies and collaboration with anthropologists. Rivera illustrated the Mayans' holy book, *Popul Vuh*, and built up an extensive personal collection of pre-Columbian art, which is now to be found in a museum in Anahuacalli, which was conceived by the artist himself, in the city's Coyoacán district.

Dream in the park: Rivera's mural *Sunday Reverie in the Alameda* (1947–48), in the foyer of the Hotel del Prado on Alameda Park, marked the high point of his career. This traditional Mexican hotel was badly damaged in the earthquake, but before it was demolished the mural was rescued and given an exhibition space of its own on Avenida Juárez. It has the effect of a burning glass in uniting vital events from Mexican history, although it only starts from the colonial times. Half a century after its creation, it still draws regular crowds of admirers.

Starting on the left, the period of Spanish rule is represented by the burning of a heretic at the stake, and by portraits of Bishop Zumárraga and the religious poet Sor Juana Inés de la Cruz. Prominent 19th-century Mexican historical figures follow, Emperor

Iturbide and Santa Anna overshadowed by Benito Juárez and his liberal comrades-in-arms. A plaque refers to the Reform Laws of 1857, which heralded a fundamental secularization of Mexican society.

Rivera portrays himself as a son of the popular illustrator José Guadalupe Posada and Catrina, a *calavera* woman (Posada's famous skeleton motif). With this he allies himself with a long-established Mexican tradition, for the *calavera* reached a wide audience in pre-revolutionary Mexico through woodcuts. Behind Rivera appear the revered Cuban poet José Martí and Frida Kahlo, Rivera's wife and a distinguished painter in

A unifying theme is provided by the representative masses in the foreground, with their balloons, sweets and fruit – symbols of a living culture in which fantasy is still part of everyday reality. The action is set within the framework of the Alameda Park on the edge of the old town, laid out in the 16th century, and its architectural backdrop. The whole work, with its futuristic mood, combines elements of the art of social criticism, Magic Realism and popular culture, whose Indian roots are essential to an understanding of a particularly distinctive form of Mexican ambiance.

In addition, there is a glistening, dream-

her own right, whose work can be admired in the house in suburban Coyoacán where she and Rivera lived for many years. Then come scenes from the Revolution, with dictator Porfirio Díaz and the mainstays of his regime, as well as a group of armed Zapatistas, and finally, on the far right, the liberal president Francisco Madero, who was at the time a revolutionary martyr.

Left, Rivera's revolutionary trinity. **Above**, viewers experience the world according to Siqueiros from a revolving platform in the Polyforum.

like quality to the light, which casts a spell over the whole mural. This capacity for assimilating material from so many different sources is one of the fundamental characteristics of mural painting. In his best works, Rivera succeeds in blending Mexican and European heritages to create a new quality.

Walls of horror: If Orozco relied on the visual traditions of his people to spread his ideas into a national art, he also recognized early on that an abstract critique of capitalism sold well. In the face of World War II, the abuse and defilement of humanity and ubiquitous violence, he developed an aesthetic of horror, at times reminiscent of Goya. His cycle of murals in the stairwell of the Supreme Court (1941) on the south side of the national palace are a stinging pastiche of society's hidden evils. The angel of justice sits in judgement on the henchmen of a corrupt judiciary. A new humanity rises from the cathartic flames.

Orozco developed this theme during the years 1942–44 in a series of murals in the church of the Hospital de Jesús (where Avenida República del Salvador meets Pino Suárez), founded in 1528 by Hernán Cortéz. While Orozco's vision of the apocalypse was still in the planning stage, the Church was secularized. The Christian theme became instead a permanently relevant expression of accusation and prosecution, a sign of protest against the terror and suffering that had been brought down upon mankind. The beast and the apocalyptic wife, the demons of darkness and destruction, are symbols of imminent danger. Orozco's art is a revolution of conscience, remote from all ideological handicaps.

Master of the mural: In contrast to this uncompromising disillusionment, a third master of the mural, David Alfaro Siqueiros strove for a political clarity. Thus he is less concerned with giving a detailed reconstruction of pre-Columbian history than celebrating individual heroes who have been seen to uphold the revolutionary cause. In his mural *Cuauhtémoc versus the Legends* (1944) in the Tecpan of Tlatelolco, a colonial building near the Plaza of Three Cultures, the Aztec hero is portrayed as the victor over the conquistador centaurs. Here too the actual course of Mexican history is reinterpreted to create a Utopian vision of the past, a technique which is in evidence in some of the artist's other works, for example the mural *Patrician and Patricide* (1945–72) in the stairwell of the baroque Customs House located on Plaza Santo Domingo.

Always an avid experimentalist, Siqueiros was responsible for introducing new materials and techniques to mural painting, including synthetic paints and the spray gun. His mural *Portrait of the Bourgeoisie* (1939) on the stairs of the Electricity Company (located at 45 Antonio Casa) is the product of his experiences in the Spanish Civil War. Its dynamic structure is reminiscent of the formal principles of futurism. The central image is that of a torch-swinging, parrot-faced political activist. The monster, intended to symbolize fascist propaganda, is seen whipping up the brown shirts into a frenzied attack on ordinary life.

A new aesthetic: The effectiveness of murals lies not only in the breadth of their vision but also the public controversies which they trigger. Their ambivalence lies above all in the fact that they make a critical claim while at the same time being dependent on public support. Many commissions only came about through the state's need to legitimize itself. Early on, individual artists warned of the dangers of fossilizing "a waxworks of Mexican nationalism" (Octavio Paz).

There was a steady stream of exciting innovations in technique, style and subject matter. Murals appeared in government ministries, schools, churches and hospitals throughout the capital. Within 50 years, thousands of works were created of widely differing standards. Ironically enough, in fact, mural painting came to be threatened more by the cheap mass production of imitations and reproductions of the great masters than by any over-protectiveness exhibited by the state authorities.

As a reaction to the official version of mural art, a new aesthetic concept developed. The second generation of muralists turned with renewed vigor to local culture, but also to universal themes. The integration of mural painting into modern architecture provided further innovative impetus, and was to become even more important after the upturn in the Mexican economy. The murals and reliefs in the Centro Médico and in the new University City were the most important forerunners of this trend.

A new factor began to appear in the debate over cultural identity, one which was only too aware of its own possibilities. In his 4,000-sq. meter (43,057-sq. ft) mosaic (1949–51) in volcanic rock on the main university library, for example – an attention-grabbing position – Juan O'Gorman outlines Mexico's contribution to world culture. The four sides of the cube are decorated with allegories and symbols of pre-Columbian culture, of the colonial period and Europe, as well as of independent Mexico and the university itself. In terms of its content, the human interest tends to eclipse the polemic of the formative phase.

The move toward modernism took a variety of paths. Siqueiros sought to preserve the revolutionary impetus in a new use of form. His *Polyforum Cultural* (1965–72) next to the Hotel de México (junction of Avenidas Insurgentes Sur and Filadelfia) is dedicated to mankind's march through history and combines architecture, relief, sculpture and wall painting. It is used as a center for revitalized strength and renewed energy.

World example: Those who are interested in learning about the significant trends in mural painting can do so in the Palacio de Bellas Artes. On the top floor are murals by Rivera, Siqueiros and Orozco. Alongside are works by other masters, most notably Rufino Tamayo, who provided an early challenge to the "three greats." His mural *Birth of our Nation* (1952–53) is a powerful synthesis of pre-Columbian Indian legends and symbols and the vocabulary of modern art. Mexico's contribution to world art stems from this same technique. Another contributory facet was a geometric trend, tending toward the

multicultural performances of various kinds and always has folk art on display.

While the interior consists of a dynamic, voluminous relief frieze of the martyrdom of the masses, which the viewer confronts from a rotating platform, the exterior is made up of a series of murals bearing motifs from both Mexican and world history. Hope for overcoming conflict appears in the shape of the legend of the new man. From the center of the intricate ceiling frieze, he glows full of

Above, *Sunday Reverie in the Alameda* is the title of this mural by Diego Rivera.

abstract, represented by Carlos Mérida, Mathias Goeritz and Manuel Felguérez, not to mention a movement of young political artists whose work was largely a reaction to actual events.

For all the contradictions of its "dualistic and static view of history" (according to Octavio Paz), the art of mural painting has provoked debate about the future of the nation. It has become a model of cultural identification, and for visitors it provides an invitation to search beyond the inconsistencies and look into the very heart of this fascinating country.

What Mexican isn't an artist? This is the home of artists in corn, artists of the *taco* and the *quesadilla*, who use their hands to create the most original delicacies, and of the roadside cooks, offering an amazing variety of food in the open street. We are men of corn, part of a corn society. Our culture is a corn culture, based on corn as opposed to wheat. We build pyramids and observatories, we make gods of sound and stone, gods hidden still behind the altars of our land.

Cantinflas, actresses like Dolores del Río, painters like Frida Kahlo. They all drew inspiration from the city's rich mythical tradition: "la Malinche," the founding of Tenochtitlán, the visions of the Virgin of Guadalupe on the hill at Tepeyac, the labyrinths of man's lonely existence... There's no artist who wouldn't come here to drink from such a deep well. In Mexico City, the artist quickly learns total, uncompromising dedication to his art.

The three great muralists – Orozco, Rivera and Siqueiros – turned the walls of the city's

We corn types are more creative than others. But the only place that we can hope to gain recognition is in the capital. There's no chance of becoming successful anywhere in the provinces.

Jalisco is a case in point: a province that has given birth to an unusual number of Mexico's most prominent countrymen: José Clemente Orozco, Juan Rulfo, Juan José Arreola, Agustén Yanez. But Mexico City draws people like a magnet, just as Paris did for a time when it was the capital of the world. Writers like Carlos Fuentes grew up on the streets of the city, together with poets like Octavio Paz, who was born in the district of Mixcoac, comedians from the slums like

palaces into one endless painting, which set out to show the people their history and make them proud of their past. José Vasconcelos, Minister for Culture at the time, swamped the country with editions of the classics, in the hope that the *campesinos* would take to reading Plato and St Augustine. Thanks to him, many Mexicans were baptized Socrates, Parménides, Temistocles and Arquimedes.

The *estridentistas* or "Extremists," strongly influenced by the Dadaists, sought to take the mechanization of the city to its limits by giving it futuristic designs like those in Fritz Lang's seminal film *Metropolis*.

The *contemporáneos*, inspired by their muse Antonieta Rivas Mercado (who committed suicide before the main altar of Notre Dame), composed perfect sonnets, while European modernism was introduced into Mexico by the likes of Salvador Novo, a master of language, the chemist and poet Jorge Cuesta, an extraordinary character of strong contrasts, the alchemist Gilberto Owen, Jaime Torres Bodet and Carlos Pellicer, poet and historian of the Olmec era, Enrique Gonzáles Martinez and Xavier Villaurrutia, the most talented of them all.

According to Octavia Paz, our civilization has never been so blind as when the intellectuals used to meet in Café Paris and allow themselves to be captivated by the beautiful María Asúnsolo and her cousin Dolores del Río. Yet in World War II, the *Taler de la Gráfica Popular* (Workshop of Popular Art) filled every street corner with black and white prints opposing fascism and tyranny.

Mexico took in many refugees from war-torn Spain as well as the rest of Europe. Many great figures landed here: painters, authors, film directors like Eisenstein, writers like Anna Segher, Katherine Ann Porter, Graham Greene, D.H. Lawrence, Léon Felipe, André Breton, Léon Trotsky (who was murdered in Coyoacán), Luis Buñuel, Antonin Artaud, who used to experiment with hallucinogenic mushrooms, Jean Charlot, assistant to Diego Rivera and a muralist in his own right, historians like Ralph Roeder, author of the essential work *Juárez and his Mexico*, archaeologists and anthropologists like Rolf Stavenhagen, who – like the travelers Alexander von Humboldt and Egon Erwin Kisch before him – contributed a fund of knowledge about Mexico which has become a precious treasure. Alejandra Kollontai and the photographer Tina Modotti are other famous names to have fallen under Mexico's spell, leaving behind them a culture we now regard as our own.

There are other artists living on our streets: the *evangelistas* under the arches of the Plaza San Domingo, who tap out letters on old Remington typewriters – and make glorious grammatical mistakes. Their clients dictate the text, which the typists then embellish with flowery turns of phrase and protestations of love. The "evangelists" of San Domingo are our *literati*. Mexicans, many of whom are unable to write themselves, queue for hours outside their makeshift offices. They'll send letters to your loved one, letters to your family,

even petitions to the Pope or the president, although you'll never get a reply.

Then there are the basket makers and the flower arrangers, the folk singers and the *mariachis*. Their name comes from the French word "marriage," since they used to perform mainly at weddings. With their amorous guitars, trumpets, violins and violas, the *mariachis* have the power to transport the listener to another world. In the past they were hired by budding Romeos to serenade their darling Juliet beneath her balcony.

Today there are no more Romeos, and those who want to hear *ranchero* songs or sentimental ballads have to go along to Tenampa, where the artists of the strings will weave enchantment all night long with their

sad chords and melancholy lamenting: "Ay, ay, ay, ay, sing, don't cry, for song, ay, ay, ay, ay, will make your heart light."

Pickpockets on the buses and the Metro are artists too, as are the bureaucrats shuffling papers, or the teachers in front of their classes. But none is a greater artist than the *merolico* – the trader hawking natural remedies in the market place. He's more persuasive than José Luis Cuevas or Octavio Paz when extolling the virtues of his corn ointment, potions to ward off the "evil eye" or cure sudden unexplained lameness, or medicinal herbs that he says induce instant abortion. Small wonder he is so popular in a vast city with so many glaring social inequalities. ∎

Mexico City has a long tradition of artists both celebrated and unsung. Left, Rufino Tamayo. Right, José Luis Cuevas.

TACOS AND CHILI: CULINARY MEXICO CITY

No visitor should miss the pleasure of Mexican cuisine or fail to sample Mexican delicacies. The wide variety of dishes stems from an intermixing of different eating habits and has some surprises even for those who think they know all about it.

The country's real culinary art has little in common with what is commonly known abroad as Mexican cuisine. Outside the country's borders one rarely finds such familiar menu specialties as *caldo tlalpeño* (a tasty

corner, but you should be careful when first trying Mexican cooking. If you want to avoid "Montezuma's revenge," don't subject your stomach to excessive strain.

The many different types of *chile* peppers are an ubiquitous part of Mexican cuisine. The Aztec Indians of Mexico and the South American Incas domesticated the chili plant about seven thousand years ago, but it is only in recent years that the flavors and uses of these many varieties have been defined for

chicken soup with avocado and vegetables), *tamales* (maize semolina croquettes), or *chiles en nogada* (peppers in a nut sauce with pomegranate seeds).

Mexico City offers a broad culinary spectrum as well as a wide price range. It ranges from the simple *taco* (a rolled maize pancake that is usually filled with meat), to the *comida corrida* (a three-course *menu de jour*), to the exquisite *mole poblano* (chicken in a dark sauce which is prepared with more than 17 ingredients – the most suprising of which is chocolate). One should definitely try the *taquerías* which can be found on any street

people outside those cultures. Columbus carried some chili plants back to Europe where Spain and Portugal adopted the chili for some dishes and passed the plants on to India and Africa where they were eagerly incorporated into the native foods. Chilis are used as spicy garnishes and very sharp condiments in cold sauces (*salsa verde, roja* or *Mexicana*) or stuffed with meat or cheese (*chile relleno de carne* or *de queso*). If you should find them too spicy, the best antidote is a *tortilla* (maize pancake) which is a surer way than an icy glass of water to neutralize a burning tongue.

Chile mulato and *chile pasilla* are similar to one another, both being nearly black when they are dried. *Pasilla* is an ingredient in one of the great dishes of Mexico City – *caldo tlalpeño*, a soup which includes chicken and avocado (*see previous page*). *Mulato* is an essential ingredient for *mole* sauce.

Tortilla is the staple food of the population, and forms part of practically every meal, not only as a side dish, but also as a main course: as rolled *tacos* with all sorts of fillings such as meat, vegetables, spices, cheese, etc.; as *enchiladas* with tomato and chili sauce; or roasted as *tostadas*.

Rice (*arroz*) and brown beans (*frijoles*) are

onions and tomatoes, fresh coriander and lemon juice), a Mexican delicacy.

There are many drinks to go with this fine food. A *tequila con sangrita* (agave spirit and a glass of spicy tomato juice) is an aperitif that can be recommended. A local wine or one of the many superb Mexican beers will go with any meal. Fruit and scented waters (*aguas naturales*) made from tamarind, melons, limes, guavas, hibiscus (*jamaica*), etc., are also particularly good thirst quenchers.

The list of Mexican restaurants in the capital (and remember that one eats relatively late in Mexico City) is inexhaustible, and it

the most common side dishes. *Puntas de filete* (fillet ends), *carne asada à la tampiqueña* (a juicy strip of broiled beef) and *huachinango à la Veracruzana* (red bass prepared according to a Veracruz recipe) are only a few select main dishes.

The curious should also try a cactus leaf salad (*ensalada de nopales*) or the crisp fried agave worms (*gusanos de maguey*) with *guacamole* (avocado paste with chopped

Preceding pages: a Mexican soup chef. <u>Left</u>, al fresco dining at the Hotel Majestic. <u>Above</u>, in high spirits at the Fonda del Recuerdo.

is difficult to make selection. Many prefer the rich atmosphere offered in the former mansions of old haciendas – favorites with the city's business community – such as the Antiqua Hacienda de Tlalpan, with its wonderful garden, or the Hacienda de los Morales. The Fonda del Recuerdo and the Restaurant Focolare are among those with live Mexican music and typical cuisine. Both offer Veracruzan specialties and folklore expressive of the Mexican's festive character. The Kino Mexikatessen, in the Palanco quarter, specializes in the "exotic" dishes of the pre-Spanish period.

OFF-DUTY IN MEXICO CITY

On Saturdays a sigh of relief runs the length and breadth of the city. Rich and poor alike yearn for the great outdoors. Those who can afford it jet off for two days to the coast, to Acapulco or Cancun, but even the hour's drive to Cuernavaca brings a change of climate. The city slickers indulge themselves here amidst the lush, subtropical vegetation. Since some of the smog has now dispersed over the provinces, the air in the city is more bearable too, and pedestrians are winning back the center.

Relaxing in the parks: There are those who don't have even a clapped-out old banger or *carcacha* to their name to drive the family out to the countryside. So they go walking or camping in the Alameda. Or husband, wife, children, uncles, aunts and grandparents will get together for a picnic in Chapultepec Park. Even before lunch, areas are already marked out with strings of balloons to show there's a children's birthday party taking place later that afternoon.

Children are kings and queens of the park on Sundays. Their little heads dive blissfully into huge mountains of pink candy floss. Spellbound, they watch the traders' brightly-colored windmills spinning. Their laughter rings out from a circle gathered around a clown, drawn there by the merry sound of his penny whistle. They can ride through the zoo on the miniature train, be rowed around the park on the artificial lake, or have their photos taken on a wooden horse, dressed as mini-revolutionaries.

On the *montana rusa,* the massive roller-coaster in the Pleasure Park (Parque de Diversiones) in the southern part of Chapultepec, parental screams compete with those of their offspring. It's a colorful change for people who spend their everyday life between gray city walls. Everyone needs some fun – adults too.

Another place to spend holidays and get

Preceding pages: taking a break on a park bench. Left, homage to King Football against the majestic backdrop of Popocatépetl.

closer to nature is Xochimilco. On Sundays the packed gondolas (*trajineras*) are propelled nose to tail along the canals. People pack huge hampers of food and crates of drink, or buy hot *tacos* and cold drinks from the *canoas* paddling up and down. Flower sellers, ice-cream sellers and steaming food stalls are all part of the service. Other boats sway along the water, filled with photographers and *mariachi* bands with their violins and trumpets, who'll tag along behind your boat for a few songs. Sometimes you'll meet another boat carrying a *marimba*, a large Caribbean xylophone, to make a Mexican pot-pourri. "Ay, ay, ay, ay – sing, don't cry."

women's sides – regularly fight it out on the dusty pitches alongside the highway.

This land was previously the bed of a lake. The suburb has developed from a giant slum into an established satellite town, and it is now the home of a huge stadium, where the top clubs in the national league play their matches. Visitors who want to see top-class Mexican professionals in a football match should find out who is playing on Saturday and Sunday afternoon in the Azteca, Universitario and Neza stadiums.

Football *à la mexicana* is whatever the players and spectators choose to make of it. The *ola*, the crowd "wave" around the sta-

King football: Many *chilangos* (city dwellers) are so exhausted by the time the weekend arrives that they want no more than to swing gently in a hammock between two trees in Chapultepec Park. Others turn to sport to let off steam – either as active participants or committed spectators. Join the convoy down Avenida Zaragoza heading toward the Puebla highway, and at Nezahualcoyotl you can sample what has become Mexico's favorite sport: football, the imported game which has become the opium of the masses. At "Neza" alone, well over 100 amateur teams – including several

dium was invented by the fans of player Hugo Sánchez.

The old Mexicans were early masters of the art of staying on the ball, even before the Europeans invaded. Their sport of *tlachtli* was in no way "just a game" but a fundamentally serious matter. The ball symbolized the sun and the team which let the sun go down – i.e. dropped the ball on the ground – was sacrificed to the gods. The rubber ball, considerably smaller in size than today's football, was not allowed to be touched with feet or hands, only with the elbows, knees, hips and bottom, but these parts of the body were protected with leather or cloth padding. The major attraction of the game, however – for only the nobility were allowed to play – seems to have been in the betting that accompanied it. Huge sums changed hands, sometimes in the form of gold, feathers, clothes – even slaves – and many unfortunate gamblers found themselves ruined for life.

Bullfighting: The Mexicans came up against the ritualistic nature of the *tlachtli* in some of the games introduced by the Spanish, for example bullfighting, also a matter of life and death. All debate for and against is futile, for the *aficionados* – those avid followers of bullfighting – are deaf to criticism. Those

The Plaza México seats 50,000 spectators, which makes it the largest bullfighting arena in the world. From December through to May, the best matadors display their courage and grace in this ring. During the summer months, the *novilleros* use the Plaza México to practise their routines.

It is far from easy to get a seat in the shade because, like the grand opera, seats at the Plaza México are booked on a season-ticket basis. You will find plenty of women and children in the audience and you may well end up sitting next to some delicate bourgeois housewife, who when asked whether she comes to these things often, says proudly:

who go to a bullfight just once, drawn by curiosity and a desire for spectacle, are unlikely to understand much of what goes on and will wonder why the deep, reverential, admiring "Olé" rises at precisely the same moment from a thousand throats.

But for the open-minded spectator, the atmosphere in the imposing Plaza México and all the trappings of the event should prove fascinating, giving as they do a brief insight into the soul of the Mexican people.

Left, "Helados!" is a welcome cry. **Above**, the line-up for the *charreada*, the Mexican rodeo.

"I've been coming since I was a girl."

Dress tends toward two different styles: classical Spanish with flat-brimmed black hat or Basque cap, and the Mexican *ranchero* look, with boots and cowboy hats. As bottles are forbidden in the arena on safety grounds, people make do with Spanish leather flasks, which they hold at arm's length in traditional style, aiming a stream of red wine into their open mouths.

Punctually at four in the afternoon a trumpet fanfare sounds and the *corrida de toros* begins with the ceremonial entry (*paseo*) of the *toreros*, all dressed in their tight-fitting, gold-embroidered suits. They are followed by their helpers on horseback, the *picadores*, then the *banderilleros* and others whose task it is to drag the dead bull from the ring by three white horses. The bull storms into the ring, and it is first teased by the *capeadores*, who wave their *capas* (short bullfighters' capes). This skirmishing is followed by the *suerte de varas*, in which the *picadores* on horseback attack the bull with lances, thrusting them into his back. From this point onwards, anyone who can't stand the sight of blood should concentrate instead on the crowd's reaction.

In the next part of the fight, the *bande-*

"cross" – the vulnerable spot between his shoulder blades – is laid bare. If the *torero* strikes this exact spot, the bull is fatally wounded. His death throes may carry on for a while, but they don't appear to hold much interest for the crowd.

The fight is over with that fatal thrust: the spectators stand, the men light themselves fat cigars and the women nibble on pistachios or eat ice cream. This is perhaps the most gruesome part of the whole bullfight.

The ritual is repeated six times in one *corrida*, each of the three *toreros* competing against two bulls. The matador is not always the victor. Sometimes the 500-kg (1,100-lb)

rilleros shower the bull's neck with three pairs of *banderillas* (long, barbed sticks decorated with bright ribbons). Sometimes the *torero* will join in at this point, before demonstrating the full extent of his skills in the *hora de la verdad* – the hour of truth. With his cape (*capote*) the *torero* leads the bull around in tight circles, rewarded by suitable applause from the crowd for particularly daredevil maneuvers bringing the bull close to the body.

It is crucial that he picks the right moment for the fatal thrust. The bull's head has to be lowered, his feet close together, so that the

bull catches him on his horns and the victory falls to the tormented not the tormentor.

Noble *charreadas*: The *charros* also put their manly prowess on public display at the Mexican rodeo or *charreada*. At the risk of insulting them, you could compare these gentlemen to North American cowboys. They share a common background as professional cattleherds, whose skill in handling horses and the lasso makes a stunning display north or south of the border.

The Spanish introduced horses and cattle to Mexico, and the traditional *charro* suit, with decorative silver buttons on the trousers and a short jacket, brings to mind the festival costume of the men of Salamanca on mainland Spain, while the sombrero resembles the wide-brimmed Andalusian hat. To the rest of the world, the proud *charro* is the popular image of a Mexican.

Charreadas are a fashionable sport in Mexico City nowadays, based around specialist clubs. For the participants, they are an expensive form of entertainment, because the horses have to be stabled and the *charro* costume, along with the elaborately decorated saddle and bridle, are unbelievably expensive. For spectators in the *lienzos charros*, the *charreada* arena on the outskirts of the city, entry is usually free.

The *jaripeo* tournament begins with the *cola de caballo*: riders enter the ring at a gallop, then bring their horses to an abrupt standstill, before turning them in a circle. Then, in a maneuver known as *coleadero*, they seize the cattle by the tail and try to throw them off balance by whirling them round. They demonstrate their skill with a lasso by rounding up wild horses, and the climax of the show comes with the daring leap from the back of a galloping horse onto an untamed wild horse. Women riders also take part in *charreadas*, although they have their own competitions and elegant side-saddles – no doubt so that they don't risk stealing the men's limelight.

Place your bets: Punters desperate for a gamble would do best heading for the race course, the Hipódromo de las Américas (Tuesday and Thursday through Sunday). There is also betting at the Basque jai-alai game in Frontón México (Plaza de la República), open every evening except Monday and Friday. This is probably the world's fastest ball game, involving either eight individual players or eight pairs. The ball is hurled and caught using banana-shaped baskets (*cestas*) and is only allowed to touch the ground or the wall once. Betting plays a large part in the activities and the gamblers, too, use a ball – a tennis ball with a slit in it to hold their stake which they throw to the bookie.

Other sporting events that the Mexicans get excited about are boxing (Saturday evenings) and *lucha libre*, all-in wrestling. Those who want to put in a spot of training themselves can take a morning jog through Chapultepec Park, or swim, play tennis or golf at one of the expensive private clubs. Some are open to visitors (take your passport and tourist card with you).

The *chilangos* are expert in enjoying themselves without feeling guilty – even in times of economic crisis. They eat out with family or friends in restaurants, where they like to pay musicians to play for them while they sing along to well-known folk songs. Ex-

travagant hosts, they like holding parties, or enjoying themselves at the various sporting events in ring or arena.

Cultural and educational pastimes are available at very little cost, because they are subsidized by the state. Entry to most museums is free on Sundays and theater and concert tickets don't cost the earth. Many make the most of these bargains. Those who have the chance to relax in their hammocks or let off steam in sport and games have refueled their energy by Monday and can hurl themselves back into the hectic everyday of Mexico City with renewed vigor.

Left, glass bottles are banned at bullfights, but there are ways round the problem. **Right**, *toreros* should show daring and grace.

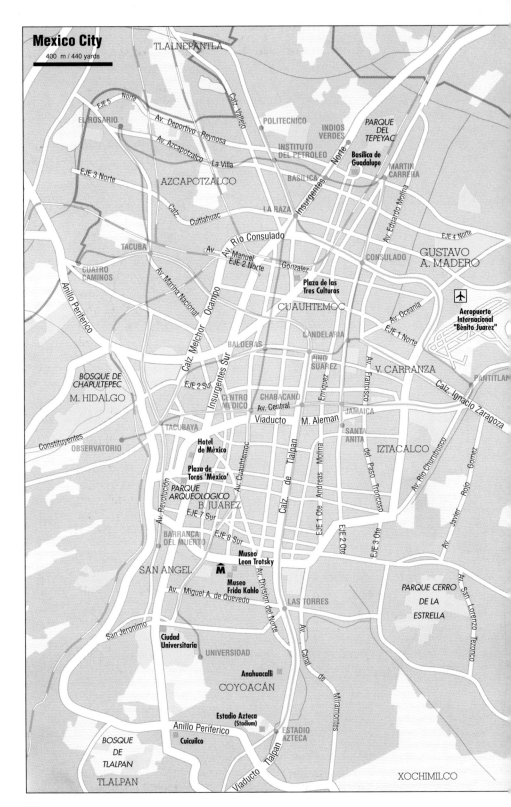

Mexico City

400 m / 440 yards

TLALNEPANTLA

EJE 5 Norte
EL ROSARIO
Av. Deportivo Reynosa
Calz. Vallejo
POLITECNICO
INDIOS VERDES
PARQUE DEL TEPEYAC
Av. Azcapotzalco
La Villa
INSTITUTO DEL PETROLEO
Basílica de Guadalupe
MARTIN CARRERA
EJE 3 Norte
AZCAPOTZALCO
Calz. Cuitlahuac
BASILICA
Av. Eduardo Molina
EJE 4 Norte
LA RAZA
Insurgentes
TACUBA
Av. Río Consulado
CONSULADO
GUSTAVO A. MADERO
Av. Manuel González
EJE 2 Norte
CUATRO CAMINOS
Av. Marina Nacional
Calz. Melchor Ocampo
Plaza de las Tres Culturas
CUAUHTEMOC
Av. Oceania
EJE 1 Norte
Aeropuerto Internacional "Bénito Juarez"
Anillo Periferico
BALDERAS
CANDELARIA
PINO SUAREZ
Av. Francisco
V. CARRANZA
PANTITLAN
BOSQUE DE CHAPULTEPEC
EJE 2 Sur
Insurgentes Sur
CENTRO MEDICO
CHABACANO
Av. Central
Enriquez
Calz. Ignacio Zaragoza
M. HIDALGO
Viaducto
M. Aleman
JAMAICA
SANTA ANITA
IZTACALCO
Av. Río Churubusco
Av. Javier Rojo Gomez
Constituyentes
TACUBAYA
Hotel de México
Av. Cuauhtemoc
Calz. de Tlalpan
Andreas Molina
del Paso Troncoso
OBSERVATORIO
Plaza de Toros 'México'
Av. Revolución
PARQUE ARQUEOLOGICO
B. JUAREZ
EJE 7 Sur
EJE 1 Ote
EJE 2 Ote
EJE 3 Ote
Av. San Lorenzo Tezonco
BARRANCA DEL MUERTO
EJE 8 Sur
Museo Leon Trotsky
SAN ANGEL
Ⓜ
Museo Frida Kahlo
Av. Division del Norte
PARQUE CERRO DE LA ESTRELLA
Av. Miguel A. de Quevedo
LAS TORRES
San Jeronimo
Ciudad Universitaria
UNIVERSIDAD
Anahuacalli
Av. Canal de Miramontes
COYOACÁN
Estadio Azteca (Stadium)
Anillo Periferico
ESTADIO AZTECA
BOSQUE DE TLALPAN
Cuicuilco
Tlalpan
TLALPAN
Viaducto
XOCHIMILCO

PLACES

Flying over the seemingly endless sea of houses into today's Mexico City visitors might wonder how they will possibly find their way around. The reality is that they are likely to stay in a relatively small portion of the metropolis: the area bounded by Chapultepec Park to the west and the Zócalo – that vast plaza which forms the heart of downtown – in the east. Much of the visitor's time will probably be spent close to the main street, the broad and beautiful Paseo de la Reforma which runs from the edge of the park, past the touristy Zona Rosa, and bisects Avenida Juárez beside the downtown Alameda Park. The Reforma has been acclaimed by novelist Octavio Paz as Mexico's "river," a "Seine in cement," and a casual stroll along its wide tree-shaded sidewalks should certainly be on every visitor's schedule.

Vast and verdant Chapultepec Park with its lakes, museums and zoo is another place to unwind from the frenetic pace of this crowded city. Its treasures include the National Museum of Anthropology, which is probably unequalled in the world. At weekends the park is inundated with Mexican families, but it seems big enough to absorb everyone and still retain much of its tranquility.

With its enormous hordes of smoke-belching buses, an efficient if limited subway system and innumerable inexpensive taxis, Mexico City is easy to get around, and there are interesting sights nearby in every direction. To help with your orientation, make an early visit to the top of the Latin American Tower (Torre Latinoamericana) in the center of downtown. Despite the ubiquitous smog it will help you get a better fix on where everything is.

Southwest are Xochimilco's floating gardens and the distinctive architecture of the university. North of the city center is Tlatelolco with its Plaza of Three Cultures bearing witness to the different civilizations which have thrived during the city's history. Even farther north is the shrine of the Virgin of Guadalupe, the Mexican national patron saint.

No visitor should miss exploring the city's *mercados*: the vast Lagunilla or Merced markets selling virtually anything, or such colorful venues as the Saturday-only Bazar del Sábado in suburban San Angel. Bordering on San Angel is Coyoacán, notable for museums devoted to Leon Trotsky and painter Frida Kahlo.

TIPS FOR SHORT TRIPS

Some travelers in Mexico, especially business people, have only time for a short stay in the capital. This chapter aims to help those travelers to use that time to the best advantage.

First, one should definitely get to know the historic city center. To get in the right mood, a good start is a substantial breakfast in Sanborn's famous House of Tiles or in the Café Tacuba, both on the Calle Madero. From there it is a very short walk to the **Zócalo** and the **cathedral**, the **Palacio Nacional** and the excavations of the **Templo Mayor**. The roof terrace of the Hotel Majestic (which also has a good Sunday buffet on offer) has a commanding view of the city's main plaza.

It is also worth walking a few blocks north of the Zócalo to the **Plaza Santo Domingo** with its old hand-set printing presses and itinerant secretaries. En route

along Calle 16 de Septiembre you might like to inspect the Restaurant Prendes which has been the favourite meeting place of Mexican politicians and business people for decades. Nearby, the turn-of-the-century Cantina La Opera is also rich in tradition. It has a genuine Mexican ambiance and is only rarely visited by tourists.

First-rate ballet: Book seats as early as possible in your visit for an orchestral concert or performance by Mexico's brilliant Ballet Folklórico at the **Palacio de Bellas Artes**, the magnificent art deco building which is a lively cultural center. Two blocks north on Hidalgo is the superlative **Museo Franz Mayer**, a private collection of art treasures from the colonial epoch which belonged to a German who emigrated from Mannheim in the 1920s.

The nighttime view from the **Torre Latinoamericana** almost opposite the Bellas Artes Palace is impressive – the sprawling valley seems to be an endless sea of lights.

Next stop after downtown should be the **Zona Rosa**, a classy district of restaurants, cabarets, galleries, jewelers, handicraft shops, and boutiques devoted to fashion and aimed squarely at tourists. It's a pleasant place to relax at sidewalk cafés and watch the life in the big city go by. Buses from downtown run along the Paseo de la Reforma (get off after you cross Insurgentes) and it's a cheap taxi ride.

There is something for everyone, for every age and for every time of day in and around **Chapultepec Park** to the west of the city. Anyone in the least interested in the ancient Indian cultures should definitely visit the **Anthropological Museum** here. Mexican history since the Spanish conquest is unfurled in the **Historical Museum** in the hilltop castle. Three other excellent museums display modern art: Museo de Arte Moderno, Museo Rufino Tamayo and the well-appointed Centro Cultural de Arte Contemporáneo.

Between these attractions there are

Bargaining i
the Bazar de
Sábado

walks in the park, with lakes, the zoo and children's playgrounds. The elegant hotels on the park's perimeter – Camino Real, Nikko and Stouffer Presidente – have live music or international discos in the evenings. The Restaurante del Lago on one of the ponds in Chapultepec Park is the place for a romantic evening with dancing

Weekend specials: If you are here for a weekend, you should visit the **Bazar del Sábado** (Saturday bazaar) in San Angel where you can mingle with the well-informed crowd admiring and buying arts and crafts from all over Mexico. Alternatively, you could take a boat trip along the canals of **Xochimilco** and afterwards have lunch in one of the old *hacienda* restaurants in the south of the city. The cultural center (**Centro Cultural Universitario**) of the national university (UNAM) also lies in this part of the city. Within its precincts are cinemas, theaters, and one of the world's best concert halls called **Sala Nezahualcóyotl**. Also near the university is the

city's biggest shopping center, **Perisur** (closed Monday), where you can find anything from a toothbrush to a tuxedo or a new car.

A lively musical evening can be spent at the **Plaza Garibaldi** where the *mariachi* bands gather, often before performing in the nearby restaurants. The *Mexico City Daily Bulletin*, a free daily newssheet found in most hotels, has information about night clubs, bars with shows and cabarets, and the journal *Tiempo Libre*, available at any newsstand, provides a weekly listing of all the city's cultural events and entertainments. **Teatro Blanquita**, almost opposite the square, is a good variety theater where, of course, all the performances are in Spanish.

Other good nightspots are the places where Caribbean music (*música tropical*) is performed, e.g. the Salón Margo, the Antillanos, the Bar León or the Peñas; night spots with Latin American folk music include the Mesón de la Guitarra, and El Condor Pasa.

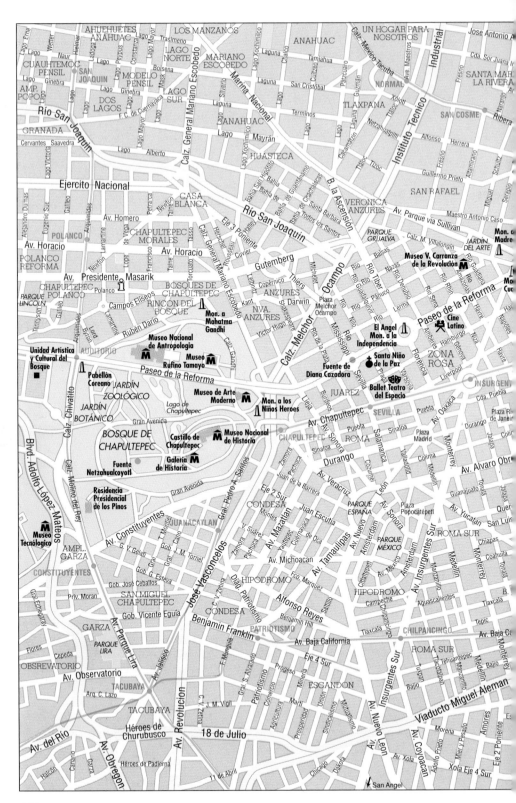

Mexico City Center

800 m / 880 yards

Matamoros
Gonzáles Bocanegra
Jaime Comonfort Nuñó
Camelia
Camelia
orte
Martinez de la Torre
GUERRERO
Mosqueta
Lerdo
Paseo de la Reforma
MORELOS AMPL
Caridad
BUENA VISTA
Jose Maria Iglesias
Buenavista
GUERRERO
Rayón Eje 1 Norte
MORELOS
Centro
Violeta
Zaragoza
Magnolia
Lerdo
Mercado de Alimentos
San Camilito
Mercado Lagumilla
República de Paraguay
Av. del Trabajo
GUERRERO
GUERRERO
Violeta
Mon. Simón Bolívar
República de Peru
Allende
Honduras
Brasil
República de Argentina
Florida
Manuel
Doblado
Gonzaleri
BACALERA
Héroes Ferrocarrileros
Plaza de Garibaldi
República de Perú
Santa Catarina Mártir
Apartado
Peña y Peña
San Fernando
Mina
Da Cartos
Mina
Bel. Domínguez
San Lorenzo
República de Bolivia
San Sebastián Mártir
José Joaquín Herrera
UCION
de San Carlos
San Hipólito
San Juan de Dios
Museo Franz Mayer
Museo Nacional de Arte
Santo Domingo
Palacio de la Inquisición
Carmen
Frontón México
Edison Terán
Av. Hidalgo
Sta. Vera Cruz
Mon. a Donceles Carlos IV
República
Secretaría de Educación Publica
de Venezuela
Plaza de la República
Pinacoteca
HIDALGO
Museo de la Alameda
BELLAS ARTES
ALAMEDA CENTRAL
Palacio de Minería
ALLENDE
Toluca
Museo del Templo Major
Ramírez
Lotería Nacional
Palacio de Bellas Artes
Av. Juárez
5 de Mayo
Nacional Monte de Piedad
Catedral Metropolitana
República de Guatemala
Justo Sierra
EMILIANO ZAPATA
Mon. a Cristobal Colon
Museo de Artes e Industrias Populares
Torre Latino-Americana
La Profesa
Plaza de la Piedad
Santa Inés
MiguelNegrete
U. H.
Av. Morelos
Independencia
Francisco Madero
Palacio de Iturbide
Palacio Nacional
Museo Nacional de las Culturas
Academia de San Carlos
Emiliano Zapata
JUÁREZ
San Francisco
16 de Septiembre
Constitución
Museo Juárez
Soledad
Victoria
Luis Moya
Dolores
República de Uruguay
CENTRO
ZOCALO
Corregidora
ZONA CENTRO
La Ciudadela
Atenas
San José
San Augustín
Palacio de Hierro (Department store)
Mayor
República de Uruguay
Zavala
CANDELARIA
BALDERAS
Ernesto
Pugibet
Vizcaínas
Hosp. y Igl. de Jesus Nazareno
Museo de la Ciudad de México
Gral. Anaya
CANDELARIA DE LOS PATOS
eo
erra
Delicias
Colegio de las Vizcaínas
Mesones
San José de Gracia
Correo
San Pablo
Av. Chapultepec
Arcos de Belen
José María
Izazaga
5 de Febrero
20 de Noviembre
PINO SUAREZ
MERCED
CUAUHTEMOC
SALTO DEL AGUA
ISABEL LA CATOLICA
Cda. del Rosario
Arena México
Fray Servando Teresa de Mier
Isabel
Fray Servando Teresa de Mier
Dr. Lavista
Chimalpopoca
Chimalpopoca
Cda. Canal
MERCED BALBUENA
Dr. Claudio
Lucas Alaman
TRANSITO
Dr. Liceaga
Lucas Alaman
Cjón. San Antonio Abad
Sur 32
Niños Héroes
Bernard
Dr. J. M. Vertiz
Dr. Pascua
Diagonal 20 de Noviembre
ESPERANZA
F. Industrial
Ote. 32
Dr. Juan Navarro
F. Alva Ixtlilxóchitl
Calz. Zoquipa
NIÑOS HEROES
Dr. Andrade
Bolívar
Lorenzo Boturini
San Antonio Abad
Lorenzo Boturini
DOCTORES
Dr. J. Velasco
José T. Cuellar
Alfredo Chavero
Cjón Cuitláhuac
Dr. Erazo
Dr. J. Terres
Manuel M.Flores
BOTURINI
Dr. Olvera
Manuel Othón
SAN ANTONIO ABAD
Dr. Balmis
Manuel Payno
Gutiérrez Náiera
Eje 2 Sur Av. del Taller
AARON SAENZ
HOSPITAL GENERAL
JARDÍN "ARTES GRAFICAS"
OBRERA
Fernando Ramírez
Av. del Taller
PAULINO NAVARRO
R. Aldama
ARTES GRAFICAS
Prof. Roa Bárcenas
Antonio Anza
Dr. Durán
J.M. Roa Bárcenas
VISTA ALEGRE
JAMAICA
Dr. Márquez
I. A. Mateos
Juan A. Mateos
Dr. Norma
Dr. Andrade
Antonio Solís
AMPLIACION ASTURIAS
Calz. Chabacano
Eje 3 Sur
Fray J. Torquemada
CHABACANO
PUEBLO
LAZARO CARDENAS
J. P. Contreras
ALGARIN
G. Esquer
Calz. G. Prieto
JAMAICA
Hernández
A. Plaza Dávalos
Hernández Dávalos
Av. Central
BUENOS AIRES
Dr. Bolaños
J. T. Medina
ASTURIAS
Ventura G. Tena
Viaducto Piedad
SANTA ANITA
CENTRO MEDICO
J. T. Medina
Viaducto Miguel Aleman
SAN FCO. XICALTONGO
STA. ANITA
PARQUE DEL SEGURO SOCIAL
ATENOS SALAS
Casa del Obrero Mundial
VIADUCTO PIEDAD
NVA. STA. ANITA
Casa del Obrero Mundial
UNIDAD ESPERANZA
ALAMOS
Coruña
Coruña
Plan de Ayala
Zapata
Segovia
VIADUCTO
Calz. Sta. Anita
Obregón
Diagonal San
Morena
Victor Hugo
MODERNA
Av. Pdte. P. E. Calles Eje
Av. 4 Sur
Bismark
SAN PEDRO
5 DE DICIEMBRE

121

AROUND THE ZÓCALO

The heart of the largest city in the world is appropriately grand: the **Zócalo**, the main square, which has always been the center of the city and of the entire country. The ruined temples and palaces of the Aztec **Tenochtitlán** lie right next to the square on which now sit the Spanish-built cathedral and government offices from which New Spain was run.

Even before the 15th century, Tenochtitlán was a magnificent city crowded with its 400,000 inhabitants, its great temple the symbolic and physical center of the Aztec empire. By the time the Spaniards arrived, two centuries after its founding, it had been enlarged and rebuilt many times.

The conquistadors, wrote historian Bernal Díaz, "saw things unseen, nor ever dreamed," and he records that four days after his entrance into Mexico, Cortéz and his chief captains were taken by Montezuma "to look at the great city and all the other towns nearby on the lake and the villages built on dry land… This great accursed temple was so high that from the top of it everything could be seen perfectly… So having gazed at all this and reflected upon it we turned our eyes to the great marketplace and the host of people down there who were buying and selling: the hum and murmur of the voices could have been heard for more than a league. And among us were soldiers who had been in many parts of the world… and they said they had never seen a market so well ordered, so large and so crowded with people."

During the reign of the Emperor Maximilian, the square – once the Aztec ceremonial center – was transformed. Trees were planted, a pavilion was built for concerts, a kiosk, candelabras, statues, benches and fountains were imported from Paris to give it the maximum French atmosphere. Now it is a huge flat surface, unimaginably spacious compared to the overcrowding which characterizes the rest of downtown, and the ideal site for festivals, parades and demonstrations. Beside the entrance to the Templo Mayor, dances are held on summer afternoons.

Everyday life for the people unfolds on the Zócalo like a series of picture postcards – an experience that certainly should not be missed. The best overall view is from the rooftop restaurant of the Hotel Majestic (entrance on Madero).

The square's modern name derives from an empty pedestal (in Spanish *zócalo*) erected in 1843 by the dictator Santa Anna for a monument to independence that was never built. After the people began to call the square "Zócalo" the name came to designate the main square in any Mexican city.

The Aztec temple: On February 24, 1978, construction workers discovered a cut stone weighing 8 tonnes, with delicate, well-preserved reliefs, behind the cathedral. According to archaeologists the decapitated figure on the stone is the powerful Aztec moon goddess

Coyolxauhqui. They also discovered that the oval monolith, which is 3.25 meters (10 ft) in diameter, marks the spot where the sacrificial victims, falling from the Great Temple, would hit the ground. Deducing that the **Great Temple of Tenochtitlán** had to be nearby they spent the next four years pulling down historic colonial buildings over a vast area, unearthing temple ruins and more than 6,000 artifacts – testimony not only to the Aztecs' cruel religious rites but also to the size of their empire.

Sculptures from Oaxaca, clay vases from the Guerrero region, burial urns from the Gulf of Mexico, anthropomorphic figurines and fish and shell ornaments – all these were part of the tribute that subjugated tribes had to pay to the Aztecs, who themselves lived primarily from fishing.

The temple sites are best explored following the path which leads to the **Tzompantli**, an altar made of 240 stone skulls representing the walls on which the skulls of the beheaded sacrificial victims were displayed. Note the colorful reliefs that decorate the houses of the "Caballeros Aguila," the Eagle Men, a military caste in Aztec society. A sculptured copy of the moon goddess Coyolxauhqui stands here. The original, whose head first came to light in 1825 in the foundations of a house being built on nearby Santa Teresa Street, is now in the museum of the Templo Mayor, designed by Mexico's famous architect Pedro Ramirez Vazquez, creator of the Museum of Anthropology and History in the Chapultepec Park. Transcending traditional concepts, the **Templo Mayor Museum** avoids display cases so that no glass barrier stands between exhibit and visitor. Unfortunately, none of the information next to the displays is in English.

Coyolxauhqui, an important goddess in Aztec mythology, can be viewed on the first floor or from above on the second floor through an opening. According to legend, she was dismembered by her brother Huitzilopochtli,

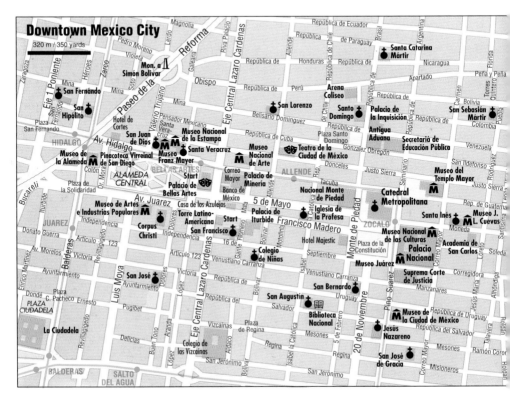

God of War, because she wanted to kill her mother Coatlicue, the earth. It was the aim of the artist who created this relief to show life and death side by side so that at close range, the goddess seems to be both alive and dead at the same time, a seeming contradiction intended to express the antagonisms within the world of the Aztec gods.

The renowned German explorer Baron von Humboldt on a visit to Mexico in 1803, with the aid of his friend the Bishop of Monterrey, had the Coatlicue statue dug from under a foot of earth at the University of Mexico. It was buried there on the orders of the Spanish viceroy, who feared that this "devilish idol" could provoke anarchistic ideas.

Exhibition halls: The museum's eight halls are arranged on four levels around a central patio with the four halls in the southern wing devoted to the legend of Huitzilopochtli, god of war, and to war, sacrifice, tribute and trade. **Hall 1** shows the migration of the Aztecs to their permanent place of settlement in Tenochtitlán; **Hall 2** demonstrates the war and the sacrifices necessary to reconcile the gods and the sun; and **Hall 3** explains tribute and trade as the Aztecs' bases of existence. In **Hall 4** the most important monoliths are on display: the eagle warrior, the god of fire and the eight standard bearers. Some of these showed traces of paint and shell-incrustations on their bodies and obsidian in their eyes when they were discovered. Up to the present day the archaeologists have failed to agree on the significance of this. Some of the recently discovered objects had already been covered by earth and thus forgotten by the time the Spanish arrived.

In the northern wing, the four halls are the realm of Tlaloc, god of fertility and water. Some pieces were found in the area of the Mixtek tribe as far as 560 km (348 miles) away. In the room marked "Fauna" are skeletons of sacrificial animals: crocodiles, turtles, eagles, pumas, poisonous snakes, snails and sharks. The seventh gallery has displays about

The Zócalo, a stage for many events.

everyday life and religion: childbirth, education, the concept of the Aztec universe and the significance of the Great Temple in the cosmology of the Aztecs. Finally, the "Conquista" hall shows the arrival of the conqueror Hernán Cortéz and his followers.

Spanish ceramics and columns built on Aztec structures illustrate the decline and fall of Aztec society. A gold bullion bar reminds us that the conquerors melted gold and precious jewelry to send back home to the motherland.

The **cathedral** of Mexico City is probably the biggest and most important Christian building on the South American continent combining, as it does, the three major architectural styles of the 16th to the 19th century during which it was built: Gothic through Renaissance and baroque to the neoclassical era. The baroque facade is framed by two neoclassical bell towers and the clock tower designed by the architect Manuel Tolsá. The layout of the cathedral is in the shape of a Latin cross, built on a square

109 by 54 meters (358 by 177 ft). Huge and impressive, with a rich repository of decorative art, its somber but magnificent interior is softly illuminated through contemporary stained-glass windows that give off a mellow, golden light.

Recycling the ruins: Hernán Cortéz had the first Christian church on the Plaza Mayor built with materials taken from the Templo Mayor. Up to 1552 the church was Franciscan, but in 1544, archbishop Montúfar began the preliminary work for a new cathedral, modeled on the one in Seville. Although the foundation stone was laid in 1573, only 50 years after the Spanish conquest, it wasn't until a century later that the cathedral could be dedicated. The basalt and limestone facade was completed only in 1689. One hundred years later architect Damian Ortiz de Castro inaugurated the bell towers. Manuel Tolsa finally finished it off, adding a dome and balustrades.

The interior of the cathedral, dedicated to the Virgin Mary, consists of one

The stone of the Coyolxauhqui.

main and two minor naves plus 14 side altars. The most significant work of art in the choir is the **Altar de Pardon** (altar of forgiveness) in the Churrigueresco style, named for the elaborate surface decoration favored by the 18th-century Spanish architect José Churriguera. Some years ago, this altar, together with the cedar-wood choir stalls, was partly destroyed by fire but has since been renovated. The choir-lattice – a mixture of gold, silver, and bronze – comes from China. The prize exhibit is the **Altar de los Reyes** in the apse, carved over a period of 10 years by Jerónimo de Balbas. The *estípites*, pillars which taper off at the base, are typical of the colonial period, and the paintings by Juan Rodriguez Juárez depict the Adoration of the Magi and the Assumption. In the third chapel to the left of the entrance is a statue of the Señor del Cacao to whom the Indians gave cacao – to them it was a valuable currency – as a sacrificial gift for the construction of the church.

The Sagrario: To the right of the cathedral, in 1749, the Spaniard Lorenzo Rodriguez began to build the **Sagrario Metropolitano**, the sacristy, in which books with the names of all believers were kept. It was Balbas, with his Altar de los Reyes, who introduced the Churrigueresco style, but Rodrigues took its most important element, the *estípites*, turning them into the most dominant feature of the Sagrario's facade. This created a harmonic, well-proportioned church front which is made to seem less stark by the use of volcanic red tezontle stone set among the gray basalt blocks. Ever since, this and other Churrigueresco elements have been imitated on hundreds of churches throughout the country.

The Sagrario's interior is very impressive, with its Greek cross layout above which rises a fine octagonal dome. As with other buildings in the city, the foundations have sunk into the soft ground of the dried-out Lake Texcoco on which the city is built.

Gilded pomp in the cathedral; the Chapel of Fear.

The beauty of the Sagrario is the way it harmonizes with the cathedral, though the two buildings are totally different in style and shape. The best view is from the center of the Zócalo. It is worth walking around the cathedral, especially toward the east where you will find a picturesque square with a fountain and a monument honoring one of Mexico's heroes – Fray Bartolomé de las Casas, the Spanish bishop who dedicated his life to defending the Indians. (He suggested, in partisan naivete, that blacks be brought from Africa to do much of the hard labor, and that contributed to the infamous slave trade.)

On the Zócalo's east side is the **National Palace** of Mexico which, since the foundation of the Aztec empire, has been the place where the political fate of the nation has been decided. The Spanish viceroys resided in the palace, and since the proclamation of the republic it has been the official residence of the Mexican president (although he actually lives at Los Pinos near Chapultepec

Park). The palace, whose precious furniture and works of art date from the days of the Habsburg Emperor Maximilian when the palace hosted visiting dignitaries, was destroyed – but immediately rebuilt – during an outbreak of insurgency in the 17th century. The last viceroys reveled in their love of French architecture and design and gave the palace its European character.

During the War of Independence the building had to serve as the military headquarters on many occasions. General Porfirio Díaz had the building modernized, installing telephones, lights and elevators. During the revolution, the palace once again was used for military purposes, and between 1924 and 1928 President Elias Calles added a new facade and a third story.

Since independence the palaceo has housed the federal government, the legislature and the Supreme Court, and it also houses a rather somber and dull museum honoring Benito Juárez, Mexico's liberal hero. But most visitors come to admire the murals on the main staircase and first floor corridors by Diego Rivera, Mexico's great muralist.

Like all of Rivera's murals these are both confusing and ambitious. On the walls of the staircase he attempts to portray the entire history of Mexico, from the creation of the world up to a future Marxist revolution. It is a personal, naive, and charming vision of Mexican history by a man in love with the Indian past. Rivera, a practicing Marxist although a millionaire – he was expelled from the Communist Party – hated the Spaniards to a ridiculous degree. But the mural, as a painting, is beautiful, full of soft and glowing colors, and somewhat like the church retablos except that instead of saints Rivera painted all the heroes of Mexico that only a patriotic schoolboy would have taken the trouble to know about.

Along the corridors, Rivera painted scenes that painstakingly represent pre-Columbian life. Utopian as they are, they reveal his extensive knowledge of

Scribes and printers in the Plaza Santo Domingo.

Indian culture. All his best works are in Mexico City. In the downtown area are two important murals, one in the Palace of Fine Arts, and the other, perhaps the better of the two, is in a special museum at the far end of the Alameda Park. But if you like Rivera, you should visit **Anahuacalli**, the exotic Aztec pyramid-palace Rivera built in the south part of Mexico City in which to house his collection of Indian art.

El Grito presidencial: The National Palace is the scene of one of Mexico's most popular festivities, *El Grito*, or The Shout. This event takes place during the night of September 16, when the president of Mexico appears on the main balcony of the palace to ring the very same bell with which Father Hidalgo summoned the people of his congregation in Dolores, beginning the War of Independence.

El Grito is a short but emotionally charged ceremony at which the president proclaims once again the independence of Mexico and the crowd in the Zócalo shouts lustily: "*Viva Mexico. Viva la independencial!*"

The other buildings around the Zócalo are of minor interest. At the south end is the **City Hall**. On the west side are private buildings of even lesser import, with the exception of the one housing that vital Mexican institution, **El Monte de Piedad** (The Mount of Mercy), an enormous pawnshop founded in 1775 by a millionaire miner to help his needy countrymen. Before leaving the Zócalo, look to your left for another landmark – the gray dome of the Palacio de Hierro department store, one block down Calle 20 de Septiembre. Once inside, you can gaze up at a superb stained glass ceiling.

Avenida Pino Suarez leads to the **Museo de la Ciudad de Mexico** in a former ducal palace, and across the street is the Hospital de Jesús Nazareno, reputedly built on the very spot where Hernán Cortéz first met Montezuma. It was the first hospital in the Americas and it still treats patients – mainly from the poor classes. In the hospital's 17th-

rt nouveau the Gran otel.

century chapel are the mortal remains of Hernán Cortéz who died in Seville but whose body was shipped back to Mexico. He is remembered by a simple plaque bearing the inscription "Cortéz – 1485–1547." He is not a hero to most present-day Mexicans.

School premises: On the Calle Ildefonso is the sombre Jesuit school **Colegio de San Ildefonso** (1740) which has served as a dormitory for students and as a place for religious exercises. It also housed a big library, and until 1975 it was Mexico's most famous public school, the **Escuela Nacional Preparatoria**. Lining the staircases are some of the first examples of Mexican *muralismo*, already displaying its typical popular and social content as well as its characteristic monumental nationalism.

Among the most famous paintings is *La Creación* (*The Creation*, 1922) by Diego Rivera, located in the school's Simón Bolívar amphitheater. It combines elements from the Italian Renaissance, symbolism and art deco as well

as Christian scenes and allegories from the sciences. Muralist David Alfaro Siqueiros has also worked on the walls of the college: in the painting *Los Elementos* (*The Elements*), lyrical scenes are found alongside odes to the solidarity of the working class. Over a period of three years, José Clemente Orozco has painted his visions of corruption, demagoguery, lack of moral integrity, fear, pain, and the tragedy of life itself.

More beautiful murals – by Juan O'Gorman, Carlos Merida and Diego Rivera – decorate the walls of the modern Ministry of Education (Secretaría de Educación Pública) on Calle Argentina, founded in the 18th century as a nuns' cloister, Nuestra Señora de la Encarnación, and remodeled since.

Iglesia de la Santísima Trinidad is one of the most beautiful examples of Churrigueresco. The church, built in the 18th century, lies on the corner of the Calle La Santísima and Calle Emiliano Zapata. The facade, with its delicate stone carving work, is particularly remarkable: busts, semi-reliefs, papal crown and keys, the twelve apostles and the Trinity.

While in the area, a little detour to the **Plaza Santo Domingo** is highly recommended. This picturesque square, with its Dominican cloister church, nestles between Calles Brasil, Venezuela and Cuba. The square is bordered by the former Customs House and the tribunal of the Inquisition as well as other buildings from which the Catholic authorities surveyed all Mexican publications and punished those who transgressed Catholic moral beliefs.

A statue of the heroine of the revolution, Josefa Ortíz de Domínguez, known as "La Corregidora," overlooks the square. Meanwhile, under the arcades, you will find the public scribes and printers seated at battered typewriters on which they compose all kinds of letters for their often illiterate clientele, ranging from love letters, to official correspondence with the daunting ministries of government.

Left, a shiny start to the day. **Right**, tour bus or taxi?

AROUND ALAMEDA PARK

The **downtown** area corresponds roughly to the old Aztec and colonial capital. Small as the old Mexico City is compared to the present day megalopolis, it is still big enough to wear you out if you walk.

Basically, it is made up of about 100 city blocks. Its boundaries, roughly speaking, are **Repúblic de Peru** to the north; **José María Izazaga Street** to the south; **Circunvalación-La Viga** to the east; and to the west what is now officially known as **Eje Central Lázaro Cárdenas**. However, what the locals call Mexico City changes every few blocks. The **Centro** goes from sordid to majestic. It is Spanish, Indian, French, romantic, and modern. It is a business district, a market place, a colonial slum and a fancy shopping area. From the 42nd-floor observation deck of the **Torre Latinoamericana** (176.5 meters /580 ft) the greater part of the infinite cityscape is theoretically visible. The view, however, is dulled most of the time by the gray veil of smog, and thus the panorama from the top of the tower is more enchanting at dusk when a glorious sunset coats everything with a pink hue and night falls with thousands of lights. It's a spectacle best savored over an aperitif or dinner at the restaurant high on the 41st floor.

Silversmiths' street: Running east from the tower to the Zócalo, **Calle Madero**, once called Plateros (Silversmiths) was renamed by Pancho Villa in honor of his hero, the slain president Francisco Madero. It's an interesting street whose occupants include the **American Bookstore** with a large array of English-language reading material, the **Museo Serfin** displaying colorful Indian costumes, and such famous landmarks as the sinking **San Francisco Church**, once part of the Franciscan monastery founded by Cortéz himself only three years after the conquest in 1524, and the

striking **Palacio de Iturbide**. This is now owned by Banamex which stages art shows in the patio. Note also **La Profesa** church which served as the capital's surrogate cathedral earlier in this century and which has sunk at least a foot since it was built in 1720. The colorful **Casa de los Azulejos**, a 16th-century house whose blue tiles were added 150 years ago when it was remodeled to house the exclusive Jockey Club, was the former town mansion of the Duke of Valle de Orizaba.

As **Sanborn's**, it may be the best-known restaurant in the city and has been famous at least since the days of Pancho Villa and Emiliano Zapata whose soldiers insisted on eating here. A photograph of the dining soldiers can be seen down the block in the **Casasola photo store** where you can pose for a souvenir photo in a vintage costume from revolutionary days and browse through archives of ancient pictures.

Diagonally opposite the tower, at the edge of the Alameda Park, is the **Palacio**

de Bellas Artes commissioned by Porfirio Díaz during his final term of office to replace the old national theater that had been torn down in 1901. The Italian architect Adamo Boari created it in dense, white Carrara marble, an adventurous undertaking right from the start considering the soft former lake-bed upon which it was built.

In 1907, during the first phase of construction, the complex had already begun to sink into the ground, and because of several hiccups in its construction it was not inaugurated for almost 30 years. First, the revolution halted construction work, then in 1916 Adamo Boari fled Mexico, leaving a completed outer shell.

In 1930 the Mexican Federico E. Mariscal was asked to finish it off. As a result, the interior of the Palacio is all post-revolutionary art deco with its geometrical functionalism. The decorator obviously reveled in colorful Mexican rather than Italian marble, creating a special, unique elegance.

The Tiffany curtain: The 2,000-seat theater's stage curtain is remarkable. It weighs 22 tonnes, and on it glitter one million opalescent glass pieces, punctiliously assembled during a period of 18 months by Tiffany jewelers. Based on a design by the Mexican painter Dr Atl (Gerardo Murillo), it shows the mountains and valleys of Mexico with the two volcanoes Popocatepetl and Ixtaccihuatl.

This spectacular theater is home to Amalia Hernández' **Ballet Folklórico**, one of Mexico's greatest treasures, for which you should hasten to make reservations as soon as you arrive. It also hosts visiting ballets, operas and famous artists from all over the world.

The **Museo de Artes Plásticas**, also in the Palacio, presents changing exhibitions in its seven halls. The upper level, right below the dome, houses the **Museo Nacional de Arquitectura**, whose lobbies and hallways have been decorated by Mexico's most famous artists. Two huge paintings by Rufino

The arduous art of spending money.

Tamayo adorn the corridors on the second floor: they are titled *Birth of our Nationality* and *Mexico Today*.

On the third floor, the muralists José Clemente Orozco, Diego Rivera and David Alfaro Siqueiros have left their heavily metaphorical works for Mexican posterity. Rivera's notorious mural is the second version of a piece that was commissioned by and for the Rockefeller Center in New York. A tremendous international scandal ensued when the original *Man at the Crossroads* was rejected and destroyed.

Across the street, only a few steps from the Renaissance Venetian post office is Mexico's most beloved monument: **El Caballito**, or the **Tiny Horse**. The sculpture, which despite its name is huge and formal, depicts the Spanish king Charles IV, who was highly unimportant. Forced by Napoleon to abdicate in favor of Napoleon's brother, Joseph, he nevertheless had the good fortune to be immortalized by great artists. Goya painted a magnificent portrait of Charles IV's family; Manuel Tolsá sculpted the Mexican Caballito.

Tiny Horse has galloped all over Mexico City looking for a permanent stable, having adorned the Zócalo, the university's patio, and then the crossing of the Paseo de la Reforma, Avenida Juárez and Bucareli Street. But as traffic volumes grew, El Caballito became a nuisance and had to be moved. Now he has nice buildings for neighbors, such as the magnificent **Palacio de Minería** (School of Mining), also a work of Tolsá and one of the best neoclassical buildings in the country. Inexpensive Sunday evening classical concerts sometimes take place upstairs.

The **Alameda** (literally Promenade of the Poplars) was in the beginning a park, a market and a site for the burning of heretics, one of the few entertainments provided during colonial days. But in the 19th century the Alameda was transformed into a romantic park full of fountains, sculpture, and the inevitable music kiosk. Every Mexican

olk art in
e Fonart
hop.

town has a central square with trees, flowers, a kiosk, and at least one monument to a solemn hero. In the middle of the noisy and chaotic capital is a fragment of laid-back provincial Mexico. The poplar grove was planted by viceroy Velasco in 1592 "for the decoration of the city and the edification of its citizens," but in this century many of the trees have lost their battle against the smog and died on their feet.

First Indian president: The main monument on the south side, with its semicircle of white columns, is dedicated to former president Benito Juárez; and in 1921 the German community donated the Beethoven monument including the composer's black death mask. Other statues include two charming, erotic girls named in French *Malgré Tout* (In Spite of Everything) and *Désespoir* (Despair).

One of the pleasures of La Alameda is to sit in a chair and have your shoes cleaned while you read a newspaper or gawk at the passers by. During the week not only tourists who are tired of sightseeing, but also ordinary working people relax on the Alameda's lawns and benches. On Sundays, the place of rest turns into a big circus, immortalized in Diego Rivera's famous mural *Sunday Reverie in the Alameda* with historic figures from different eras (pictured on page 85). Up to 1985, this monumental fresco, covering 72 sq. meters (775 sq. ft), was the pride of the Hotel del Prado until the latter was hit by the earthquake. The mural was saved in a spectacular rescue mission and given its very own exhibition site next to the Alameda Park on the Avenida Juárez.

The face and life of the city was changed dramatically by the earthquake. A string of famous hotels once dominated the center. In addition to the Hotel del Prado, there were the Hotel Alameda and the Hotel Regis, both of which no longer exist. A part of the nightlife has died with the hotels. Like a phoenix, the Torre Latinoamericana rose from the debris, and during the earthquake its special construction allowed it to sway flexibly, saving it from serious harm.

La Alameda is flanked by two important streets – **Avenida Juárez** and **Avenida Hidalgo**, the former lined with hotels, restaurants and stores that cater to tourists. At the western end of La Alameda is a museum in the former San Diego church, the **Pinacoteca Virreinal**, housing colonial paintings. Included are works of such colonial masters as Echave, Juárez, Cabrera and López de Herrera. Mexican colonial painting, derived from Spanish and Italian styles, is not to everyone's taste. Always religious in subject, it tends to be somber, though consistent in quality.

Folk art is also to be found along Juárez at the **Museo Nacional de Artes e Industrias Populars** in the former Corpus Christi Church of 1724 (44 Avenida Juárez). In addition to the museum on the first floor, a sales exhibition on the ground floor assembles specialties from all over the country: grotesque dance masks, painted ceramics which

Siesta in the park.

branch out into "life trees," colorful lacquer work, silver jewelry, earthen figurines ranging from the comical to the obscene (called *Ocumichus*), chess boards and sculptures made from onyx, Indian woven textiles and embroideries with vivacious colors and patterns, and fantastic woollen pictures made by the Huichol Indians. The museum store is run by the Mexican Indian Institute (Instituto Nacional Indígenista).

Avenida Hidalgo has a completely different atmosphere, being modest and more genuine. Two small colonial churches (**San Juan de Dios** and **Santa Veracruz**) face a tiny square and preserve some flavor of the old days. Nearby is the **Hotel Cortéz**. This was not the residence of Hernán Cortéz at all, but an inn, once Santo Tomás de Villanueva, built by the Augustinian fathers in the 18th century and now with a pleasant patio to relax in.

On Hidalgo check out the incredible **Franz Mayer Museum**. An inveterate collector, Mayer was born in Mannheim, Germany. He spent 70 years of his life in Mexico and on his death donated his whole art collection to the Mexican people. His collection is a joy to behold: room after room of period furniture, stylish pottery, tapestry, rugs, silver objects and paintings, all laid out in a manner that must surely have delighted its benefactor as much as today's visitors. The fine **Museo Nacional de la Estampa**, the museum of Mexican prints, is located almost next door on the Plaza Santa Veracruz.

A few blocks north is the **Plaza Garibaldi**, although you can more readily find the plaza by walking up San Juan de Letran past the post office and **Teatro Blanquita** (topnotch variety shows). This is a great place to return to at night when costumed *mariachis* gather with their instruments seeking people to play for, and when lively bars, nightspots and burlesque theaters are in full swing. Check out the long row of mini restaurants in the Mercado de Alimentos San Camilito, all cheap and all serving *tacos* or other indigenous fast food. The square is dotted with statues of *mariachi* heroes Pedro Infante and José Alfredo Jimenez (who had successful singing careers in 1950s movies).

There are some very interesting markets in the city (*see the followng short feature on Markets*). Among the best are **La Merced**, by the Merced station on Metro line No. 9, and **Lagunilla**, at Calles Rayon and Allende.

The rather formal **San José** market on Ayuntamiento at Dolores and the infinitely more interesting and funky **Artesianias de la Ciudadela** on Ayuntamiento at Balderas both have a wide variety of colorful hand-crafted souvenirs of glass, soapstone, wood and tin, at surprisingly low prices.

On Fray Servando Teresa de Mier is the **Mercado de Sonora**, known for its wide array of medicinal herbs and the alleged witches who sell some of them (*see page on Sonora Market*).

West of the Alameda, at Avenida Hidalgo and Paseo de la Reforma, the

he
onument
the
evolution.

colonial church **San Hipólito** stands on the spot where the Spaniards were defeated by the Aztecs on the *Noche Triste*, the Sad Night, August 13, 1521, when they tried to skip out of town. This small church is the only landmark commemorating the Spanish conquest that Mexico is so keen to forget.

Continuing down the Calle Puente de Alvarado, one reaches the **Palacio de Buenavista**, a classical town mansion of the Spanish architect and sculptor Manuel Tolsá. It is now the home of the **Museo de San Carlos**, an exquisite collection of Mexican and European paintings – from Gothic to Impressionist. Rembrandt, Tintoretto and Rubens are among the illustrious artists represented here.

Tomb of presidents: The open-domed edifice of the **Monumento a la Revolución** rises from the Plaza de la República. The 67-meter (220-ft) high monument to the revolution was constructed from the ruins of the unfinished parliament. The huge blocks of stone, arranged in a strictly geometrical pattern, are interrupted by four openings, with the light streaming in and the wind howling through them. Four presidents, Madero, Carranza, Calles and Cárdenas, have found their final resting place in the four corner pillars which are crowned by massive sculptures.

The revolution interrupted Porfirio Díaz's grand scheme to make this edifice the legislative palace, a sort of Latin American Eiffel Tower, and the gigantic, empty iron structure was left to rust for years until an enterprising architect transformed it into this imposing monument to the revolutionary movement. Beneath it is a fascinating (free) museum which includes a collection of irreverent cartoons in which the building assumes many amusing forms. It helps to have at least some slight knowledge of Spanish in order to appreciate the museum's enormous exhibition of newspaper stories and documents, but there are also drawings, photographs, weapons, uniforms and furnishings.

Bull fighting is still popular with *los capitalinos.*

140

SONORA MARKET

Step into the last door of the Sonora Market and you are greeted by the aromas of unusual herbs, pungent spices, incense, and candle wax. You will find lodestones, spiritual sprays, Stars of David, rosaries, crucifixes, rabbit legs, *ojo de venado* (deer's eye), ribbons, threads, feathers, dried hummingbirds, voodoo dolls and eggs. Buddhas vie for space with skulls and statues of Christ, the saints and the Virgin Mary.

The shops sell wreaths of garlic adorned with saintly images. They avert the evil eye or *mal de ojo*, caused intentionally by a witch or unintentionally by a person with a strong gaze. Throughout Mexico the evil eye is considered a leading form of childhood disease, so you can buy a deer's eye or *ojo de venado* to protect your child.

The matriarch of magical stalls has been here since the Sonora Market opened in 1956. Marina Magaña, at Local 204, gives consultations from noon to 7pm, assisted by her nephew, Manuel Valadoz. According to Manuel most of their clients are women and most come with problems concerning love or money: they want magic to bring back the husband who left them for another woman; to make a husband or boyfriend toe the line; or to cure a streak of bad luck.

A wreath of garlic or an aloe plant adorned with saints and sometimes packets of mustard, linseed, wheat or rice at the entrance assures good luck in your home or business. But should you suffer a streak of bad luck, the answer is a *limpia* or cleansing. You can seek the assistance of a witch but, according to Manuel, in most cases this do-it-yourself procedure is just as effective.

With a special branch, you must cleanse yourself, starting from the top of your head and continuing down to your toes. You then stomp on the branch to rid it of the bad luck it has absorbed and kick it away, backwards. Repeat the cleansing process using an unlit candle of the seven powers. Then light the candle, say the prayer printed on the package and make your wish. According to Manuel, the candle sometimes cracks from all the negative vibrations it has absorbed.

The final step in this cleansing process is the sloughing bath, or *baño de despojo*. In

four quarts of water crumble rosemary, basil, a thin bark called *cascarilla*, St Mary and rue. Add some ground cinnamon and *abrecamino* (open the way) lotion. Apply this mixture all over the body while praying for the bad luck to end and good fortune to return. Some people use a whole egg instead of the herbal mix for this last process, and sometimes the negative vibrations absorbed by the egg are so strong that the contents turn black and putrid.

Black magic, according to Manuel, is somewhat more complicated. It can be used for either good or evil, but is basically more

potent than white magic. One popular black magic recipe calls for making a packet with a photo of the person, some strands of his or her hair if possible and a piece of their clothing. To the packet add some ground *palo dominador, palo venamé* and *amanzahuapo* – all available at Marina Magaña's stall. Tie it up with red embroidery thread and make a doll out of a soft wax called *cera de campeche*. Stuff the wax doll into the packet and cover. Then light a large red votive candle, say a special prayer and make your wish.

When the candle has burned down, wrap the wax doll in a piece of your clothing and keep it well hidden. Results should be seen in about a week to 10 days. ∎

Above, miraculous remedies for all ailments from the Mercado de Sonora.

There is nothing you might wish to buy in Mexico City for which you might conceivably have to enter any of the city's modern supermarkets and department stores. Everything necessary for daily life is offered for sale in one or another of the more traditional street markets.

To bargain on the street, to make your purchase from an itinerant vendor or a trusted *marchanta* is no furtive delight – it is an open passion of the Mexicans. Shopping is part of the daily activity of the Mexican housewife or her maid. Who knows whether the Indian or Spanish heritage is the more significant in

repeatedly tried to keep the streets and squares free from commercial activities. They have built many indoor markets in those areas where the vendors' stands accumulated. The indoor markets were also introduced in an attempt to control the hygienic conditions under which foodstuffs were sold, but the majority of vendors who cannot afford to rent a place inside continue to spread over the streets and sidewalks.

Some markets in the city are especially interesting for travelers. Among these are La Merced, the former great market which, with its 7,000 stands, covered 110 streets and

this? In any case, we know from contemporary reports that the Spanish conquerors were amazed at the size of the great Aztec market of Tlatelolco when they set eyes on it.

The word *tianguis*, still used as a synonym for market, comes from the Indian *náhuatl* language. *Tianquistli* means "every five days," the cycle of the pre-Spanish weekly market. Today it indicates a particular day of the week when a street within a neighborhood is closed off by market stands with their colorful sun shades or the *mercado sobre ruedas*, the market on wheels.

There is supposed to be a law which prohibits the obstruction of vehicle and pedestrian traffic by street vendors. The city fathers have

five squares in the old city center. Now it is mostly collected under one roof, reached by Metro line No. 9 at Merced station. Visitors emerging from the underground into the center of the market are greeted by the overpowering odor of onions.

La Merced is a colorful, turbulent world of its own. All the country's fruits and vegetables are represented – sometimes artfully piled into pyramids by the vendors. Here you can become acquainted with *chirimoyas* (sugar pears), *jicamas* (a bulbous fruit), *tunas* (cactus figs) and the spicy *cilantro* (coriander herb), as well as many varieties of chiles. This corner of La Merced is only one of six sections. In addition, clothing, sweets and flowers are sold here. Then there are, of course, the *comedores*, the delightful small market restaurants that are scattered throughout the area, and the perfect place for lunch.

The Mercado de Sonora with its *herbolaría* (herb market) is surely one of the most mysterious parts of La Merced (*see separate feature*). Here the vendors sell homeopathic medicines against every sort of illness in hundreds of large and small sacks, and here superstition also flourishes. The merchant-sorcerers are ready to offer aid for nearly every imaginable problem – difficulties at work or in the marriage bed; protection from the evil eye or a variety of other curses. Magical properties are attributed to snake skins, shark's jaws or deer's eyes.

Sensitive souls would do better to avoid the adjacent animal market. They would be sorely tempted to free a small kitten from its cage next to fat pigeons or perhaps to adopt a puppy just so they could release it from its wooden crate. Or perhaps they wonder who might buy a poisonous tarantula or snake – and to what end the animal's fate.

Most visitors end up going to the flea market La Lagunilla (Sunday only; on the right hand side when driving down the Paseo de la Reforma in the direction of Tlatelolco). Here it is not only junk that is displayed: you can also find valuable antiques. Next to bombastic Victorian-style beds hang art nouveau figures beside martial swords and old pistols or a treasure chest full of old coins. The green camouflage suits that are on sale could probably be put to good use by the dealers themselves when the police make their raids in search of *fayuca* (smuggled contraband), which they often do.

Folk art and handicrafts from all regions of the country are also on sale. The Ciudadela Market, with its small businesses and stands, is centrally located near the old citadel (Avenida Balderas). The Bazar del Sábado, in San Angel (Plaza San Jacinto) is open as its name suggests only on Saturday. While shoppers browse through the various stands filled with expensive handicrafts non-shoppers can enjoy a Mexican-style meal on the patio of an old mansion. Outside in the square artists exhibit their paintings or sculptures and in the adjoining plaza are the regular stands of the modest provincial traders.

For how long has the fat *marchanta* from Xalitla been coming here with her colorfully

painted *papel amate* (bark paper) hanging in a row? The Indian masks and embroidered blouses and lovely dresses are also gaily colored, making a feast for the eyes and a danger for the purse – not only because of the temptation to collect souvenirs but because one can easily lose one's wallet in the seething crowd.

The Mexican markets, with their wealth, color, delicate scents and strong smells, may be an extravaganza for the foreigner. For the people who move about behind the sales counters they are a matter of economic survival. Just the location of the stall is the end result of a complicated game. It is not enough to pay the required stall fees to the local administration; powerful merchant *caciques* allow only those who pay protection money to sell their wares (*cacique* was originally the Indian word for a chief or local tyrant). The city has virtually no control over these market czars who often have thousands of dependent vendors on their books.

The Indian women fresh from their villages appear to be quite defenseless in these markets, ignorant of the hierarchical structure. They sit on the sidewalk with small piles of limes or peanuts in front of them, a child in their arms. The city dwellers call them *marías*, a condescending term for Indian women. These women wait patiently, not only for a few pesos, but as if to understand somehow what it is that is behind the incessant movement in this vast city. ∎

Above, greengrocers at their stalls. **Right**, markets are good places for handpainted crafts.

PASEO DE LA REFORMA AND ZONA ROSA

Tall buildings line the grand **Paseo de la Reforma**, which is among the world's more charming boulevards. At the hectic crossing place of the Reforma, Juárez and Bucareli is the distinctive art deco tower of the **National Lottery Building** where public draws take place three nights each week. Attendance is free, but the draws are not very interesting to watch. At almost every intersection, as in other parts of town, the itinerant lottery ticket salesmen can be seen with their sheaves of tickets on long sticks. They carry lists of winnings numbers from previous lotteries which are also displayed at the booths from which tickets are sold.

From the crossroads the Reforma marches grandly along. Bucareli is Mexico City's Fleet Street, the street of newspapers, and Avenida Juárez becomes **Ejido**, at the end of which is the bulky **Monument to the Revolution** with its fascinating (free) museum. Across the street is the Frontón México, that sports cathedral to jai-alai, a Basque ricochet ball game that is one of Mexico City's great passions but interesting to watch for only a short time unless you participate in the betting. Bookies who take your bet will throw you a slit tennis ball in which is tucked the betting slip and into which you tuck your bet before throwing it back.

Three blocks northeast on Alvarado, the Museo de San Carlos has a collection of European paintings including some 19th-century Spanish works.

The construction of the Paseo de la Reforma was begun by the short-lived Emperor Maximilian, who envisaged it as a Mexican Champs-Elysées: a broad majestic avenue stretching from Zócalo to Castillo de Chapultepec, the castle to be broadly based on Maximilian's own Castle Miramare in Trieste, Italy.

The emperor did not live to see the magnificent thoroughfare completed, as

Preceding pages: street scene. **Left**, the Paseo de la Reforma. **Right**, a tree becomes another monument on the Paseo

146

he ended up in front of a firing squad in 1867. Ten years later, by an irony of fate, the avenue was to be named after the presidential triumph of Benito Juárez, the man who ordered the emperor's execution. Juárez was himself responsible for the reform laws of 1861, which called for the division of property between church and state.

Even before it was finished, Paseo de la Reforma witnessed an age of splendor: huge French-style residences with horse-drawn carriages, Parisian fashions, Italian millinery, and distinguished gentlemen riding down on their fiery steeds from the castle mound to Zócalo, right up to the front of the cathedral and the Palacio Nacional.

The Mexican writer Octavio Paz described the Paseo as Mexico City's river, a Seine in cement, majestically crossing the best part of town. But, alas, the Paseo's success and Parisian appearance were also its undoing. The French-looking mansions were torn down to be replaced by skyscrapers, as the horses and carriages were replaced by the automobile. Polluted air ruined the trees and plants. Yet even today, the Paseo is still a beautiful street. And so are its monuments, whose subjects include **Columbus** by the French sculptor Charles Cordier and, at the crossing of the Reforma and Insurgentes, **Cuauhtémoc** – the last Aztec emperor and first Mexican hero who ruled during the siege of the city by Cortéz. Cuauhtémoc became the perfect romantic hero, valiant and doomed, and this monument to him seems like something out of opera. He stands like a Roman senator wearing a feather hat, at one of Mexico City's busiest crossroads. The Cuauhtémoc monument has its own fountains, where children love to splash until the police come and haul them out.

The next monument, the glittering **El Angel**, is perhaps the most beautiful of all, balancing on the chubby toes of its right foot. Its wings outstretched ready for take-off from the top of an elegant Corinthian column, it commemorates the country's independence. In the angel's right hand is held a laurel wreath, and despite its rounded breasts, like two golden oranges, and the obviously feminine features, we still – with macho pride – give the figure the masculine title "El Angel."

The angel rises out of a *glorieta*, a circular garden or traffic circle that takes an infuriatingly long time for a pedestrian to walk around. *Glorietas* are even more infuriating to motorists unfamiliar with local driving etiquette and who have been known to circle several times before being able to take their preferred exit. One sculpture that has disappeared from the Paseo de la Reforma is Charles IV's El Caballito (Little Horse), which newspaper sellers used to climb to watch the military parades and demonstrations. It now sits in front of the Museum of Art on Calle Tacuba. The lovely, fountain-enshrouded *Diana Cazadora* (Diana, goddess of the hunt) was briefly censored by the city's moralistic contingent but the voluptuous nude, known to all

e glittering
Angel.

simply as Diana, is now back in the center of its own *glorieta*.

To the northeast, the Paseo is less exciting and less fashionable with traffic circles that are often clogged, undistinguished monuments and a huge housing development called **Nonoalco-Tlatelolco**. Otherwise unimpressive, it is worth a visit because of the Square of Three Cultures (**Plaza de las Tres Culturas**) which marks an archaeological site where the foundations of an Aztec temple have been excavated. In this square in 1968, in the shadow of the colonial **Church of Santiago** and the rather bland **Ministry of Foreign Affairs** building, occurred a national disaster. Police and army troops shot and killed a number of students and others protesting against police brutality and a lack of democracy. Understandably this incident has not been forgotten.

The Zona Rosa: When high society degenerated to mere café society in the 1950s, and the aristocracy became the jet set (managing by a bit of work and the magic power of money to live in Mexico exactly as they did in Paris, Madrid or New York), Mexico City's Zona Rosa came into being – a district of elegant restaurants, smart boutiques and glitzy galleries.

Pâtisseries and designer shops sprang up in the French-style houses, built with attics and pitched roofs against the snow (this in a land which has no winter). Bespoke tailors appeared to make suits for politicians, not to mention the plastic surgeons, snipping away at the bodies of politicians' wives. There are branches of all the famous foreign couturiers and parfumiers, as well as Italian shoemakers, Swiss pâtissiers, Viennese chocolate shops and German delicatessens. The boutiques offer cigarette-holders, key rings, wallets, room scenters, picture frames and Japanese flower arrangements. Floral stylists thread little wires through chrysanthemum blooms to make the petals stand out like arrows. Florists show tortured-looking Bonsai trees, and the shop windows are full of

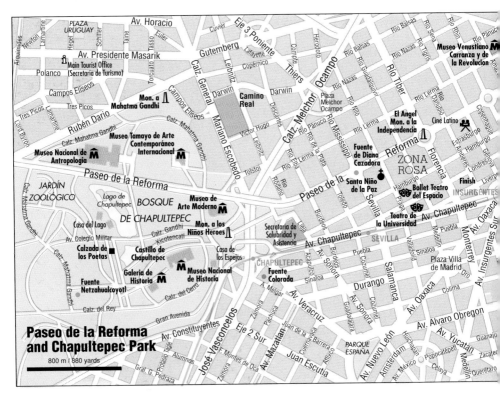

Chinese figures, ashtrays and glassware artistically arranged on twisted trunks and dwarf-like branches.

Zona Rosa, the area between Paseo de la Reforma and Avenida Chapultepec, was for a long time the choicest part of town but is losing some of its attractions to the Polanco area, east of Chapultepec Park. The Zona Rosa, like a little Europe, with streets named after its continental cities – Florence, Stockholm, Dresden, Strasbourg, Rome, Lucerne, Hamburg and London – is crammed with eating places, the most interesting of which are the sidewalk cafés on Copenhagen or Genova. Local residents go to the Zona specifically for eating, shopping and people-watching, and as long lunches are a Mexican institution it is a good place to unwind.

Check out Amberes street, little changed from its 1960s upscale ambience, for exclusive jewelry, sweaters or the whimsical, tinted sculptures and jewelry of Sergio Bustamante, a Mexican artist of Indian and Chinese origin

who studied architecture before turning to his amusing specialty. Gucci is at the corner of Hamburgo, Los Castillo has intriguing silver inlay chinaware. The entrance to the glitzy Plaza Rosa mall is across the street, crammed with miniscule stores. On Londres is the Plaza Angel, a mall specializing in antiques, some with a Mexican motif, such as quaint pictures of saints and miracles on tin, and sculptural colonial furniture. Its central patio and walkways are filled on Saturday mornings with a popular flea market where you'll surely find some trinket or fascinating old book or vintage postcard to treasure. Across the street is the **Mercado Insurgentes**, whose persistent but friendly salesmen should not deter you from inspecting the extensive array of silver, sarapes, embroidered clothing and all kinds of souvenirs. One side is totally devoted to a series of cheap and clean food counters.

The *konditori* (café) tables meander across the pavements, and waiters run to and fro with open sandwiches of Ger-

ting al
sco in
na Rosa.

man black bread and liver pâté, salmon or herring, real German sauerkraut and large tankards of beer. The Focolare and other top restaurants are like precious caskets lined with velvet. There's a popular Sanborns at the corner of Niza and Hamburgo and various tearooms and Viennese-style coffee houses.

First to appear in the Zona Rosa was the Hotel Genève (now **the Calinda**), to which tourists flocked by the thousand. Silversmiths (*tane*) and craft shops appeared at its side and clung there through the passing years. Cluttered basements were transformed into elegant, exclusive shops.

In one such basement in the Amor building in Abraham González street, the Galería de Arte Mexicano was founded with exhibitions by Rufino Tamayo, Diego Rivera, José Clemente Orozco, Juan Soriano, Leonora Carrington and Carlos Mérida – all great Mexican artists. The gallery has since moved to the San Miguel Chapultepec area, with an established clientele.

The shops behind these elegant facades were from the start rather snooty. Porfirian ladies descended the creaking wooden stairs from their second floors and opened bookshops, picture-framing studios, galleries selling religious art, furs or leather goods. Then pizzerias began springing up, complete with checked tablecloths and glasses of beer, or gondolas and Chianti. The **Fonda del Refugio** opened its doors.

It was above this bar that Carlos Fuentes lived and here that he wrote his novella *The Death of Artemis Cruz*. At one time Fuentes was a familiar face in the district, along with Antonia Souza, the manager of the gallery which exhibited all the young painters who were later to become so famous: José Luis Cuevas, Franciso Toledo, Manuel Felguérez, Pedro and Rafael Coronel. José Luis Cuevas painted his first short-lived mural in a building in the Zona Rosa, and later he staged many artistic "happenings," which scandalized the district's devout churchgoers.

Left, modern day Aztec. **Right**, the French touch

The art of the Zona Rosa today, packaged and confined as in so many other places of this kind, is actually less interesting to view than that of **Sullivan Park** (sometimes known as the **Jardín del Arte**) a few blocks away. Here, between Calles Sullivan and Villalongin, a Sunday afternoon art show is always packed with visitors inspecting the casual display of sculptures, paintings and engravings, more than a few of them attended by the artists themselves.

Although the cuisine of the Zona Rosa was international, everything that happened on Niza Street happened – and happens still – in English. Many Mexicans followed the tourist herds to Zona Rosa, among them a group of intellectuals known as Los Divinos (The Divine Ones), who somehow managed to mouth the word *revolución* while in the same breath ordering giant crabs in garlic sauce in the Ballinhaus.

José Luis' **El Parador** on Niza Street is a Spanish-style traditional bar, where you can eat first-class cuisine, prepared by the same Pueblan angels or nuns who invented the black *mole*, which the French call *poulet au chocolat* (chicken with chocolate).

One of Zona Rosa's curiosities is the huge circle where the **Insurgentes Metro Station** is located and which is jammed with stalls of every type. In other cities, a subway station is just a subway station, no more, no less. Here it is a pretext for exhibiting urban space on a grand scale. (By the way, don't visit the Mexico City Metro during rush hours. The reason is obvious. Go during off-hours.)

The Metro is clean and some of its stations are fascinating. One called **Pino Suarez** boasts an Aztec pyramid, the real thing. It's no trouble getting around on the Metro: wall maps are clear and easy to follow. (*Note: a detailed Metro line map is reproduced in the Travel Tips section.*)

At almost 28 km (17 miles) long, the Insurgentes is the longest avenue in Mexico and possibly the world.

Id jewelry display.

THE TRAFFIC: SURVIVAL IN CHAOS

The traffic light is green but the police officer holds up the traffic with her hand. Multi-toned horns honk and continue until the first police motorcycle patrols have driven past, clearing the way for a limousine: a politician who wants to get to his appointment on time.

As the procession glides past, the horns instantly sound together – three short blasts, two long – *chinga tu madre* (fuck your mother). For a Mexican this is the maximum insult, an expletive more easily sounded by a horn than spoken. People who, only moments before, had been cursing each other with horn signals

network. However, by the time a project is completed, the problem is three steps ahead of the planners. The development of Mexico City's infrastructure is hopelessly behind the real expansion rate. The city is growing by approximately 3,000 people per day, almost a million new inhabitants every year.

In the late 1960s the Anillo Periférico connected the suburbs of Satélite in the northwest and Villa Coapa in the southeast with the downtown Paseo de la Reforma area. People criticized the extravagance of such a luxuriously wide street, but today these regions are part of the metropolis and the five lane

and hand movements typical of the Mexican car-driver, are instantly united against a collective opponent – the tangible sinner blamed for the traffic jam.

Traffic jams are part of everyday life in the Mexican capital, and not just because politicians override the lights. Defective vehicles can block traffic for hours. In the rainy season, heavy rainfall makes the overloaded drains shoot water back into the streets. Vehicles stuck in the water hold up others. Thousands of trucks, oil tankers and trailers that provide services for the city form yet an additional, enormous burden.

Mexico has made great efforts to keep up with the demands on the city's transport

Periférico has long been too small for the ever increasing traffic demands.

The Paseo de la Reforma, the imperial parade built by Maximilian, links the city center with Mexico City's most exclusive residential neighborhood, Chapultepec, as far as the federal highway to Toluca. All of these streets have been widened over the years but they still remain too narrow to allow anything resembling an even traffic flow.

In the middle of the 1970s, the *ejes viales* (principal routes) were built to provide the city with north–south and east–west connections. Numerous houses and green areas were sacrificed. Despite early protests and demonstrations, today one cannot imagine the Mexican capital without the *ejes viales*. All the major streets have been widened over the years, but they still remain much too narrow to cope with the demands of the automobile and delivery transportation.

The road construction measures of the last couple of decades have helped considerably, but they are just as ineffective at reducing the transport chaos in what is probably the world's largest city traffic problem. Helicopters fly daily across the city during the rush hour to provide radio reports of the traffic situation for drivers, while also providing an effective police support system to critical points throughout the city.

According to conservative estimates, over three million motor vehicles, often with old, but more usually defective, exhaust systems,

circulate daily through the Mexican capital. They are responsible for a substantial part of the 11,000 tonnes of air pollutants which are emitted daily, contributing to the destruction of the atmosphere in a city once praised for its excellent air quality.

The blankets of smog are causing serious health problems too – especially when, in the cooler winter months, the thermal inversions in the Valle de México prevent the air movements that are so needed to carry the smog away from the city.

Even the significant increase in public

Left, a dangerous post. Above, entrepreneurs sell goods and services at red traffic lights.

transport over the last few years has done little to help the traffic problem. Although the Metro will eventually be expanded from three to nine lines, it has not grown fast enough to meet demands. And most of the day the buses and *colectivos* (minibuses) are hopelessly overcrowded.

Musicians, singers, and vendors push their way through the crowds on the buses and subway trains, do their business between stations and collect their money. One can also buy all sorts of different things at street intersections while waiting for the light to turn green: chocolate, chewing gum, lottery tickets, rear view mirrors for cars or a Popeye doll for the baby.

At the junction itself, children play and juggle, dressed as clowns. Sometimes they concentrate so hard on their performances that they do not notice the lights changing to green and must run for their lives without receiving a single peso for their performances. Cyclists and moped drivers are even rarer in the heavy traffic than pedestrians, since they are in even greater danger. The main reason is the continuous changing of traffic lanes. The worse the jam, the more frequently the drivers move pointlessly from one side of the street to the other, and the more frustrated everybody becomes.

Mexican automobile drivers use instinct more than traffic rules – which many do not know – yet the system functions amazingly well. Although accidents are part of everyday life in a huge city, they are relatively rare. The Mexican driver expects aggressive driving and knows how to handle it. He is only irritated when he cannot drive any further. "*Ni modo!*" (So what!) said one man about the hopeless traffic situation and proceeded bravely into the evening's traffic turmoil. "I've long ago given up going to the theater. Either one gets there too late on account of the traffic or one can't find a parking place," notes another with resignation.

The government has tried to restrict automobile use to control the problem. Every car is prohibited from entering the city on one day in the week. The day is determined by the last number of the car's registration plate. Following a trial period of four months, the program has been extended indefinitely because of its obvious success.

Unfortunately, many of the more affluent buy two or more cars and subvert even these measures. And, as the city grows still further, the public transport system is bearing up badly under the strain. ∎

CHAPULTEPEC PARK

Visit **Chapultepec Park** – the largest wooded area in Mexico City and one of the few places for open-air relaxation in the capital. It is also a place of great historical importance. In pre-Columbian times, the city's drinking water came from Chapultepec – the lake that surrounded Mexico-Tenochtitlán attracted Mexico's rulers. It is believed that the famous Indian king Netzahualcóyotl had a palace there. The summer home built there by Viceroy Matías de Gálvez eventually became Mexico's military academy. During the Mexican War the invading Americans attacked the military school, known as **El Castillo**. Some teenage Chapultepec cadets died rather than surrender to the US forces that captured the city in 1847. They became great national heroes. ***Los Niños Héroes* monument** – tall white marble pillars crowned with bronze eagles – stands at the entrance to the park.

Divided into three areas, covering 670 hectares (260 sq. miles) in all, Chapultepec Park is not only a place to unwind – to bring a picnic at the weekends, or go for a walk or a jog. People also come to take advantage of the wide-ranging cultural and sporting facilities on offer.

Dotted around Chapultepec Park's 810 hectares (2,000 acres), which no amount of careful tending can save from the ravages of air pollution and overuse, there are a range of attractions: man-made lakes, the zoo, theaters, a children's center (*Centro de Conviviencia Infantil*), a botanical garden, sports pitches and a funfair, and some first-class museums including the world famous National Museum of Anthropology, one of the outstanding buildings in the world.

Attractive and relaxing as the park is in the daylight hours, it is not to be recommended for visits at nighttime any more than the urban parks of most visitors' hometowns. By night, its population is quite different from the daytime one.

Numerous stories and legends have grown up around Chapultepec, the "grasshopper hill." In 1266 the Aztecs held their first "new fire" ceremony here. The extinguishing and relighting of all fires heralded a new calendar every 52 years. In 1325, Chapultepec was declared a "holy place," and a temple was erected on Chapulín Hill.

Montezuma Ilhuicamina ordered the building of the first aqueduct in 1465 to carry water from the Chapultepec springs to Tenochtitlán. Montezuma Xocoyotzin (Montezuma II) was concerned only with his personal well-being and had an opulent palace built, surrounded by swimming pools and fishponds. Here he would come to relax after hunting in the Chapultepec woods.

On May 26, 1521, these woods were the scene of a bloody battle between the Spanish and the Aztecs. The conquistador Hernán Cortéz took the Chapulín with the intention of laying siege to

receding
ages:
ntrance to
e Museo de
rte Mod-
no. **Left**,
culpture at
e Museo de
te. **Right**,
e Castle.

Tenochtitlán, and by destroying the aqueducts he cut the enemy water supply. Then he fortified the hill to defend himself against Mexican attack.

A Spanish resort: After the country had been overrun, the viceroys followed the example of the Aztec rulers and used Chapultepec as a kind of spa resort. On the site of the Aztec palace they erected a summer residence, as well as a pilgrimage church.

In 1537 Emperor Charles V decreed, at the request of Viceroy Antonio de Mendoza, that the hill and woods of Chapultepec belonged to the capital of New Spain and should be used for the edification of its inhabitants. Cortéz's stronghold was turned into a gunpowder factory, which blew up in 1784.

At the behest of Viceroy Bernardo de Gálvez, construction began on a castle on the Chapulín. It was completed three years later. Shortage of funds meant that the castle and its woods came under the hammer for 130,000 pesos in 1788. Count Revillagigedo intervened to try and prevent the sale. In a desperate attempt to raise the necessary funds to finish the castle, festivals and bullfights were organized.

After the declaration of independence in 1810, both the castle and the woods were declared public property and in 1826 Mexico's first president, Guadalupe Victoria, announced the creation of a botanical garden. Meanwhile the castle remained empty, until in 1841 it was turned into a military academy. During the French and North American invasions of the 19th century, the capture of Chapultepec was an important strategic goal. During the 1847 US invasion, when 900 Mexican soldiers and 47 cadets of the military college attempted to defend the castle, six young cadets lost their lives.

Chapultepec Castle is inhabited by the ghosts of Maximilian of Austria and his empress, Charlotte, whose story reads like a 19th-century popular novel. The tragic prince, who under the auspices of France became short-lived emperor of

"Young Heroes" monument near the Castle.

158

Mexico, made the castle his imperial residence and had both interior and exterior substantially rebuilt and improved, as befitted his status. He also initiated the construction of a street connecting the park with the city, but it was only completed as the Paseo de la Reforma after the end of his fateful three-year sojourn as emperor. But when the French army left for home in 1867 the forces of Benito Juárez defeated Maximilian who was captured and shot. Charlotte went insane and died years later in Europe, forever dreaming of the adventure in Mexico that went wrong.

With the re-establishment of the republic, the castle was designated the seat of the president and General Porfirio Díaz was the first to take up official residence in 1876. Lázaro Cárdenas, the popular president of the revolution, whose puritanical streak was displayed when he closed the city's brothels and gambling houses, did not wish to surround himself with such luxury. During his period of office (1934–40) he moved into the modern Residencia Presidencial de los Piños on the western edge of the park. This remains the official address of the Mexican president to this day.

Cárdenas designated the castle as the **Museo Nacional de Historia**, but as rebuilding took until 1944, it fell to General Manuel Avila Camacho to perform the opening ceremony. The castle, a 20-minute steep hike up from the park, is a good place from which to see Mexico City in all its grandeur – provided there isn't too much smog.

The museum's artifacts include Maximilian's carriage and the plain, black coach in which Juarez entered the city after the emperor's defeat. There are also important Mexican murals, including the vivid Siqueiros hall painted with themes of the revolution. In the castle's main western wing, 20 rooms are devoted to Mexico's history, from the conquistadors to the revolution. The paintings also include works by European artists who traveled through Mexico in the 19th century and left a

apultepec's rge lake.

permanent record of their impressions. Other murals include Juan O'Gorman's vision of independence and José Clemente Orozco's violent interpretation on the theme *Juarez, the Church and the Imperialists.*

In the east wing (Alcazar) you can visit the rooms used by the Mexican dictators when the castle was the presidential seat. The chambers where the Habsburg emperor dwelt with Charlotte are furnished in period style with some pieces purchased at a later date. There are also two full-length portraits of the unfortunate Maximilian and Charlotte who were respectively 32 and 24 when they arrived in Mexico.

The Escalina de Carlota, the Charlotte Steps, named after the empress who was described by one historian as "brooding, haughty and highstrung," lead back down to the park. Beneath the castle, architect Pedro Ramírez Vázquez's **Galería de Historia** is also known as Museo del Caracol because it is shaped like a snail. Its display is built around an accessible presentation of the Mexicans' historical battle for freedom.

Artistic pilgrimage: Not far from the foot of the castle is the sleek, steel-and-glass edifice of the **Museo de Arte Moderno**, also designed by Ramírez Vázquez. It is the perfect setting to display contemporary trends in Mexican art. Among the museum's most important collections are works by Dr Atl, Orozco, Rivera, Siqueiros, Kahlo, Tamayo and Goitia and later works from the second half of this century. Especially notable are two small but beautiful permanent exhibits: one is dedicated to the great Mexican photographer, Manuel Alvarez Bravo, and the other features a collection of wonderful landscape paintings by the 19th-century Mexican artist José María Velasco.

The **Museo Rufino Tamayo** on the other side of the Paseo de la Reforma is housed in an expensive and clever building conceived by designers Abraham Zabludosky and Teodoro González de Léon. Inaugurated in 1981, the museum

Chapultepec Park.

houses Rufino Tamayo's outstanding international collection, as well as his own work, which includes a splendid portrait of his wife, Olga. The main body of the museum is built around two vast exhibition spaces, housing paintings, drawings and wall-hangings by some 150 contemporary artists from around the world, among them works by Picasso, Dalí, and Francis Bacon as well as Mexican artists. Between them lies a covered patio, reserved for sculptures. The rooms on the second floor are devoted to changing exhibitions. The museum also has an auditorium in which are staged various cultural events, and a cafeteria.

The Museo Rufino Tamayo now enjoys worldwide fame as another impressive example of the excellence of Mexican museum architecture. This reputation for excellence has come about largely in response to the neighboring Museo Nacional de Antropología designed by Pedro Ramírez Vásquez. The museum was opened in 1964. The next chapter relates some of the history associated with the building.

Outside the museum the Paseo de la Reforma continues west to enter residential areas occupied by well-to-do Mexicans, neighborhoods such as Lomas de Chapultepec, Bosques de las Lomas and **Polanco.**

On the left, before the Paseo de la Reforma crosses the highway known as the Periférico, is the **Auditorio Nacional**, the city's largest assembly and concert hall. The whole complex is known as the Unidad Artistica y Cultural del Bosque and houses several theaters and administrative offices.

Behind the anthropological museum (and its massive car park) is the Centro de Arte Contemporáneo, belonging to the television company Televisa. Televisa has an extensive collection of modern art and holds international exhibitions in these premises.

Los Lagos: Across the Paseo de la Reforma from the anthropological museum is the largest of the park's man-

made lakes, which at the weekends teems with rowing boats. The Casa del Lago on the lakeside belongs to the National University and is the venue for cultural events like plays, concerts and exhibitions. On Sunday in particular this more traditional part of Chapultepec, between the castle and the lake, is the province of casual strollers, traders selling pink candyfloss and brightly colored windmills, and photographers with model horses and pony traps for the children. The nearby zoo is home to more than 2,500 animals of over 300 species. A major attraction is a family of pandas, whose young were born here.

On the far side of the Periférico, the second part of Chapultepec Park was opened in 1972. From the highway you can see the massive roller-coaster (*montana rusa*) in the adults' pleasure park. Next door is the electricity company's **Museo Tecnológico**, which is devoted to developments in technology. To the southeast, beside another small lake, the **Museo de Historia Natural** provides a guided tour through the history of evolution. A miniature railway (*Ferrocarril Escénico*) chugs around the artificial lake, passing through a tunnel of terror and a tunnel of love. On the banks of the other lake in this part of the park you will find the select Restaurant Del Lago.

Resting place of the famous: Between the second and third sections of Chapultepec stretches a huge cemetery, the Panteón de Dolores. Eighty-nine eminent Mexicans are buried here in the **Rotonda de los Hombres Ilustres** (on Avenida Constituyentes), founded in 1876 by Porfirio Díaz. Among them are the best of the muralists: Orozco, Rivera and Siqueiros, as well as the composers Jaime Nuñó and Agustín Lara.

The third part of the city's great park contains additional leisure attractions. In the sea-water aquarium called **Atlantis**, sealions and dolphins perform their tricks for the public. And in **Aguas Salvajes** you can safely simulate riding the rapids. The only real danger is accidentally getting too close to the archers who have a practice ground nearby. Barbecues are banned in this more remote part of the park.

The smart Polanco area north of the park is being touted as a trendier place to spend time than the old Zona Rosa, but this is largely because more shops and restaurants have opened for the benefit of the affluent residents of the area. It is much less compact than the Zona Rosa and therefore more confusing to walk around, although most of what's interesting can be found on or around Polanco's main drag, **Avenida Presidente Masaryk**. This runs parallel to, and about half a mile north of, the Paseo de la Reforma and can be accessed easily by taking the Metro one stop from Auditorio (just east of the National Auditorium in the park) to Polanco. There's a Sanborn's on Masaryk, right opposite the headquarters of the Secretaría de Turismo, and a pleasant, fountain-filled park a few blocks away on Horacio between Hegel and Lope de Vega.

Left, some friends never talk back. Right, a boy and his toys

THE MUSEUM OF ANTHROPOLOGY

Water signifies life in the ancient cultures of the highlands. Through water, the rain god Tlaloc guaranteed bounty to believers. A massive monolith of Tlaloc at the entrance to the Museo Nacional de Antropología (Anthropology Museum) is a reminder of this belief. The seemingly unfinished block-like statue with circles for eyes, was brought here in the 1960s amid continuous downpours, which some said was a protest at being moved from his original location. The museum's magnificent inner court of pink stone with water falling down the single column holding up the striking roof canopy, was inspired by the Mayan ruins at Uxmal.

The Anthropology Museum has proved to be an inspiration for a whole generation of modern Mexican museums. The flat-roofed building was designed by a team of architects under Pedro Ramírez Vásquez and opened in 1968. Before then the art treasures of pre-Columbian Mexico had been collecting dust in warehouses, and the sculptures of the Aztecs were either walled into or buried under public buildings. But now, clearly displayed on the ground floor of the museum, a selection of first-class art from ancient Mexico leads visitors through the millennia of Indian high culture. On the second story there is displayed a collection of contemporary Indian art.

To whet the public's appetite for the Indian artifacts displayed within, there are regular performances in the museum courtyard of a spectacular ritual dating from the pre-Spanish era. In the past such rituals were celebrated in many areas of Mexico to honor the god of spring and fertility, Xipe Totec.

Today the tradition of the *voladores* or "flying men" is preserved mainly by the Totonaken on the Gulf Coast and in the Sierra de Puebla. The *voladores* climb a tall pole, wound around with

Preceding pages: crowds gather around a street entertainer. Below, the Museum of Anthropology

ropes which are fastened on to a rotating wooden frame. The *capitán* takes his place at the top of the pole, playing a flute and beating on a drum. When he gives the word, the four fliers, who have each tied themselves to the end of a rope, somersault backwards from the wooden frame. The ropes unravel from the pole and after 13 revolutions of the frame the men land safely on the ground. Multiply 13 by the number of fliers and you get 52, the old Indian "century."

The museum is extremely large and takes time to savor, but be sure to take in the marvelous **Sala Mexica**, the jewel of the museum dedicated to Aztec art and history. All these halls are on the patio level, but there is more: on the second floor is the **Ethnology Museum**, describing the life of Indians and decorated with contemporary murals.

To the right of the museum's entrance, the hall devoted to an **Introduction to Archaeology** has a useful map of the Mexican regional cultures and artistic landscape. The next gallery, the **Sala de Orígen** deals with man's occupation of the New World. During the last two periods of the Ice Age until about 18,000 BC, big-game hunters migrated across the Bering Strait, which was then a land bridge between Siberia and North America. They came in pursuit of mammoth and bison. We know from excavations that they finally reached the southern tip of Tierra del Fuego about 8000 BC. The Ixtapan mammoth find, not far from present-day Mexico City, produced evidence about the way of life and hunting practices of these big-game hunters.

Around 8000 BC the climate changed when precipitation became less frequent and savannahs turned into steppes and then deserts. Herbivores like the mammoth or the giant sloth lost their subsistence base. Along with the improvement in hunting techniques, this climatic catastrophe led to the extinction of those giant beasts whose bones we admire today. Under these new ecological conditions the desert cultures came into

being, and the hunters started to concentrate on stalking small animals or gathering seeds and fruits.

The cultivation of maize: The first cultivated plants appeared in Mexico around the fourth millennium BC. Avocados, pumpkins and tomatoes were grown and maize was developed from the cross-fertilization of different grass types. But it was the classic triad of foods – maize, beans and pumpkins – that formed the basis for the rise of pre-classical Mesoamerican cultures in the second millennium before Christ.

The variety of clay maternal figures representing fertility and the now famous acrobat with wildly contorted limbs, hint at the increasing importance of the arts to the new society. In this period the social preconditions for an artisan class first emerged, with the artists specializing in working clay, stone, obsidian, bone, wood or shells.

Eventually a powerful priestly class emerged, and it is their urban architecture and handicrafts that are on display

in the **Hall of Teotihuacán**. The way that human likeness was depicted in stone masks, the small clay figures and, above all, the image of the rain god Tlaloc, was tightly circumscribed by these priests.

Tlaloc appears on urns and clay vases and on brightly colored frescoes in the large pre-Columbian city of Teotihuacán which, along with the reconstructed facade of the Quetzalcoatl pyramid, give an idea of what the original ceremonial center must once have been like. The pottery was all made without potters' wheels, which were introduced by Spanish invaders.

Also in the hall is a depiction of happily dancing skeletons, which was saved from a palace on the periphery of the city. The rain god crouches over the dancing dead, spewing forth colorful streams of life-giving water which came from paradise to the dry world of the high valleys of Teotihuacán.

In the middle of this hall is a 4-meter (13-ft) high statue of Tlaloc's wife Chalchiuhtlicue, at the same time magical and vaguely threatening.

After the fall of Teotihuacán (AD 600), the power monopoly of the priests was destroyed and a warrior civilization prepared the way for the rise of the Aztecs. In the Hall of the Toltecs, jaguars and coyotes, which at one time guarded the entrance to the temple platforms, appear to spring at the visitor. The Atlantes who carried the roof of the temple of the morning star god are carved as likenesses of these warriors: fully armed with the *atlatl* (a kind of discus), shield and spear. The Toltecs preserved the skills of the Teotihuacán craftsmen. Priceless inlay work, such as the warrior head which shows through a coyote's jaws, alabaster vases, and large stone face masks were found among the ruins of the capital, Tula.

Tyrannical Aztecs: The great sculptures of the Aztecs are impressively displayed on the front side of the **Hall of the Mexicas** across from the main entrance to the museum. A replica feather head-

Xochipilli, the Aztec flour prince.

168

dress gives an impression of the splendor of the Aztec kings and nobility.

A reproduction of the *Codex Boturini* describes the migration of the tribe from their mythic ancestral home, Aztlan, to the Lake of Texcoco, while other pages of the book tell, in pictures, of the defeat of their neighbors and one-time masters. Codices, primitive fold-out "books" filled with hieroglyphics written on bark paper or sometimes deerskin, are understandably rare. Filled with records of such matters as religion and astronomy, they are still largely obscure.

Sacrifices of blood and human hearts took on great significance among the Aztecs. As the warriors pushed farther and farther into new territories, so the gods became ever more greedy and tyrannical. Even though the sacrificial knives and bowls were very artistic, they served a cruel purpose. Here there are also reproductions of the painted lists which recorded the tribute of the subjugated peoples, who sent their prisoners for sacrifice to their gods.

The colossal statue of Coatlicue, the Aztec mother goddess, is among the most impressive in the hall. The two snake heads which replace the human head signify the gender duality of this deity. A complex array of symbolism is contained within the goddess's form: a snake skirt, wild cat's paws with eyes, two human hearts and two pairs of human hands on the breast, a deaths-head, feathers, a double mouth and multiple sets of eyes.

The "sun stone," commonly but mistakenly called the "calendar stone," is filled with a similarly diverse concentration of symbolism. It depicts a tribute to the sun god, Tonatiuh, whose face can be seen in the middle of the slab, and it dominates the other exhibits from the middle of the hall.

The bloodthirsty god was once colorfully painted, like the whole stone. On both sides of the face are claws that clutched human hearts. The claws with eyes inserted between them also form faces, and they themselves are part of

the central face with its two rectangular wings extending from top to bottom.

This sign of olin, which is further qualified by four discs indicating the date "4 olin" shows the day on which the world of the Aztecs, the fifth world according to their beliefs, would come to an end. The four previous worlds are signified by the wings of the symbol. Three other dates and the four directions of the heavens are represented by a symbol cluster within the figure. Beginning anticlockwise from the apex, an outer ring shows the symbols for the 20 days. Snakes and deific images on the edge of the sun stone depict the various attributes of Tonatiuh.

Superb animal sculptures such as coiled rattlesnakes, oversized grasshoppers, jaguars, coyotes, and lizards, are another defining feature of Aztec art. Using only a very few strokes, these artists were able to capture the essence of these symbolic animals in highly polished stone sculptures.

Before visiting the other side of the

museum with its exhibitions of the cultures of southern and western Mexico, try the museum's very good restaurant with its respectable Mexican menu. Or alternatively have a rest by the fountain in the courtyard. The bulrushes in the waters there are meant to resemble the environment of Tenochtitlán as it was once, on the swampy islands of the Lake of Texcoco.

Olmec influences: The visitor to the **Hall of Oaxacan Cultures** is greeted by a reproduction of fabulous, almost abstract, wall patterns from the Mixtecan palaces in Mitla. A map here provides an overview of the mountain landscape of Oaxaca, where the Zapotecs and the Mixtecs lived. In the wide, fertile valleys of Oaxaca, since the first millennium BC, these cultures expanded around the most important of their ceremonial centers, Monte Alban.

The *Danzantes*, fragments of large stone reliefs depicting dancing figures, were sculpted around 600 BC and convey the unmistakable influence of the early Olmecan culture of the Gulf coast. One can imagine the role of shamanistic practices and the ritual use of drugs depicted in these reliefs from the grotesquely distorted limbs and the hands pressed against the abdomen.

The Zapotecs of Oaxaca took great care in the construction of the tombs of their priests. Clay urns in the form of the gods stood on cornices above the tomb entrances. A replica of one of the famous tombs from Monte Alban is also shown here.

In the **Hall of the Gulf Coast**, the exhibits date back to the earliest days of the Olmec culture. The ingenious Olmecan stonemasons created the enormous heads, perhaps as portraits of some of their chiefs, using only stone age tools and techniques.

Deified jaguar-human beings or "baby-face" figures with mongoloid features were principal themes among the puzzling peoples of this pre-Christian civilization. The highly valued jades and emeralds they found were often

Olmec era head.

made into polished ceremonial hatchets. In a famous archaeological find, near the important site of La Venta, a group of small jade figures was found among a setting of stone megaliths. It is believed that these figures had some sort of ritual significance.

A model of the Totonac temple of El Tajín is also on show here. Of a very high artistic quality are the *hacha*, *palma* and *yugo* stone sculptures exemplifying elements of the ritualistic ball game around which so much upper-class leisure was centered.

The complex **World of the Mayas** forms the central theme of the next gallery. The pinnacle of classical Mayan culture from the 3rd through to the 10th century can be seen in the diverse artifacts and replicas: finely worked sandstone stelae from Yaxchilán with depictions of priest-kings and complex symbol texts; colorfully painted, lifelike clay figures from Jaina island near Campeche; jade and shell jewelry from the lowlands; and fantastic pyramid and palace architecture. Later the center shifted to the Yucatán peninsula.

With a new wave of immigration, pilgrimage centers like those adjoining the sacred Cenote, the well of Chichén Itzá, experienced new importance. A copy of the Toltec city of Tula was built, where the Mayan rain god Chac stood alongside the Toltecan Quetzalcoatl.

In stark contrast are the cultures of **Northern and Western Mexico**: in the last two galleries of the ground floor, the ceramics on display read like a library of the daily life of the Indians set in clay. Depicted here are animals, acrobats, ball players and complete scenes of indoor and outdoor life. The essence of this art, as it was found in their graves, suggests that for these people nature and daily life had replaced the gods as their main concern.

The upper story of the museum offers an excursion through the contemporary life of Mexico's Indians, the exhibits including traditional costumes, festivals, handicrafts and traditions.

the Hall of
e Mexicas.

XOCHIMILCO

The most colorful photos of Mexico City are usually taken in Xochimilco. At weekends, the traffic is as busy as it is on the roads, but here the gondolas are painted with cheerful designs, their canopies wreathed in flowers, and the Mexicans certainly don't sit still in well-behaved rows listening to the driver's commentary. Instead they hold rowdy parties on board the rocking gondolas, liberally supplied with *tacos*, beer and tequila, to the strains of a hired *mariachi* band performing raucous renditions of *Las Mananitas*, the Mexican birthday serenade.

If you want to experience this side of choice. Look a little closer and you'll realize that nowadays the floral decorations are made of paper, but the names they frame are all the more flowery as though to compensate: Graciela, Lupita, Angelita, Isabel, Esperanza, Carmelita...

"*Xóchitl*" is the Aztec (*nahuatl*) word for flowers, and "Xochimilco" translates as "in the flower fields." Flowers and vegetables are still grown here, but no longer in the legendary *chinampas*, the "floating gardens" of the Aztecs that so impressed the Spanish invaders. Only one motorboat is allowed to chug around what remains of the "Venice of the

Xochimilco, you should choose a Sunday to visit. But be prepared to join a steady stream of cars heading out of the city for the countryside – the journey may take you an hour. By Metro you simply zip along to Taxqueña station and change there onto the quaint tram (*tren ligeno*) to Xochimilco.

Once at Xochimilco, you're faced with the dilemma of choosing between the 2,000-odd *trajineras* (that's what they call gondolas here) working the waterways. Of the five quays or *embarcaderos*, Nativitas is the biggest and best known. It's here that most of the market stalls and food stands are congregated at the weekends. Maybe the name of the boat, hiding among the flowers, will help with your

New World" – and it belongs to the Mayor of Xochimilco. On this boat you can travel through the canals, where the air is heady with the scents of camomile and carnations that waft from the banks out into the lagoon.

In 1890 the travel writer Ernst von Hesse-Wartegg found some of these same "curious islands" drifting against his boat: "A tangle of long dark roots, quite independent of the seabed, forms the base of the floating bodies. The fertile clouds of dust that blow from the stubble fields during the dry season, together with the accumulation of decaying plant and animal matter, in time laid down a layer of soil, the wind brought plant seeds, and thus the green islands were created...

They move around the lake in the wind… run aground on the banks in heavy storms, one on top of the other, soon growing into each other, and when they tire of their vagrant life, they form part of the proper mainland."

The fertile black soil of the *chinampas* always gave a high yield, irrespective of the rainy season. There were harvests up to four times a year. The people who lived on the banks used to anchor the little islands with posts so that they could work them. Sometimes they also built their huts on the islands and let themselves float around the lake. Not only did they carry their homes with them like snails, but also the land on which and from which they lived. It was this independence that von Hesse-Wartegg so envied in the great *chinampa* farmers.

In the past they used *canoas* (dug-out canoes) to carry the harvest to market in the center of the city. During colonial times, the largest of these barges would have been anything up to 15 meters (50 ft) long, capable of transporting several tonnes of maize.

Today, 190 km (120 miles) of Xochimilco's canals are still navigable. The German Rowing Club "Antares," with a long tradition in Mexico, trains here. A section of the canal was widened to create the course for the 1968 Olympics. Many of the canals are barely passable, so completely are they covered with water hyacinths, which the farmers happily scattered on their fields as fertilizer. But agriculture is slowly returning to Xochimilco. Homes are appearing on the *chinampas*, and now machines are working at clearing the canals of their carpet of plants.

Meanwhile other dangers are threatening Xochimilco. The problems of the city's growing population are spilling over into the surrounding countryside. A quarter of the city's water supply is drawn from the ground-water to the southeast of the city, above all from Xochimilco. It's not hard to envisage a time when these reserves will be exhausted. Some canals have already dried up.

At the same time, large areas of Xochimilco are subject to flooding during the rainy season. In 1987 UNESCO declared Xochimilco part of the "cultural heritage of mankind" and the Salinas government initiated an ecological protection program for the canal system. On the one hand this called upon the popula-

tion of Xochimilco to take action to help themselves – by keeping the canals clean and planting more trees, for example. At the same time, the government plans recommended the installation of a sewerage system and the construction of overspill lakes to counter the danger to the city of flooding. Finally, private investment in the scheme was to finance a massive leisure park.

The people of Xochimilco remain skeptical, however, suspicious because under the aid program they will have to surrender over 1,000 hectares (2,500 acres) of land for the planned projects. They are preparing to fight. Since the revolution of 1910, the authorities here are no longer afforded the blind respect they once were where land is concerned – the land on which one lives and works.

From the back of beyond, where you'd be lucky to catch a hazy glimpse over the distant snow-covered peaks of Popocatépetl and Iztaccíhuatl (at their most imposing on a winter afternoon), the one motorboat slowly makes its way back toward the center of Xochimilco. Narrow *canoas* rock past it, laden with red and white geraniums. Unlike the gondolas they have no names, but aphorisms along their sides bear witness to the people's almost fatalistic attachment to their watery environment: *Soy feliz entre las flores* (I'm happy among the flowers); or *Navegar es mi destino* (I was destined to be a sailor). The Xochimilco flower market does great credit to the ancient name of the city. ∎

Left, during the week, Xochimilco is a peaceful place. **Right**, waiting for customers in an enticing rainbow of painted gondolas.

COYOACÁN
AND SAN ANGEL

Coyoacán and San Angel are among the most beautiful of the hamlets once felt to be some distance from the city but now encompassed by its sprawl. Coyoacán is much older than San Angel, and its residents have a stronger sense of tradition. But in both these suburban communities you can detect the intertwining of three different cultural epochs: the pre-Spanish, colonial, and modern styles.

The route to San Angel is very straightforward – southbound along Insurgentes for about 20 km (12 miles). Ten blocks before San Angel you'll spot the busy mosaic facade, Mexican-mural style (incorporating lots of people) of the **Teatro Insurgentes** on the right : the theme is *The Theater in Mexico* and the work was created by Diego Rivera. The enormous hands have bright red lacquered fingernails and are partially covered in crimson lace. They seem to hold up the composition of the great comic actor Mario Moreno, Cantínflas, taking from the rich and giving to the poor.

The borders between the two communities have long since disappeared and both are dominated by colonial architecture. In contrast to Coyoacán, which is very mixed, the population of **San Angel** is far more homogeneous and the residents belong primarily to the wealthy upper middle class. Many Germans arrived here in the first half of this century, and as a result there are several places where German cuisine and delicacies can be purchased.

San Angel has somehow managed to retain much of its earlier atmosphere and charm with crooked, cobblestoned streets and secretive mansions, many hidden behind high walls and fabulous gardens. The charming **El Carmen** church has tile-covered domes and a serene 17th-century cloister. Today it houses both the socio-anthropological and ethnological departments of the

Preceding pages: Dieg Rivera created this mural for th Teatro Insurgentes Left, romantic Coyoacán.

Mexican Institute for Anthropology and History. The rest of the cloister with its fine courtyard serves as a museum, housing colonial art and an intriguing collection of the mummified bodies of priests, nuns and nobles.

Don't miss inspecting the spectacular **Casa del Risco Fountain**, a national monument made of hundreds of gaily colored plates, cups, saucers and vases, most of them centuries old, set into the wall of the house of the same name.

Every Saturday a handicraft market, known as the **Bazar del Sábado** fills **San Jacinto square**, a sort of upper-middle-class Indian market place. Usually packed, which makes getting around a squeeze, this much-visited bazaar is attractive to many because artists are often here selling their own work. Prices and wares range from the quaint and cheap to the grand and expensive.

In the patio of the bazaar's main building you can eat and drink to the soft sound of *marimba* music or simply gaze at the things offered for sale: pictures; clay, onyx or wood figures; pottery, clothing, and jewelry. Even if you want to resist the many distractions and buy nothing, a Saturday excursion to the Bazar del Sábado can be a fun and stimulating experience, as it has been for at least three decades.

Also on the plaza is the **San Angel Inn**, a former *hacienda* and a place full of aristocratic appeal that has a fine restaurant at which to eat. It is mostly frequented by wealthy Mexicans, people who are nostalgic for the charms of a departed era.

Diego Rivera's **pre-Hispanic collection** is housed in an immense building designed by the celebrated muralist. "I return to the people the artistic heritage I was able to redeem from their ancestors" is the dedication that Rivera had inscribed in the entranceway and which gratifies the visitor of today.

San Angel has numerous art and antique shops and many galleries featuring artists from all over the world as well as Mexican artists with pre-Span-

ft,
edding
lls.
ght, idyllic
sting place.

ish roots. In one gallery, in an elegant colonial house, the artist, a Huichol Indian, receives visitors. He wears the traditional attire of his people: a shirt and three-quarter-length cotton trousers which are loosely cut and richly embroidered. His hair is long and he wears handmade leather sandals on his naked feet. Next to him stands his wife, a delicate, blond Polish woman. The couple explain that they live in a traditional Huichol village and have only come to the capital on account of the exhibition. In his pictures, made of wool threads in bright natural colors, the artist integrates those symbols that were created and used by his ancestors long before the Spanish conquered Mexico.

A beautiful route between the twin communities of San Angel and Coyoacán is the Callejón del Monasterio, a narrow, tranquil lane with high walls. A parallel street also leads from the Avenida Insurgentes Sur past the **Peña El Condor Pasa**, an artists' pub boasting Latin-American music and poetry readings. Nearby on Insurgentes Sur is the **Monumento Alvaro Obregón**, a monument which stands on the actual spot where the revolutionary president was murdered in 1928.

Wandering the small, sleepy streets of **Coyoacán** it is easy for visitors to imagine themselves in another era. Behind the green of the trees, palms, and ivy and the bright blossoms of the bushes and shrubs, are some of the most beautiful colonial houses in the city with facades that are decorated with huge portals made from carved wood, often interrupted by narrow, wrought-iron balconies. Not infrequently, poor cottages can also be seen alongside the villas, since rich and poor often live side by side in this district.

The name Coyoacán goes back to the pre-Spanish epoch. It is derived from the *nahuatl* word *Coyohuacan* meaning "place of coyotes." Statues of these lean, mean beasts sit beside the fountain in the Plaza Hidalgo and the Jardín, which form the heart and the social center of

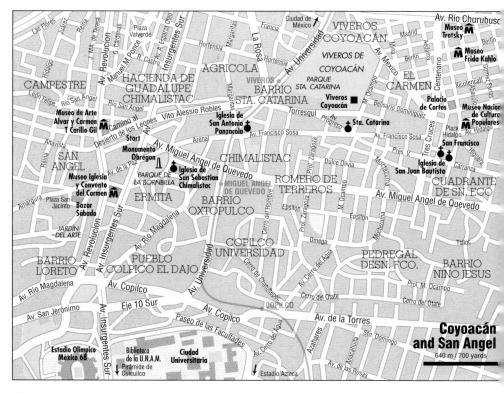

Coyoacán and San Angel

640 m / 700 yards

Coyoacán. Shoeshiners, peddlers, organ grinders, and ice vendors flank the fountain, and it's nice to watch all this activity from one of the numerous cafés.

Nearly 100 years before the Spanish conquest, the Aztecs conquered this area and subjugated the former metropolis of Tenochtitlán. Hernán Cortéz found the inhabitants of Coyoacán to be willing allies, and he set up his headquarters among them. The supposed house of his traitorous consort Malinche is pointed out to visitors.

Intellectuals and artists: Many famous artists, politicians, and intellectuals have lived and died in Coyoacán, among them the highly original painter Frida Kahlo whose anguished life as the partner of Diego Rivera was often the subject of her work. The **Frida Kahlo Museum** (the house where she was born in 1910 and in which she lived, off and on with Rivera, from 1929 until her death in 1954) is filled with her paintings and a great deal of the pre-Columbian art that she collected. The memorabilia includes many of the couple's love letters and some of Frida's colorful Indian dresses.

The rooms have been retained in their original style, and the walls are decorated with numerous paintings by both artists. On boxes, cabinets, and shelves is a harmonious collection of household appliances and folk art of Indian origin. The collection symbolizes the attraction which both artists felt toward traditional Mexican culture, and demonstrates their zeal as collectors. Most remarkable are the many papier-mâché figures in the shape of skeletons or devils with red or black horns. The figures accompany the visitor from the entrance to the patio.

At Coyoacán, too, is the mournful **Leon Trotsky museum-memorial**, a tribute to that first great heretic of the communist faith. It was in this fortress-like home on August 20, 1940, that Trotsky, despite heavy steel doors and round-the-clock armed guards, was assassinated by a Spanish communist, apparently at the instigation of Josef Sta-

the Bazar
l Sábado.

lin. The interloper, who supposedly came to woo Trotsky's daughter, stabbed him to death with an icepick. In the rear garden is **Leon Trotsky's tomb**, designed by Juan O'Gorman.

Two other museums are worthy of note: the **Museo de las Culturas Populares** (Museum of Popular Culture) which is to the left of the church of San Juan Bautista in the **Calle Hidalgo**; and the **Museo de las Intervenciones**, which documents the history of foreign intervention in Mexico, in the former **Churubusco Cloister**. The latter can be reached by taking one of the large taxis with the sign "Metro General Anaya" from the Kahlo Museum.

Today, Coyoacán is still favored by artists and intellectuals who come to places like the **Parnaso** in search of like-minded people. In this bistro-like café with an adjoining bookshop they sit over a cappuccino conscientiously studying the daily papers. A few streets away, soldiers guard the residences of several former Mexican state presidents.

For many Mexicans, Coyoacán is also the part of the city where you can buy the best ice cream. Next to elegant restaurants there are small, modest taverns. Unpretentious though these places may seem, everyone knows that only here can you get the best *pancita* (pig's stomach) or the best *pozole* (a type of casserole) which is prepared in a huge pot in the open entrance of the restaurant. Even elegantly attired businessmen come a long way through the morning traffic to begin their workday with a hearty breakfast in Coyoacán.

There are many ways of getting to Coyoacán. Buses, taxis and the Metro make the trip as far as the **Plaza Hidalgo**, in the heart of the district. The Metro also stops at the **Viveros**, a large parkland. A walk from here to the center of Coyoacán can be an experience in itself, offering a distinctive view of the area.

Green lungs: Viveros translates literally as nursery, but for many it is the essential "green lungs" of the southern part of the capital, allowing the locals to

breathe. A rich Mexican named Miguel Angel de Quevedo (an important street is named after him) gave this huge area to the city, with his will stating that should the grounds be used for any other purpose they would revert to the private possession of the family.

In view of the high real estate prices in Coyoacán, the Quevedo legacy is the best guarantor that Viveros remains protected against development. In the past 20 years, several state research institutes settled on the edge of Viveros. However, after lengthy court battles, they were forced to move and their premises were demolished.

In the middle of Viveros is a garden-like market in which the most varied kinds of flowers and plants are sold. On the way out of the market is a small, cobblestone lane leading to the dreamy **Jardín Santa Catarina**, a shady garden scattered with restaurants and handicraft workshops in colonial style.

Colonial mansions: The **Calle Francisco Sosa** runs directly past the garden and is one of Coyoacán's most beautiful streets. Numerous art dealers, galleries, and antique dealers are housed in the street's lordly colonial villas. Francisco Sosa opens into the great park, **Jardín del Centenario**, which adjoins the Plaza Hidalgo with the much remodeled 16th-century **San Juan Bautista** church

Unfortunately, the large area of Viveros and the many smaller gardens are not enough to keep the air of Coyoacán clean. As the trees of the Jardín del Centenario began to die, artists used the opportunity to make original sculptures out of their remaining trunks and branches.

At the weekend, the park belongs to the children. Every Saturday and Sunday, the Jardín changes into an enormous open-air theater when Miko arrives with his big suitcase from which he magically takes rabbits' tails, wolves' furs or a little red hood. Every weekend hundreds of children join Miko, and wait breathlessly for their turn, laughing, shouting, clapping and singing.

n Angel
wer
arket.

THE MODERN UNIVERSITY CITY

Mexico's National University (known locally as the **Universidad Nacional Autónoma de México**), and often referred to as **UNAM**, can be reached along Avenida Insurgentes Sur or by Metro to the Universidad stop. The main part of the university was built in the 1950s under the supervision of Carlos Lazo to plans by Enrique del Moral and Mario Pani. Flamboyant may not be a word usually associated with universities, but it's not too out of place here. The campus has become a tourist site in its own right, largely because of such buildings as the 10-story library covered with murals by Juan O'Gorman. And, of course, it is of special interest to those with an architectural bent. There are always visitors wandering around taking photographs, and the public are welcome to patronize the various inexpensive university cafeterias.

First university: As early as 1553, South America's first university was opened in Mexico by Viceroy Luis de Velasco. After several changes of site the university ended up in the Zócalo, but it had to move again when the new Supreme Court was built in 1935.

Plans for the revolutionary new complex were helped by several factors. Under the presidency of Miguel Alemáns (1946–52), Mexico had opened itself up to industrialization. A national architecture based on simple lines and constructed according to the latest techniques was consistent with the modern drive for profit. The country was also endeavoring to espouse modernism. The neocolonial style that was still in favor in the Zócalo for the centers of power was considered obsolete elsewhere.

The ground plan of the campus is based on a wide square, around which cluster the groups of faculty buildings. The strict geometry of the modern blocks is broken up by an asymmetrical layout. Thus the white towers that house the natural science and psychology departments face one another across the edge of the main walkway.

The **Chancellery** is a particularly lavish building, designed by Mario Pani, Enrique del Moral and Salvador Ortega. The 15-story tower block comprises a vertical and a horizontal section, embellished with Siqueiro's bas-relief *The People for the University, the University for the People* (1952–56). The relief is an amalgam of painting, sculpture and glass mosaic.

The right-hand corner of the Chancellery adjoins the **Library**, designed by Gustavo Saavedra and Juan Martínez de Velasco and renowned worldwide for Juan O'Gorman's monumental mosaic, which expresses a vision of Mexico's past and future. The library has space to house over two million books. Beneath it are administrative offices and reading rooms, while a pond and a terrace hewn from the volcanic rock and decorated with pre-Columbian motifs create a pleasant setting. The library embodies two very different trends, which are united to experimental effect in UNAM. There is the international style, seen as synonymous with progress, together with the urge to access Mexico's own age-old culture in order to find acceptable solutions for today's problems.

Grassy courtyards: Colorful building materials, the covered walkways essential during the rains, the grassy inner courtyards based on the patio house, the involvement of educational artists – all are part and parcel of Mexican tradition. Particularly Mexican is the coordination of several styles, the ability to integrate and assimilate different trends.

A concrete example of stylistic extremes coexisting in one building is the pavilion of the Institute of Cosmic Ray Research, which was designed by Félix Candela and J.G. Reyna (1953). There are also the sports facilities to the south of the campus, especially Alberto T. Arais' *Frontones*, which draws on pre-Hispanic traditions.

The integration of art into the campus

became a hallmark of UNAM. It's not a question of individual components but the clever juxtaposition of similar elements, seen for example in the medical faculty building. Designed by Roberto Alvarez Espinosa, this features Franciso Eppens' glass mosaic *Life, Death and the Four Elements* (1952). Steps are used to accentuate the different levels of the lava field. The visitor is offered a continually changing perspective, enriched by vegetation and sculptures. The apparently loose layout rests upon a strict design.

City within a city: UNAM is a complete city in itself, with over 100 buildings, numerous squares and its own infrastructure of museums, shops, chapel, botanic gardens, post office, bus station and campus service industries. For this reason it is also known as Ciudad Universitaria (University City). The university reflects the explosive growth of the megapolis. Originally planned for 26,000 students, more than 300,000 are now studying there. Over the years many new buildings have sprung up, notably for the natural sciences, most of them conventional constructions without any architectural pretensions. UNAM has left its mark on a wide area, with a network of housing blocks, bars and supermarkets. It has turned into the most ambitious project of post-revolutionary Mexico and has long been a place of pilgrimage for art and architecture historians. Its international influence is undisputed.

The **Olympic Stadium** on the west side of Avenida Insurgentes also counts as part of UNAM. This is the work of architects A. Pérez Palacios, R. Salinas and J. Bravo (1953). Structurally, it resembles a cone-shaped volcano with a giant oval bowl sunk into the crater as an arena. The exterior is decorated with a mosaic relief by Diego Rivera, using motifs from the history of sport.

Arts center: To the south of UNAM on a slight incline is the arts center. It is bordered by Avenida Insurgentes and the **Periférico Metropolitano**, and

Mosaic riddl on the library.

186

scenically framed by the nearby volcano Xitle, Mount Ajusco, the UNAM buildings and the whole panorama of the Mexico valley. On rare clear days the twin volcanoes Popocatépetl and Iztaccíhuatl join the scene, too. In contrast to the building of UNAM, where the whole terrain was planned, the natural topography here was largely left untouched and instead integrated into the design. Geometric similarities to pre-Hispanic places of worship, especially Teotihuacán, are far from coincidental. The ground plan lies around a similar longitudinal axis. These bearings confirm the complex as part of UNAM.

The north side is defined by the **Unidad Bibliográfica** (the National Library, Hemerothek), the south by the concert hall buildings, the theater, cinema and dance center. A transverse crosses between the concert hall and the northern edge of the dance center in the right-hand corner. This transverse runs across the square in which Rufino Tamayo's totem-like sculpture stands,

leading into the **Centro Universitario de Teatro**, a little off to one side.

The sloping entrance of the theater building, as well as the northwest side of the Centro Universitario de Teatro, run parallel to the axis, which appears to divide the concert hall in two. The point of intersection of this axis and the transverse points to the significance of the square as the center of this site. Framed by terraces, walkways, entrance halls and vegetation, the square provides a scenic space for open-air events.

The plans for the arts center were drawn up by a team of architects from UNAM, under the leadership of Orso Núñez Ruiz-Velasco, Auturo Treviño Arizmendi and Arcadio Artis Espriú. The concert hall, **Sala Nezahualcóyotl** (1976), named after an Aztec poet prince, admits daylight only through the windows and doorway in the entrance hall, which leads to a flight of steps. It was designed for optimum acoustics and, next to the Amsterdam Concertgebouw, is one of the most successful concert

halls in the world. Almost every day of the week there are performances by the UNAM Philharmonic or a visiting international ensemble on the stage in the center of the wood-panelled auditorium.

The theater complex houses the Teatro Juan Ruiz de Alarcón and the smaller Foro Experimental Sor Juana Inés de la Cruz (1979), named after two writers from the colonial period. The theaters seat 430 and 250 people respectively. The high-rise section houses the fly tower. Two entrances lead up a flight of steps and into a foyer. The ground plan is elegantly mirrored by the interior, which in turn reflects the functional purpose. Thus an exciting alternation of right-angles and 45-degree angles in both ground plan and elevations creates a constancy of form, crucial to the overall impact. This formal principle is common to all constructions which are built around a variety of focal points.

The building opposite also links two functional areas by a common foyer: the Miguel Covarrubia ballroom and the Miguel Chávez recital room, used for chamber music. In addition the complex houses two cinemas, a bookshop and the center's administrative offices. A diagonal toward the square passes through a high foyer into a series of passageways which form the heart of both complexes, their layout determined by the fall of light and shadow.

Clever orchestration: The Unidad Bibliográfica is physically set apart from the complex but closely related in terms of texture, color and style. It houses a large part of the million-volume national library founded by Benito Juárez in 1867, as well as treasures from the ancient university and secularized monasteries and valuable early literature. An old books department is located in the old town in what was once the monastery of San Agustín, the previous home of the National Library.

Massive cuboids adorn the facade of the library. A flight of steps leads up to a small courtyard. Across this runs a glass entry into the foyer. The fortress- **Villa in the Pedregal lava field.**

like quality is moderated by the three-dimensional outer skin, which isn't much in keeping with the internal structure. The lofty inner courtyard of the five-story building is particularly unusual, and is adorned with sculptures by Frederico Silva and Hersúa.

The interaction of the parts that make up UNAM's whole becomes clear by passing through them. Walk through the campus and it opens out around you, but drive around it and it blossoms to particularly aesthetic effect. According to your position, individual buildings come into view, only to disappear again into the lava field.

Head down Avenida Insurgentes for another mile or so to reach the sculpture park, **Espacio Escultórico** which, though separated, is regarded as part of the university complex. Once discovered, however, the visitor quickly realizes that the park successfully bridges architecture and topography. Established in 1978–80 it is the result of a collaboration between the Mexican artists Helen Escobedo, Manuel Felguérez, Frederico Silva, Hersúa, Sebastián and Mathias Goeritz, a German. It includes a lava field framed by colored blocks of concrete, a kind of Mexican Stonehenge of almost earth-force energy.

This collectively planned space for quiet reflection is also an answer to the nearby **Round Pyramid of Cuiculco**, a meeting place firmly rooted in Mexican culture which was covered in lava for thousands of years until its excavation in 1922. Goeritz achieved a worldwide reputation for his Towers of the Satellite City (1957–58), which you pass on the way out toward Querétaro. He also instigated the **Street of Friendship**, an imposing avenue of sculptures created by artists of all continents which runs alongside the Periférico right up to the Aztec stadium.

The modern dilemma: Besides the arts center, which is one of the city's main attractions, a series of ambitious construction projects is concentrated in the south. From the artistic tension between tradition and the avant garde, Mexico's architects are developing a distinctive style of their own. An example is the elite **Colegio de México** on the road to Ajusco, a university founded in 1975 to plans by the architects González de Léon and Zabludowsky.

Mexico has invested its volatile fortune in oil dollars in modern administration blocks, clinics, schools and highways, as well as hotels, banks and shopping centers like **Perisur**. The current economic crisis is necessitating more modest projects.

In individual districts – like **Pedregal**, with its luxury villas, less imposing purpose-built estates for the middle classes and sprawling slums on the outskirts for the poor – the social injustices are drawing increasing attention. The scope for city planning has been exhausted by the pressures of the megapolis. The splendor and high-flown rhetoric of modernism only serves to conceal the threatened collapse of the overpopulated valley of Mexico.

Perisur
shopping
paradise.

Three cultures, separated by several meters of earth and centuries of time, come together just north of the city in the quarter of Tlatelolco: the Aztec period with its pyramids, the colonial era with its 17th-century church of St James of Tlatelolco right in the middle of the grand esplanade, and the modern era with the tall, airy buildings of the Foreign Ministry.

Tlatelolco is the surest proof that Mexico City is a city built in layers. Here one sees the walls, altars, steps, the *tzompantli* (the stone skull scaffolds) next to the colonial church of St James which seems as if it would conceal

ans. At the time the verdict on Aztec sculptures and gods was, if you believe British writer D. H. Lawrence, a colorful heap of detestable and disgusting stuff, and the ceramic and silversmith works hideous and uninteresting – so much so that one look at them made one depressed.

According to the description of the Franciscan teacher and chronicler, Bernardino de Sagahún, the children of the Aztec nobility were taught in the imperial school of the Santa Cruz cloister, right next to the church of St James, by his fellow Franciscans. Today, the cloister serves as the Foreign

everything around it. In fact, it was the will of the Spanish conquistadors that any pre-Hispanic art be buried. They believed that the gods of fire, water, and fertility were in union with the devil, and that these evil spirits must be driven away from the Indians. Conversion to Christianity meant destroying all that existed previous to the conquest, obliterating it, putting everything to the torch.

It is common knowledge that the Spanish not only annihilated the indigenous peoples but with them destroyed a whole way of life and a highly developed and differentiated culture. They thereby destroyed art which was much more than an object of fascination for archaeologists, anthropologists and histori-

Ministry's historical archive where many valuable documents are preserved.

Tlatelolco not only records the Aztec empire but is also witness to its decline and the new race which thereby came into being, the *mestizos*, the people of today's Mexico. According to the historian, chronicler, and scholar Siguenza y Góngora, in 1692, the starving people (*mestizos*, poor Creoles, and Indians) rose up against the white colonial masters who were eating all of their sacred staple food, maize. The Spaniards' answer was a massacre here on this plaza. Tlatelolco was to be the scene of a bloodbath which overshadowed the end of the 17th century.

The square is not only of great historical

significance for Mexico, it is also the home of more than 80,000 people living in a public housing complex originally encompassing 102 buildings. The complex was built in the 1950s according to the latest scientific and engineering concepts. The residents cross the Plaza de las Tres Culturas daily without paying much attention to what they are walking through. Children walk to school; students to the university, passing peddlers with their lottery tickets promising great fortunes: "Look, isn't this a beautiful number!" In the Jardín, the small park of Santiago Tlatelolco with stone benches and balustrades, you can buy balloons, ice cream and miracle cures.

The square was also the grave of the 1968 student movement that preceded the Olympic Games. On the "Night of Tlatelolco," the

government's security forces shot at demonstrators. Tlatelolco became a death trap for the assembled students because no one knew where to run once the shooting began. The pre-Hispanic ruins were covered with the shoes and blood of fleeing protestors. Some ran for cover in the colonial church but the Franciscans refused to open the doors. The windows of the Foreign Ministry buildings were smashed by a hail of bullets.

Just as the *mestizos* revolted against the viceroyalty, injustice, and poverty in 1692, the student rising of 1968 was against the

<u>Above</u> and <u>right</u>, the Plaza de las Tres Culturas was the setting for several catastrophes.

government. With the help of the one ruling party, the Partido Revolucionario Institucional (PRI), the revolution had been usurped and in its place a financial oligarchy was established which worked hand-in-hand with the US. Those who had once worn sombreros and wielded rifles for the revolution became politicians, bureaucrats and civil servants, members of the new business, social and intellectual elite. It was in their interest to thrust Mexico into prominence on the world stage; make her presentable and dress her in the finest available clothing.

When the Olympic Games came to Mexico in 1968, the government spent millions on modern accommodation for the athletes as well as on the Olympic Stadium and other facilities. At the same time, the students carried banners that condemned the poverty and oppression of the ordinary people and demanded justice and freedom.

As the demonstrators began to cry "People unite!", the government stood up and took notice. The students tried not only to sabotage the games (rumors circulated that bombs had been laid in the stadium) but wanted also to expose the government before world opinion. On October 2, 16 days before the official opening of the XIX Olympics, there was a bloodbath on the Plaza de las Tres Culturas in which children, pregnant women, students and the elderly were killed. (The English newspaper *The Guardian* said there were 325 dead.)

But this was by no means the last tragic event for this part of Mexico City. In 1985, Tlatelolco was threatened with the most powerful earthquake in Mexican history. The quake didn't break up the plaza but the concrete residential blocks of the surrounding area were seriously damaged. Above all the "Nuevo Leon" came crashing down – a building that played an important role in the 1968 uprising when the leader of the students addressed the masses on the plaza from the third floor window.

For Mexican author Octavio Paz, Tlatelolco is a sacred and mysterious place, which seems destined to witness the human sacrifices that greedy and choleric gods demand time and again. Here are celebrated sacrificial rites, rites of vengeance, human sacrifices by the people of the sun who loved rituals. Religious celebrations, ceremonies of life and death, games, dances and fireworks spring from this place, rise to the sky from below, from the plaza, the market, the Zócalo, and the Plaza de las Tres Culturas. ∎

THE VIRGIN OF GUADALUPE

To North Americans and northern Europeans, even if they are Catholics, Latin-American piety is something exotic. A visit to Mexico City's Virgin of Guadalupe can highlight that special Mexican mix of religion and patriotism.

The vast site of the shrine 6 km (4 miles) north of Zócalo consists of an enclosed atrium of 46,000 sq. meters (55,000 sq. yds) facing six churches and chapels at the foot of the park-like **Tepeyac**. The summit of the hill is crowned by another church. The Metro stations of Basilica and La Villa are both but a few blocks away, and as you depart the station you'll see the curved roof of the new basilica and the old one it replaced slightly to the north. Designed by Mexico's top architect Pedro Ramírez Vásquez (who was responsible for the acclaimed Museum of Anthropology) it is regarded by some as a *monstruosidad*, but has nevertheless been hugely popular from the day it was completed in 1976.

Two one-way streets, continuations of the Paseo de la Reforma, lead to the gates to the shrine: the Calzada de Guadalupe and the Calzada de los Misterios with its prayer stations presenting the 15 "mysteries of the Rosary." The pilgrim, who naturally makes his way from here on foot, can pray 10 *Ave Marias* and one *Pater Noster* in between each of them. On December 12, a national holiday, thousands of penitents make the pilgrimage to Guadalupe on the anniversary of the Virgin's 16th-century manifestation, and at any time of the year you'll see penitents crawling up the approach on their knees and quite often enthusiastic, chanting, banner-waving processions filing into the enormous square.

There is almost always a service taking place in the vast basilica itself, but people wander in and out, admiring the stained glass windows, the marble stairs,

Preceding pages: the climax of th Guadalupe cult is the midnight mass on December 12. Below, dancers in front of the basilica.

latter-day chandeliers and fluted ceiling of burnished wood. A slowly-moving pedestrian walkway carries an endless stream of admirers past the giant-sized portrait of the Virgin high up on one wall. This spacious building can hold as many as 10,000 people at a time. The old basilica – much more aesthetically pleasing to those with a traditional eye – dates back to 1533, but it had become too small to accommodate the enormous crowds that visit on every day of the year. Besides, it was beginning to list noticeably as – like many other buildings in the capital – it continued to sink into the ground. For some years it served as a museum, with a fine collection of colonial paintings, but at present it is fenced off as it undergoes renovations. Behind it, on top of the hill, is a small chapel. In front, beside the pedestrian bridge, is a string of shops and stalls selling religious images, incense, food, toys and lottery tickets.

Juan Diego's manifestation: The legend of the icon differs from other similar legends in so far as the Virgin did not appear to a young boy or girl, but to a 57-year-old man. This man was one of the first converts of the 12 Franciscans who had come to Mexico in 1524, and he had taken the name Juan Diego at his baptism. On the morning of December 9, 1531, on his way to church, Juan passed the Tepeyac and saw a vision of a dark-haired, brown-skinned woman who demanded that a church be built on the hill, reinforcing her message by causing roses to bloom on the barren hillside. The vision appeared five times altogether, finally convincing the obdurately skeptical Bishop Zumarraga of her authenticity by causing her image to appear on the inside of Juan Diego's coat.

Today the picture of a young woman with light brown complexion but not very pronounced Indian features is ubiquitous in Latin America. She has entirely replaced the first Virgin of Guadalupe, the miraculous dark statue of the Madonna with Child from Extremadura. Tradition says that the

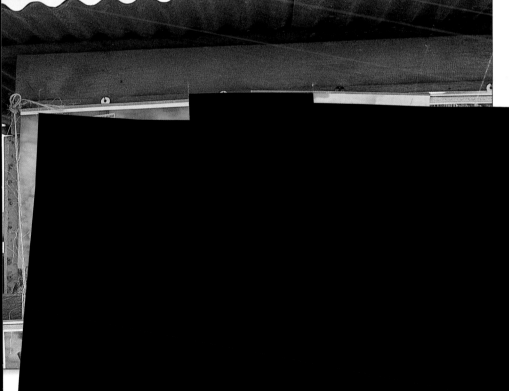

icon immediately caused miracles: first, the healing of Juan's uncle; then the healing of a young Indian, injured during a procession to place the image in the new shrine. Since then there have been countless healings and rescues from spiritual and material need as well as other help for which the Virgin has been responsible. Votive images, now on display in the museum near the old basilica, testify to the infinite misery as well as the infinite hope of man.

Soon the Virgin of Guadalupe proved helpful not only for individual believers, but took on the role as patroness of the City of Mexico, the whole country, and finally all Latin America. The first opportunity to demonstrate her power arose in September, 1629, when torrential rains as well as the rising lake threatened to flood the city. The icon was carried in a holy procession from the Tepeyac to town and the danger was diverted. Ever since then Guadalupe has been the official "First Protectress" of the city against floods.

In the end there was little else to do but call upon divine assistance to fend off the epidemics (smallpox, plague, cholera, measles, etc.) which the Spanish brought to the city and which severely reduced the Indian population. By 1520, when the Aztec capital was rebuilt after a disastrous flood, its population of more than 350,000 made it one of the three largest cities in the world. Today it is the largest.

Shared symbol: In time, Guadalupe became the symbol of the newly developing Mexican identity. When appealing to the brown-skinned Mary, the Spanish, *mestizos* and Indians in their misery all forgot their feelings of hostility. The *criollos* or creoles, particularly the Spanish born in Mexico, were devoted to the Virgin whose image rose from Mexican soil.

From the middle of the 17th century the cult of the Virgin of Guadalupe became a commitment to Mexican identity as well as to political and spiritual independence from Spain. In 1810,

Left, endless streams of pilgrims. Right, shrines are everywhere in Mexico.

waving the banner of Guadalupe, Father Hidalgo waged the Mexican struggle for liberation. Since independence in 1821, Mexican politicians and revolutionaries alike have called upon her for protection for their side. Even today, no trade unionist would neglect to celebrate the Virgin's December feast day, and well in advance, pictures of the Patroness are decorated with flowers and candles throughout the country. Indian groups dance in front of the churches, most of them wearing costumes which date from before the Spanish invasion. Some dress in baroque velvet and silk or as Christians and Moors in fierce battle dress.

Adjoining the old basilica is the church of the Capuchin nuns who founded a cloister here. Further on is the place where the first prayer station for the Virgin was erected. Today's structure, the third, dating from 1695, is modest and dignified. Next to it is a fountain for the refreshment of pilgrims. The fountain chapel **Pocito**, a playful circular

structure with three domes covered with blue and white tiles, dates from 1791.

The visitor who climbs one of the two 50-meter (165-ft) high stairways to the hill's summit gets an impressive view of the area. The church, now on the original sacred place marked by a pile of stones topped with a cross, adjoins a cemetery with fascinating gravestones. Once the ramps and gardens were laid out in the 18th century, the hill became a favorite place for Sunday excursions.

Anyone who wants to see how the site most probably looked in the pre-Spanish epoch can set out by car and inspect two well-restored Aztec temples. The pyramid of Tenayuca, 6 km (4 miles) northwest of downtown, is guarded by 138 especially threatening snakes, a living echo of the row of serpents' heads along the pyramid's base.

Not far away is the small village pyramid of **Santa Cecilia** where you can see the temple construction and the sacrificial stone. Today it is a quiet and peaceful place for reflection.

MEXICAN NIGHTS

At night Mexico valley is a gold and silver carpet of lights. From the observation tower on the old road to Cuernavaca, from several restaurants on the arterial road to Toluca or just from the top floor of the Torre Latinoamericana, there is a marvelous view over the world's third largest city glowing from 300,000 twinkling street lamps. Seen from above, the streets with their night-time traffic are shimmering, moving streams of light.

An evening stroll through the streets of the Centro Histórico (old town) with its colonial architecture offers a muted contrast to the glaring neon signs, while filtering out from the bars, *cantinas* and cabarets comes music and the babble of voices. The Zócalo is especially attractive by night. All the historic buildings on its perimeter are carefully floodlit: the cathedral, the Palacio Nacional, the old and new city halls, the Gran Hotel and the Nacional Monte de Piedad.

Street life: In the historic city center, people meet in the street to go for a traditional *merienda* (an early evening snack of pastries and sugary drinks). Popular haunts are the famous **Café Tacuba** for its delicious cakes, sweets and *antojitos* (Mexican appetizers); the **Super Leche**, for biscuits, cakes and hot, milky coffee, and **El Moro**, where you can feast on hot chocolate with sugary *churros*.

At this time in the evening there's even an avid audience for many of the lectures, tours and meetings in the Museo Nacional de Arte, the Palacio de Minería, the Palacio de Bellas Artes, the Museo de la Ciudad de México and the Colegio Nacional.

The people of Mexico City are often described as bohemians because they relish the varied nightlife their city has to offer – the bars, restaurants and clubs where they can listen to romantic songs and sing along if the fancy takes them.

In private, too, they organize parties or dances every Friday and Saturday, either in their own homes or in halls or even out of doors. The slightest excuse is enough: a birthday, Mothers' Day, Fathers' Day, Godfathers' Day, a christening, a girl's 15th birthday (a special anniversary in Mexico), weddings and even divorces.

Mexico City's nightlife may be less dramatic than in some other world cities yet it still has its own special charm. In arts centers and theaters evening performances usually begin at 7.30pm. In the nightclubs, business doesn't get under way until around 10pm at the earliest. If you arrive before then, there'll be nothing happening.

Hotel bars: Most nightclubs are located in the big hotels, and others are scattered across the city – in the center, to the south, in Zona Rosa and Ciudad Satélite. The highest concentration is in the center of Coyoacán, along Avenidas Universidad and Insurgentes where you'll often encounter street performers. It is said the best coffee in Mexico can be found in Coyoacán's **El Jaroche** on Calle Allende from which the aroma of roasting beans pulls in strollers from blocks away.

One of the most popular bars is **Hijo de Cuervo**, a bit pricey and popular with journalists and a younger crowd. Also especially lively at night are the various shopping precincts and leisure centers such as **Perisur**, **Plaza Universidad** and **Plaza Satélite** on Paseo de la Reforma and, last but not least, Avenida San Juan de Letrán.

Just across from the Plaza Garibaldi, on Lázaro Cárdenas, is the venerable **Teatro Blanquita** whose variety shows frequently offer enough to amuse even those who can't understand Spanish. The cabaret there is all that remains of the *Teatro de Revista Musical* (Mexican Revue Theater), the last bastion of the magical variety shows from the 1950s, which produced some of the greatest names in Mexican cinema like Cantinflas, Tin Tán and Resortes.

Every day a whole assortment of artists appear at the Teatro Blanquita to give of their best in song, dance or comedy routine, to perform a few magic tricks or entertain the audience with humorous sketches. Artists of international repute regularly receive top billing here, and good tickets can be very much in demand.

Almost every one of Mexico City's hundreds of good hotels boasts an excellent bar. Sometimes, especially at weekends, it can be difficult to find a seat, particularly if the bar also has live entertainment. The prices charged in all these establishments are subject to controls laid down by the Ministry of Tourism and the city administration. It's probably useful to remember that getting drunk is easier at high altitudes and Mexico City is more than 2,200 meters (7,200 ft) above sea level.

Mexico City's nightspots come and go like mayflies. There are always some closing down and others opening up. Sometimes they shut for a short period only to reopen later with a better program of entertainment. *Capitolanos* seem to favor big hotels, which are often the best places for drinking, dining and dancing. Tourists might well consider sampling one of the ubiquitous nightclub tours that offer a taste of several places with minimal inconvenience.

Mexicans love dancing and there are a lot of nightspots in the city where they can indulge night after night to their heart's content. These include ballrooms in Cuauhtémoc, dancehalls in Benito Juárez, various clubs in Zona Rosa and cabarets on the Avenida San Juan de Letrán, Avenida Juárez and Avenida Insurgentes. There are also lots of discotheques in the southern districts of Tecamachalco, Naucálpan and Ciudad Satélite. Salsa clubs with live bands, usually from Colombia, play at various clubs around town. Often, on certain nights, there is no cover or admission charge before 10pm.

World music: The city's many stages offer programs of both Mexican and

Folk night in "Focolare."

international music and ballet which are among the very best. These include the Palacio de Bellas Artes, the Auditorio Nacional, the Sala Nezahualcóyotl, the Sala Ollin, Yoliztli, the Premier de San Jerónimo, the Conjunto Marraquesh, the Teatro de la Ciudad, El Patio and the Magic Circus.

The **Ballet Folklórico de México** has appeared alongside world-famous artists like Herbert von Karajan, Zubin Metha, Alexander Schnaider, Pablo Casals, Pedro Vargas, Lola Beltrán, Sara Vaughan and Cindy Lauper. The London Symphony Orchestra has also made guest appearances.

The Ballet Folklórico productions, which specialize in regional dances, are events that the first-time visitor to the city should not miss. Tickets are often bought up in large batches by the tour companies, so they are sold early for the three weekly performances. It is usually advisable to make your plans and book your seats well ahead of time.

In addition, Mexico City has a vast number of museums, galleries, arts centers and cultural meeting places that host events in the evening: exhibitions, chamber music recitals, jazz, blues, rock and folk concerts, poetry readings, film festivals and lectures on everything from science to art history.

These venues are scattered throughout the city, but are mainly concentrated in the districts of Cuauhtémoc, Miguel Hidalgo and Coyoacán. The most important are the **Foro Coyoacanense**, the **Hijo del Cuervo**, **El Juglar**, the **Librería Gandhi**, the **Librería del Sótano**, the **Casa de Cultura Jésus Reyes Heroles**, the **Librería Parnaso** and the **Foro Cultural Luis Buñuel**.

Traditional burlesque: The program for the 60 or so theaters dotted around the city features Mexican and international plays of all kinds and all periods, on every day of the week except Monday (theaters closed). Theaters like the **San Rafael**, the **Manolo Fábregas**, **Insurgentes** and **Silvia Pinal** are devoted to Broadway-style musicals.

ternational
ounds on the
ance floor.

In other theaters like the **San Jerónimo**, the **Reforma**, the **Hidalgo**, the **Tepeyac**, the **Julio Prieto**, the **Cuauhtémoc** and the **University Arts Center** (in the Sala Juan Ruiz de Alarcón), the classics of world literature are brought to the stage, from Shakespeare and Cervantes, Tirso de Molina and Molière through to Tennessee Williams, Ionesco and Fernando Arrabal. But that's not to say that first-class Mexican playwrights like Sergio Magaña, Vincente Leñero, Hugo Argüelles, Ignacio Retes, Emilio Caballido, Luis Basurto or Victor Hugo Rascón Banda receive short shrift.

Even if the language barrier deters the foreign visitor from a trip to the theater to see a local work, Mexico's leading actors still deserve acknowledgment. Ignacio López Tarso, Hector Bonilla, Ofelia Guilmáin, Carmen Montejo, Rosenda Monteros, Sergio Jiménez, José Alonso, Helena Rojo, Susanna Alexander and Diana Bracho are just a few of the names that strike a chord with Mexican theater audiences.

The majority of theaters in Mexico City, however, cater for the *chilangos'* love of burlesque. There are innumerable second-rate theaters running these kinds of shows from late evening through to early morning. Most of these vaudeville theaters are in the districts of Cuauhtémoc, Miguel Hidalgo and Benito Juárez.

There's always a wide choice of movies on offer, Mexican and international, old classics and the latest releases at the city's 150-odd movie theaters, especially at the weekends. The best movie houses (see *Travel Tips in the back of this book*) are in Cuauhtémoc, Benito Juárez, Miguel Hidalgo, Coyoacán and Ciudad Satélite. The second- and third-run cinemas tend to be found on the city's outskirts and in the various outlying districts which have now become part of the metropolis.

Sport, too, plays an important role in the nightlife of Mexico City. Week in, week out, throughout the appropriate seasons, baseball and football matches, boxing and wrestling take place in **Parque del Seguro Social**, the **Estadio Azteca** and the **Estadio Olímpico de la Ciudad Universitaria**, while in the **Arena México** (also known as the Coliseo) and the **Plaza de Toros México**, the *toreros* and *matadors* line up for classical bullfights.

Frontón Mexico, right behind the Monument to the Revolution, is the scene of jai-alai games almost every night. The Spanish conquistadors brought this fast-paced game to Mexico from the Basque region of Spain and the ball – clocked at 160 kms-per-hour (258 miles-per-hour) – is said to be the fastest in any sport.

Each game matches a pair of two-man teams and lasts about one hour. Most of the enthusiastic spectators are businessmen who are there to gamble. Betting slips are thrown to them tucked in the slit of a tennis ball, into which they insert their payment. Most night-time events are listed either in *The News*, Mexico City's daily English-language

Prendes restaurant, downtown.

newspaper, or *Tiempo Libre*, which appears weekly.

Despite inflation and the country's perpetual economic crisis, the city's exclusive restaurants are well patronized in the evenings. It's therefore advisable to book your table in advance. Don't worry about parking: when you arrive an eager doorman will take your keys and park the car for you.

A wide choice of restaurants covers Chinese, Japanese, Italian, German, French, Polish, Cuban, Arabian and, of course, Mexican cuisine. There are restaurants specializing in vegetarian dishes, others in fish and seafood. The city's oldest and best known eating places are on Paseo de la Reforma and Avenida de los Insurgentes, in Zona Rosa, San Angel and Ciudad Satélite. There are countless top-class restaurants where you can really dine in style. You shouldn't go home without having tried Mexican cuisine.

The **Plaza Garibaldi**, a few blocks north of the main post office, is one of the most picturesque squares in Mexico City and is famous for its gatherings of *mariachi* musicians – most of them awaiting gigs. People come here to listen to the *mariachi* groups who have grown to symbolize Mexican folklore, and engage them to play a traditional *serenata* (a moonlight serenade of seven songs). Musicians in *charro* costume stand ready to climb into a customer's car for the chance of performing somewhere else, in another part of the city, no matter what the occasion.

It's a fascinating square, dotted with statues of such *mariachi* heroes as Pedro Infante and José Alfredo Jimenez who had successful singing careers during the 1940s and 1950s when Mexican cinema used Plaza Garibaldi as a setting in movies of this period.

But its special atmosphere is also due to the *cantinas* and restaurants around its perimeter, where folk groups appear night after night. Fiesta Méxicana is celebrated here around the clock, whatever the climate or season. Drinks in the

e Zócalo is
favorite
eeting
ace at
ght.

bars and night clubs surrounding the square can be fairly expensive. An adjoining food hall contains dozens of booths whose highly competitive proprietors may try to bully you into favoring their particular establishment. The steaming food stalls sell *tacos*, *tortas*, *tamales*, *atole*, *sopes*, *birria*, *pozole*, and other tasty examples of Mexican cuisine. All such dishes are extremely cheap, but you might want to exercise some caution in sampling them until your stomach has adjusted to its new environment.

The plaza offers a cross-section of Mexican folk music, not only *mariachi* groups but also Norteños (from the north), musicians from Veracruz and *marimba* xylophone players from Chiapas, while balladeers give their renditions of songs old and new by Mexican songwriters like Tata Nachos and Juan Gabriels.

At the top side of the square is the Camilito Market, a tunnel-like market hall where snack counters lure visitors with typical Mexican *antojitos* (appetizers) and hot dishes. Everyone can find something to their taste in the surrounding restaurants and night-time bars, where the waiters execute the most amazing balancing acts with their trays.

On Plaza Garibaldi you can also sample those famous Mexican drinks: tequila from Jalisco, *mezcal* from Oaxaca – complete with the worm – and *pulque* from the states of Mexico and Hidalgo. They're all distilled from the *agave* plant and either drunk on their own or served with hazelnuts, walnuts, pine kernels, chunks of celeriac, watermelon or red cactus fruit.

Legend has it that the spot on which Plaza Garibaldi now stands was dedicated in pre-Hispanic times to the goddess of the *maguey* (agave art). Later the square was known for a long while as Plaza del Baratillo. It was only in the 1930s that it was given its existing name in honor of the Italian revolutionary Guiseppe Garibaldi, who sided with Mexico during the French invasion.

A *mariachi* band at the Plaza Garibaldi.

The square's musical traditions date back to 1925, when the famous *cantina* **Tenampa** opened its doors. Because of the rather scant custom, the bar's owner, a Jalisco man, decided to invite one of the *mariachi* groups popular in Jalisco at the time to the big city. (The word *mariachi* comes from the French *mariage*.)

Originally the groups comprised four musicians playing a combination of instruments, including guitar, bass guitar, harp and psaltery. More and more ensembles moved to the capital. In the beginning they used to play in the middle of the Zócalo to get themselves noticed, but they ran into problems with the police – street music was still illegal at that time. Eventually Plaza Garibaldi was officially sanctioned as their regular performance spot.

At present there are more than 100 *mariachi* groups in Mexico City. They've grown in size over the years with some containing up to 20 players. They've also added more instruments like violins and trumpets, and the traditional threadbare suit has also changed. Modern *mariachis* wear a handsome wide-brimmed *sombrero* and a full *charro* costume, usually with a jaunty tie and silver buttons marching down the jacket and trousers.

In the 1950s Plaza Garibaldi became known as the Mexican Broadway for theatres such as Follies and the Carpa Margo, where performers like Cantinflas, Palillo, María Victoria and Tin Tán used to appear.

Part of this frivolous, light-hearted world persists to this day, for the Plaza's sphere of influence reaches as far as the Lagunilla district, where there are more than 40 nightclubs. The city's best variety house, the Teatro Blanquita is just a block away.

Just as lively as Plaza Garibaldi by night is the adjoining **Plaza Santa Cecilia**, named after the patron saint of musicians. Every year on November 21 a midnight serenade is offered up to the saint by over 1,000 *mariachis*.

ariachis ke a tequila eak.

Massive pyramids, ornate colonial baroque, snow-covered volcanoes, sub-tropical gardens: whoever chooses the Mexican capital as their base will find interesting excursions in every direction.

Any organized short program for Mexico City itself normally includes a trip to the pyramids of Teotihuacán. The drive gives an impression of the expanse of the city, the landscape of the high Valley of Mexico, and the cultural accomplishments of the pre-Spanish cultures. Our text breathes life into the great city of Teotihuacán with its ceremonial center. On the way to the ruins of the old Toltec capital of Tula in the north of Mexico City, visit the convent of Tepotzotlán, where the Churrigueresco style of architecture is seen at it best.

Have you ever been at an altitude of 3,880 meters (12,500 ft) with an automobile? In Mexico you can. When you drive over the pass between the two volcanoes Popocatépetl and Iztaccíhuatl toward Tlamacas, it almost seems possible to touch the summit of "Popo." The air is quite thin here. To look into the crater of Popo requires a fairly long walk.

One hundred kilometers (60 miles) below Mexico City lies Cuernavaca, a sub-tropical garden paradise. A winding mountain drive takes you from here to the picturesque town of Taxco, where hundreds of workshops turn what silver is still mined into surprisingly chic jewelry and vessels.

The art of the Talavera potters is to be found in the city of Puebla. Their work decorates the facades of houses and churches with tile pictures. Once the "City of the Angel," Puebla is today the home of the Mexican Volkswagen factory – the "City of the Beetle." In the vicinity you can climb the pyramids of Cholula and see ultra-baroque village churches with pre-Spanish murals.

To the west, take a trip to the highest city in Mexico, Toluca (2,680 meters/8,800 ft) straight up. It's worth going there just to see the huge Indian market. The volcano Nevado de Toluca can be negotiated by car as far up as its crater lakes.

TEOTIHUACÁN

Visitors are allowed to climb the Sun and Moon pyramids of Teotihuacán. The task, however, often so completely exhausts them that sunburn is sometimes the only souvenir of their visit to Mexico's most popular attraction. This strange landscape of ruins, with the threatening serpents' jaws and the singing jaguars needs a whole day to explore leisurely, and as it often rains on summer afternoons it is wise to start out early.

From Mexico City the continuation of anonymous Indian sculptor who interpreted the symbols of Christ's passion in Aztec style. The bus does not stop at Acolman; you'll need the Indios Verdes bus for that. There are many 16th-century churches and monasteries all over Mexico, but few can be visited as easily as Acolman, and in no other place are a major archaeological center and a beautiful colonial monument to be found, side by side.

The first stop should be the museum by the

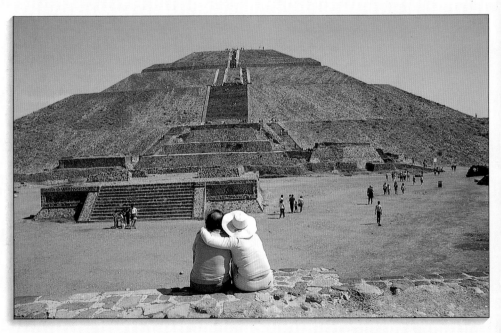

Insurgentes Norte, leads to the exit of Teotihuacán and Acolman, 50 km (31 miles) northeast of the city of **Teotihuacán**. The trip can be made by bus or rental car. A few minutes before the turn-off, look out on the left for the fortress-like **San Agustín de Acolman,** an attractive 16th-century church and monastery with a delightful medieval interior. The church is located in an ample atrium; large enough to accommodate the great number of converts who went there for instructions but who could not yet be received inside the church itself. In the center is a remarkable mission cross, carved by an entrance. The bus leaves visitors at the western side at Gate 1 where you'll pay admission plus a fee for any camera you are seen to be carrying. Walk up past the multitudinous stalls to the museum, which contains a scale model of the site and some reproductions of items found there (the originals are in the Teotihuacan Hall of Mexico City's Museum of Anthropology).

Upstairs is a small café and an exorbitantly expensive restaurant, so you might want to consider bringing fruit and sandwiches. There are restaurants in the area but almost none of them can be reached without a car.

Teotihuacán, the city of Quetzalcoatl, is a major archaeological center, one of the best preserved and most beautiful in the country. It is not spectacular in the same sense as are the Mayan cities, lost in tropical green; Teotihuacán's beauty is subdued, even sober. Huge (13 sq. km/15 sq. miles) as the site is, it can seem crowded. Sometimes it seems there are as many vendors as visitors. These peddlers are ubiquitous and not even the remotest corner is free of them. They are amiable but a pest, like mosquitoes that must constantly be fended off.

Place of pilgrimage: Over 2,000 years ago, pilgrims began to visit this site: most of them above sea level, the land is dry and brown. This is true particularly in winter, the high season for tourists.

Unfortunately, nothing but a few dismal trees are left from the erstwhile dense forests, and the lakes have disappeared, too. All that remains from the city of Teotihuacán is a skeleton unearthed by archaeologists, dried and bleached by the sun. We know very little of the religious life of the Teotihuacán. We do not even know what the people called themselves or the city they lived in. Teotihuacán, "place of the gods" or "place where gods are made" is the name the Aztecs gave to this holy and mysterious site. Even

came on foot but the rich and noble were carried by sedan, and all those who lived on the banks of the glittering and life-giving shallow lakes that then dotted the high valleys of Mexico came by boat.

Between the lake and the Valley of Teotihuacán there was a fertile marsh area. Bordered by mountains on three sides, the valley opened toward the southeast, leading far into the humid plains and to the ocean. Here, more than 2,000 meters (6,500 ft)

Left, the Sun pyramid in Teotihuacán. **Above**, view of the "Street of the Dead."

the names Sun and Moon pyramid, date from the Aztec era, 700 years after ancient Teotihuacán had perished.

This place of the gods was the first urban development on the American continent, quite distinct from the previous ceremonial centers. Teotihuacán became the model for all later cities and municipal states. From the peak of the pyramid, the grid of the city's layout is visible: the wide, mile-long north–south axis, the so-called "Street of the Dead" (so named because many skeletons were discovered along its length when it was excavated) leads south from the Moon pyramid.

Occasionally there are frescoes to be seen in covered spots along the walls.

In the east, the **Sun pyramid** marks a perpendicular axis. The quarters are separated precisely into smaller and bigger squares. Even the suburbs comply with the pattern, and the river traversing the area was divided into matching canals. South of the river were the administration and trade centers. East of the Street of the Dead was the citadel. It is thought this is where the priests and honoraries probably resided. In the west, where the museum now stands, stood a walled-in complex of buildings with apartments, stores and warehouses surrounding

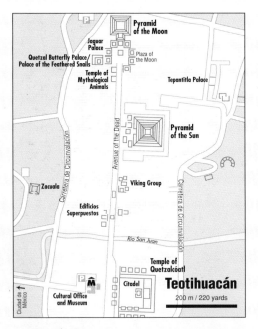

the big market square. The city had approximately 100 temples.

Living and working: Few archaeological sites are as thoroughly surveyed and examined as the city of Teotihuacán. No fewer than 2,000 residential sites have been mapped, and more than a million ceramic pieces, obsidian splinters, stone tools, bones, and debris have been registered. In some buildings you can see how the Teotihuacáns lived. One-story apartment blocks housed several families. An inner courtyard with a small temple was surrounded by patios and covered hallways that were separated from the street by walls

without windows. The flat roofs were accessible for daily use, and fountains and a drainage system were also incorporated. The floors were made of a concrete-like mixture, the walls of stone and mortar or of clay tiles, whitewashed on the inside and the outside. On houses in the heyday of Teotihuacán were pictures of people leading happy lives.

Many of these apartment complexes served as workshops as well as homes. For example, several artisan families who made arrowheads and knives from obsidian would live in one block. Their neighbors might specialize in making mirrors and jewelry from the black volcanic glass.

There were also many household-workshops of potters and ceramic-ware makers who specialized increasingly in delicate figurines which could be used either as room decorations or for domestic worship; or they made fine pottery like the thin, orange-colored ceramics that were exported as far as what is today Guatemala. The patient research of the archaeologists has unearthed many items of everyday life. Teotihuacán was a center of the arts and crafts as well as of trade. Since the city grew and flourished for more than 600 years, extending its influence ever wider, it served as a model for the construction of other cities and their administrations. There were warriors but no fortresses around the city, and there are no reports of conquests.

A number of construction workers were constantly needed in the metropolis: carpenters, painters, weavers, jewelers, the makers of feather head-dresses, and stone cutters who carved the typical stone masks of Teotihuacán. Business people and traders lived together, too. Their storerooms, which were filled with goods from everywhere between the Atlantic and the Pacific, can still be identified. Export and import were probably carried out by whole clans who lived together, like the artisans who passed on their craft from generation to generation.

In some neighborhoods, there were even foreigners who would pass their customs down to their grandchildren as in cosmopolitan cities today. The houses of the rich and prominent were also one-story buildings with a design not much different from the rest, although more richly ornamented, judging by the colorful, lavish murals that have been discovered.

Everyday life: In its heyday in the 5th century the city covered an area larger than that of imperial Rome with a population as high as 200,000 or more plus thousands of pilgrims during the holidays, all of whom had to be housed and fed. People made the long journey here from as far away as the blossoming ceremonial centers of the Mayas in what is now Yucatán, attracted by the flair of the first and biggest city.

Today, the two pyramids dominate the landscape. The Sun pyramid with its 248 steps has about the same square base area as

tial phenomena and buildings have discovered connections with the position of the sun and the constellations, yet without being able to recreate the entire system on which the city worked.

The **Moon pyramid** – at only 45 meters (150 ft) it is smaller than the Sun pyramid and easier to climb – is flanked by a dozen small temples including the Palace of Quetzal-Mariposa with well-preserved murals and bas reliefs of *mariposas* (butterflies) and *quetzals* (tropical birds) nearby. Noteworthy is the Palace of the Jaguars which has been well restored leaving traces of the original red, green, yellow and white

the Cheops pyramid in Cairo, but only half its height, 63 meters (200 ft), since the crowning temple and the outer layer of smooth stone has been lost. Its silhouette seems to be modeled after a mountain which appears on the southern horizon.

The pyramid of the Moon, overlooking a plaza at the northern end of avenue, is likewise a diminutive replica of the Cerro Gordo mountain. These similarities cannot be coincidences. Astronomers who have examined the relationships between landscape, celestial

Above, palace architecture in Teotihuacán.

symbols that represent birds, maize and water.

Cave of the oracle: As recently as 1971, during the installation of the nightly sight and sound shows at the foot of the Sun pyramid, a previously unknown entrance was discovered. A natural hallway, about 100 meters (320 ft) long, leads to a cave whose floor has the shape of a four-leaf clover. The cave, which probably used to be partitioned off in four sections, is almost exactly beneath the peak of the pyramid. The cave contained a spring whose water was carefully channeled to the outside. For centuries a small and simple temple marked the place where people came to consult the oracle in the cave.

This particular cave actually pre-dates the pyramid with the latter erected above it around AD 100, and the Moon pyramid constructed as a counterpart not much later. As the city continued to grow, the marshy land to the south had to be drained and the forests cleared, all of which resulted in the spring drying up and the cave losing its significance. Nothing but a few clay fragments were left behind when it was sealed.

The center of the city extended from the Sun pyramid above the cave to the citadel further south and the great market quarter

ancient Mexican gods. The name, as with the others, was the invention of the Aztecs; *Coatl* means serpent and *Quetzal* (the 'qu' is simply the Spanish way of writing a 'k') is the shiny green bird of paradise, but it also means "precious."

This precious bird-serpent, the plumed serpent, is one of the many symbols for the Mexican dualistic world view in ancient times: heaven and earth, air and flowing water, birth and death are united in one being. In later centuries, the plumed serpent also became the symbol of power and dominance. One theory maintains that in Teotihuacán former fertility deities were

across from the citadel. A new temple, which is today called the **Temple of Quetzalcoatl**, was erected on the empty square in the middle of the citadel.

Human sacrifices: Even in Aztec times Teotihuacán was regarded as an awesome mystery. Compared to the gods of the later city founders like the Toltecs or the Aztecs, the gods of Teotihuacán seem to have been almost benevolent. The name is an Aztec one meaning "the place where gods (rulers) are made," the original name having long since been forgotten. Quetzalcoatl, the feathered serpent, may be the most confusing of all the

complemented by Quetzalcoatl when an elite of priest-politician-warriors built the citadel around the new temple.

The elaborately carved stone sculptures that adorn the steps of the temple of Quetzalcoatl are predominantly of serpents' heads with wide-gaping jaws and threatening teeth. The eyes of the sculptures are made of obsidian with a feather collar alternating with the mask of the rain god. In between, the bodies of snakes wind around the slabs, and the whole was painted with bright colors. There is a reconstruction on display in the museum near the entrance.

Drugs and symbols: Further murals are constantly being discovered and restored on the edges of the city. The most famous painting is that which decorates a patio in Tepantitla, a residential and palace complex a little bit outside the current archaeological site. Reconstructions can be seen in the museums in Mexico City and Teotihuacán. A number of competing interpretations exist for the images. At first the masked figure in the center was identified as Tlaloc, the rain god, and the happy scenes in the lower part of the painting accordingly as Tlalocan, the paradise of the drowned and others given to the water. Today, however, experts tend to see the main figure as mother and fertility god. She sits above the sign for a cave, indicating the original site of Teotihuacán.

Above her bird-of-paradise head-dress rises a lavish creeper. Those who know how deeply ingrained the usage of hallucinogenic plants is in Mexican cultures will recognize the white leaves of the *Rivea Corymbosa* bindweed, a plant which prefers humid river banks. Its seeds were the Aztecs' sacred *ololiuhqui*, which is today called the seed of the Virgin Mary. Correctly prepared, the plant promotes a change of consciousness which allows the initiated to see the future. The cave, the spring, the oracle, the goddess of fertility, these are the foundation elements of the first city on the American continent.

Decline and fall: Around the year 650, six centuries or so after the first settlement, the decline of Teotihuacán began. Serious droughts seem to have occurred, probably a result of the destruction of the surrounding forests, and the standard of building and craftsmanship sank visibly as the number of inhabitants also decreased. Nomadic barbarians from the north started to infiltrate and the combination of land erosion, drought and plague, plus some sort of internal conflict – possibly between the religious and the military hierarchy – led to the state's downfall.

No-one has been able to discover where the surviving original inhabitants moved, but only about 2,000 peasants, holy men,

grave robbers and highwaymen remained. Grass grew to cover the temples and houses, and bushes and trees even hid the pyramids themselves until the first serious excavation of the site began in 1905 when the archaeologists found the remains not only of the ancient Teotihuacán civilization but also of both the Toltec and Aztec empires which followed in its wake.

Don't fail to explore the surrounding countryside. Nearby is Otumba, where the Aztecs were defeated by Hernán Cortéz in one of the decisive battles of the Spanish conquest. Farther to the northeast is Ciudad Sahagún, one of Mexico's industrial experiments. The

region is typical of central Mexico; desert plains and hills in which the main product is the cactus plant from which *pulque* is extracted. It is the national beverage: peculiar tasting, frothy, beerish and loaded with vitamins. It is said to be very nourishing – the best excuse in the world for a favorite drink. During colonial times and in the 19th century, big *pulque* plantations were developed. The manor houses of such plantations were magnificent. Some survive – such as **Xala**, near Ciudad Sahagún, which has been transformed into a hotel and preserves something of its early grandeur.

Left, well-preserved jaguar fresco. **Above**, atmospheric feather-collared serpents' heads on Quetzalcoatl temple.

Querétaro Road, an extension of the busy freeway known as the Periférico, starts in the northwest part of the city near the bullring known as **Cuatro Caminos** and crosses the sprawling industrial and middle-class northern suburbs. Along the way are the **Satélite Towers**, five tall, slender and brightly colored structures that were designed by Luis Barragán and Mathias Goeritz and must surely rank among the world's most attractive water towers.

The old Chichimec pyramid in the northern suburb of Tenayuca is well worth a visit before leaving the city – resembling, as it does, a smaller version of the Great Temple of Tenochtitlán. A serpent wall symbolizing the four points of the compass surrounds the structure, which once served as the model for the great Aztec pyramid in Tenochtitlán. Santa Cecilia, a very well-preserved and restored Aztec pyramid, also lies on the same highway. Together with the small museum, the entire site manages to give a lively impression of one of the thousands of small village shrines.

About 26 km (16 miles) north, right at the toll gates, is **Tepotzotlán**, famous for its magnificent church and monastery, one of the jewels of colonial art. It was *the* place chosen to house the national museum of the art of the viceroyalty, a collection of paintings, sculptures, arts and crafts and objects from daily life displayed in an environment every bit as stunning as the site itself. Among the favorite halls is number 15, which has a colorful carving of St James (Santiago), patron saint of Spain and one of the most popular saints in Mexican colonial art. In hall 19 is a wondrous painting of the Virgin of Bethlehem, attributed to the Spanish master Murillo.

Change of clothes: The church is flanked by chapels, one of which – dedicated to **Our Lady of Loreto** – contains a replica of the house in Nazareth where the Virgin is supposed to have lived. The chapel of Loreto has an eccentric neighbor, the **Camerino** (the term for a dressing room in a theater), in which the clothes of the Virgin's images were changed at different times of the year and whose ceiling is decorated with angels, flowers, shells and paintings.

In the 16th century the monastery was designed to serve as a school for the Indians, later becoming a Jesuit seminary before being converted into a museum and cultural center. It is about 90 minutes by bus from the capital, a good destination for a Sunday trip.

Families sit in the plaza enjoying their lunch for hours. Later on, they browse through the market in the village square or doze in the sun. Tepotzotlán is surrounded by rolling hills, and the air is cleaner and fresher than in Mexico City. The elegant steeple of the seminary church reaches into the peaceful sky. Nowhere in Central Mexico does Mexican rococo appear more splendid than in the church of Tepotzotlán, built over the course of 90 years and consecrated to St Francis Xavier (**San Francisco Javier**).

The church has a single deliciously carved and graceful belfry, and the interior is a medley of golden *retablos*. The *retablo*, a gilded wood structure, grows and multiplies itself like an exotic tropical plant, covering the walls and transforming them into a mysterious, glittering surface. This results in an inspired way to frame paintings and sculpture. Inspect the charming *retablo* of Our Lady of Guadalupe, which has paintings by one of the masters of the colonial era, Miguel Cabrera. Each *retablo* tells a religious story with each saint and image there for a reason, organized as precisely as the seating arrangements for guests at a banquet: obviously it helps to know who those saints are and how they are related.

"Even if all testimonies of the Churri-

saying that it is the light gushing through the dome onto the glittering, shimmering splendor which breathes life into the statues and ornaments – everything seems to be rising, pulled upward in a whirl of mystical ecstasy. In counterpoint to the gorgeous symphony of the 11 altars in the main church is a delicate but equally impressive chamber-piece in the Loretto chapel. Here, two Indian cherubs smile between the sun, the moon and the stars, and the dome is supported by a blissfully dancing angel.

Toltec warriors: About 50 km (31 miles) north of Tepotzotlán is **Tula**, an archaeological center which played a major role in

gueresco were to disappear, this room would be sufficient to establish the glory of the ultrabaroque," says art historian Manuel Toussaint about the interior of St Francis Xavier in his work on Mexican colonial art. He continues to describe this masterwork of sacred art in lyrical metaphors, comparing the church to an underwater grotto filled with corals and pearly shells, like a palace created by a fairy's magic wand. Toussaint is right in

Left, Churrigueresco facade of the church of Tepotzotlán. **Above**, the church's highly ornate gilded ceiling.

Mexico's pre-Columbian life. Tula (from the Aztec *tollan* which means "place where rushes grow") was founded around the beginning of the 10th century when Teotihuacán had been destroyed and Tenochtitlán still lay in the future. Thus Tula is another link in the chain of cultured settlements that preserved the spirit of civilization in the Mexican highlands. Tula was founded by King Ce Acatl Topiltzín (Our Lord One-Reed), who was a member of one of the nomadic tribes known as Chichimecas. Tula became the capital of the Toltecs, a cultured people. Ten Toltec kings ruled Tula for 312 years – until Tula was destroyed by Chichimecas. There is no written history of Tula, but myths abound.

There are no restaurants – and very little else – at the ruins, so you'll probably stop at the tiny town of **Tula de Allende**, with its 16th-century church and Franciscan abbey, a few minutes' drive away.

The interesting excavation museum right at the entrance to the archaeological site displays examples of the rough-hewn and often threatening sculptures as well as ceramics from the diverse trade contacts of the Toltecs. It also has an illustration of the layout of the maze-like residential quarters in Tula and the Toltec architecture in Chichén

here is the **Temple of the Morning Star**, whose true name is the tongue twister Tlahuizcalpantecuhtli.

Behind the lower gallery, covered in pre-Columbian days by a roof supported by columns, is a pyramid some 9 meters (30 ft) high. It supports *atlantes*, or columns, Tula's most important contribution to Mexican art. They represent Quetzalcoatl as the morning star – the planet Venus. Ancient representations of Quetzalcoatl depict him as a Toltec warrior, armed with arrows and the *atlatl*, the throwing board which gave the spear more power and impact, a version of which is still in use today for the hunting of wildfowl. This

Itzá (Yucatán peninsula). Wandering through the dried out cactus-scape of the site to the excavations of the ceremonial district, it is hard to believe that a town of some 10,000 inhabitants could have existed here. The buildings visible today, however, date from much later, namely from the final phase of the short-lived Toltec empire, which disintegrated around the year 1200.

The cult center consists of a sprawling ceremonial square bordered on its east side by a big pyramid and on its west side by a large open field where the sacred ball game was played. The most important building

weapon is typical of the Toltec warrior and unique to the New World. Padded armor and a shield of undressed leather, which the warriors carried on their backs, offered protection from the enemy arrows. The head-dress consisted of a box-like hat decorated with *quetzal* feathers and a descending bird on the front. A butterfly pectoral adorned the warrior's chest representing the belief that those who died in battle or as sacrificial victims were changed into birds or butterflies at their rebirth. According to legend the gentle god-king Quetzalcoatl – who abhorred human sacrifice and offered up only snakes, birds and butterflies – was bested by the black magic of his rival Tezcatlipoca ("the dark god of the night sky"). This prompted Quetzalcoatl and his followers to move to the east and further on to the Yucatán peninsula where they erected the ceremonial city of Chichén Itzá (literally "mouth of the well"), an exact replica of Tula. According to later reports this migration supposedly happened just before the year 1000. Archaeological findings corroborate this theory.

Of the other structures in Tula that have survived the centuries, perhaps the most interesting is the **Coatepantli**, or Wall of Serpents, raised along the north and west sides

poor. The town used to be on a mountain ledge overlooking the river of the same name, and research has shown that the people used the most simple methods of irrigation to maximise the benefits from their water supply: dams slowed down the draining of rainwater, and the river water was led to the fertile fields on its banks via canals. With this technology the subsistence of the population must have been guaranteed, and their methods of agriculture were followed slavishly by the Aztecs themselves.

Most recent excavations in Tula, however, also discovered the Toltecs' wide trade network: the tradesmen brought ceramics from

of the pyramid. Almost 2 meters (6.5 ft) tall, it is crowned and decorated with that universal motif of ancient Mexican art – the serpent in motion. In what is known as the **Burnt Palace**, near the pyramid, is the Chac Mool, another typically Mexican art form. The Chac Mool is the reclining figure of a priest.

Trade and change: Visiting Tula today, it is difficult to imagine the life of the former inhabitants, because the land is now dry and

Costa Rica, Nicaragua and from the Gulf Coast of Campeche; they brought shells from the Pacific Coast and turquoise from the most northern parts of Mexico. Bartering and tribute formed the mainstays of their trade-based economy.

Today a fire-damaged palace right next to the main temple in Tula is open to visitors. The heat of the fire turned the clay into bricks. The fire destroyed Tula to a large extent, but unlike Teotihuacán it was never abandoned and, during the era of the Aztecs, Tula, which was then known as Tollan, rose to some prominence.

Left, the large statues of Tula once carried the roof of the temple of the morning star. **Above**, the warriors of ancient Mexico worshipped the jaguar.

In the past, Mexico City's two local mountains, **Popocatépetl** (Smoking Mountain, 5,452 meters/17,890 ft) and **Iztaccíhuatl** (White Lady, 5,286 meters/17,340 ft) were a backdrop to the Mexican capital, some 60 km (40 miles) away. Nowadays its a talking point if the pair are not obscured by smog.

Popo (the Mexican abbreviation) is still an active volcano, albeit the last eruption was in 1802, but Izta no longer even has a crater.

In 1519, the Spanish conqueror Hernán Cortéz had to cross the pass that lies directly between the mountains on his way to Tenochtitlán. From the top of what later became Paso de Cortéz (2,650 meters/8,690 ft), an attempt was made to reach the summit of Popo, to show the Aztecs that the gods themselves couldn't harm the brave Spaniards. For the Indians believed Popo was an awesome god, and they honored Izta as his wife. Another legend says Popo was the home of the evil spirits, and the earthquakes and the terrible rumblings that accompanied a volcanic eruption were their death throes in its fiery innards. Whatever the tale, the native people fervently believed that an ascent of Popo was physically impossible.

Reaching the edge: Owing to fierce volcanic activity, the Spanish turned back just below the edge of the crater, but this aroused considerable admiration among the population. In the end it was Francisco Montaño who succeeded in reaching the edge of the crater in a second expedition in 1521.

But even that didn't satisfy Montaño. He had his companions lower him down in a basket into the steaming jaws of the volcano, to gather sulphur deposits from the rocky walls. At that time there was urgent demand for sulphur for use in the manufacture of gunpowder. Cortéz later noted in his report to Emperor Charles V that all in all it would probably be simpler to have had the gunpowder sent out from mainland Spain.

Preceding pages: Iztaccíhuatl and Popocatépetl. Left, "Popo" with snow cap in January. Right, ridge on the Iztaccíhuatl.

Today the ascent of Popo is far less spectacular, owing to more sophisticated equipment and minimal volcanic activity. Nevertheless, the whole thing is far from being child's play. There may be fewer technical problems, but there is still the unaccustomed altitude to be accounted for. Anyone attempting the climb should be physically fit and have spent a few days beforehand in average to high altitudes to adjust their bodies to the thin air, which yields little oxygen.

The best time for the trip is November to January, and those who like idyllic solitude on their mountain walks are advised to avoid the weekends, since Popo is also a favorite destination for local walkers and climbers.

The famous volcanoes can be seen on the Puebla road, which is a continuation of the great avenue Calzada Ignacio Zaragoza. This is the backbone of proletarian Mexico City that begins near the airport and runs by a sprawling community called **Netzahual-cóyotl**. Once the *calzada* leaves the urban area, the road to Puebla enters a beautiful but cold and rainy mountain area. The volcanoes loom very close. The route to those snow-capped wonders, Popocatépetl and Iztaccíhuatl, is via the Amecameca road through a pleasantly pastoral land. After crossing the mountains, the road descends into the ample valley of **Puebla.**

There is no shortage of public transport from Mexico City. The famous Cristóbal Colón line and ADO run regular services from the bus station to **Amecameca**. They leave every half hour, and the journey takes about an hour. From there you take a taxi, either to **Tlamacas** (about 25 km/15 miles away) for Popo, or to **La Joya** for Izta. There are also several travel firms in Mexico City

single day but do it in two stages. Bear in mind, however, that the bivouac shelters intended for overnight stops are in an appalling condition, and unless you fancy spending the night in a sardine can, your own tent, insulated mat and sleeping bag are essential.

The usual route via Tres Cruces is the simplest. Apart from the usual climbing equipment, you won't need anything more than crampons and ski poles. A very early start is advisable for two reasons. First, the fine-grained lava sand and snow will still be frozen hard, which makes the going considerably easier. Second, by midday the mountains are usually shrouded in cloud. So set off

where you can book package tours that include guided mountain walks.

Sardine cans: Tlamacas lies on the edge of the tree line at an altitude of about 3,882 meters (12,740 ft) and is the starting point for Popocatépetl. There are two hostels here: the newer Albergue de la Juventud and the old one some 50 meters (165 ft) below. Both offer reasonably clean overnight accommodation as well as sanitary facilities. The new hostel also has hot showers and a restaurant. It's best to bring your own food supplies, but you can hire crampons and ice picks.

You are advised not to tackle the trip in a

from Tlamacas before sunrise, along the gentle path over the lava sand, the lights of the city twinkling away to the northwest.

An awkward steep section follows, where you'll find yourself forever slithering backwards and struggling forwards. After about three hours you reach the derelict shelter at **Tres Cruces** (4,400 meters/14,440 ft, tent essential). Just beyond begins the long, monotonous snowy slope which takes you right up to the **Labio Inferior**, the lower lip of the crater (5,254 meters/17,240 ft), a four to five-hour walk.

From here you can look down into the

seething volcanic crater and watch the acrid clouds of sulphur billowing up from the depths of the earth. The yellowish-reddish-black sides of the crater complete the vision of hell. On no account should you attempt to climb down as the sulphur-gatherers used to – there's a real danger of suffocating.

From here you can continue for an hour along the rim of the crater to the main peak, the **Pico Mayor**. A shelter has been erected which has been called the world's highest bottle bank, and not only for its shape.

The descent is much quicker if you use the same route – you can slide over the snow and sand back to Tlamacas in two and a half

saddle. Follow the red trail past the Portillo gap, bearing left and then right along the flanks of the main ridge to tumbledown shelters. This will take about four and a half hours. The first shelter is at 4,760 meters/ 15,620 ft and there are two others further on.

Set off as early as possible the next day for the one-and-a-half-hour climb over rough rocky ground to the first peak (5,020 meters/ 16,470 ft) then onwards via steep paths to the **Rondillas** (two hours). Watching the sunrise more than compensates for the effort.

A two-hour walk along the southern ridge brings you to the flat plateau of the main peak, called **Pecho** (Breast). Allow five hours

hours. A steeper and more difficult alternative for climbers who feel they haven't worked hard enough is via Cañada del Venturillo Pico Mayor (allow five to six hours), but crevasses make a rope essential while negotiating this route.

The White Lady: The haul to the top of Izta is longer and an overnight stop is inevitable. From La Joya the path heads toward Amaculécatl across a grassy slope to the first

Left, a beautiful view thousands of meters up in the sky down into the deep crater of Popocatépetl. **Above**, the "White Lady" conquered.

for the descent. Incidentally, there are no buildings in La Joya, but 3 km (2 miles) further on at the Torre Rastramisora television station there is an old construction workers' cabin which makes a primitive shelter.

Both peaks are also ideal for hang gliding. From Popo, for example, you can launch off from the edge of the crater, hopefully to land at the Tlamacas hostel or on the Paso de Cortéz. Needless to say the thinness of the air at high altitudes should discourage all but the fittest from attempting the ascent, and all potential visitors should check the weather forecast before setting out.

When Insurgentes Sur becomes the highway to **Cuernavaca**, it is probably the busiest thoroughfare in Mexico because Cuernavaca is *the* weekend resort for the capital. It is where the Mexico City *capitalinos* look for pure air, nice weather, privacy and the bliss of silence: an escape from the cacophony of Mexico City.

Once there, a fortunate few can take refuge in a mansion, encompassed by high walls and protected from the hot sun by huge shade

be covered in one to two hours, depending on traffic. To the east, the twin volcanoes Popocatépetl and Iztaccíhuatl will seem to move closer as the journey progresses. Once beyond the Tres Cumbres Pass, a glorious view will unfold over the wide fertile valley of Morelos. Bordering this valley to the east are the curious rock formations at Tepoztlán, a picturesque little place with a delightful Sunday market. To the south of the valley loom the Guernos mountains.

trees, laurels from India. Because of its altitude – 610 meters (2,000 ft) lower than the capital – and its beautiful climate, Cuernavaca has always attracted the élite of any society. Aztec emperors built palaces here. Cortéz built a pleasure dome. But for the visitor Cuernavaca can be disappointing: aside from mansions and good hotels, the city has relatively little to offer. The climate here is temperate through most of the year – sunny but not too hot.

Leaving the urban sprawl by way of the Avenida Insurgentes Sur via the motorway, the 90-km (55-mile) trip to Cuernavaca can

Montezuma, Cortéz, Emperor Maximilian, the fugitive Shah of Persia – they all loved the "eternal spring" that seems to reign at Cuernavaca (1,542 meters/5,060 ft, population 300,000), the capital of the state of **Morelos**. Artists, wealthy citizens and retired Americans have also chosen to settle in this garden town, with its bright flowers and hedges. In fact, the most frustrating aspect of this otherwise beautiful city is the way that most of the flower-filled gardens in which residents take such personal pride are tucked away discreetly behind high walls and thus are never seen by casual visitors.

Originally the village here was called Cuauhnáhuac, which more or less means "on the edge of the forest." The Spanish mispronounced it *cuernavaca*, meaning "horned cow." After the Aztecs seized the valley in the 15th century, their emperor Montezuma I established his summer palace, complete with extravagant water fountains and pleasure gardens. Later Cortéz introduced the cultivation of sugar cane to this area. Mexico's "sweet valley" also attracted the unfortunate Emperor Maximilian. After the fierce battles of the revolution, peace returned to the tranquil provincial town. But Cuernavaca's era of peace and quiet, as captured in

one of the outside galleries, especially his portrait of Zapata. The foundations in front of the building date back to the pre-Hispanic times of Tlahuica and may have been part of an ancient ceremonial ground.

Avenida Hidalgo leads straight to the great **La Asunción cathedral**, dating from the early 16th century and one of the earliest churches in the Americas. It was built to a monumental size to impress the power of the Catholic Church on the indigenous people. Built like a fortress in a garden, it is fairly unadorned except for some curious frescoes depicting the persecution of Christian missionaries in Japan, and believed to have been

Malcolm Lowry's novel *Under the Volcano* are long gone. At the weekend the traffic is sometimes as bad as it is in the capital.

In the main square, the Plaza de Armas is dominated by the towering Cortéz Palace. It was substantially rebuilt over the years, fell into ruin and in 1970 underwent thorough reconstruction. Today the palace houses a history museum. The main attraction is Diego Rivera's famous frescoes on the walls of

Left, **Cortéz Palace stands defiant.** **Above**, **poinsettia and bougainvillea in the garden paradise, Cuernavaca.**

done by a convert from that country who lived here in the 17th century. A rare statue believed to be of Cortéz sits in the church at the entrance. At one time the Franciscans had a monastery in the precincts, and the skull and crossbones above the portico is the symbol of their order. A side entrance leads into the quiet cloister of the former Franciscan monastery. A *mariachi* mass takes place in the cathedral every Sunday.

In the Franciscan cloister, the **Museo Casa Robert Brady** has an interesting collection of Mexican art and Asian handicrafts. A group of paintings of Indians at work in pre-colonial days can be seen in the nearby **Palacio Municipal.**

Directly opposite the cathedral are the **Jardines Borda**. These baroque gardens were laid out in the second half of the 18th century by Manuel de la Borda, a priest who was the son of Taxco's silver prince and traveler, José de la Borda. Once surrounding the 18th-century home of Taxco's richest silver magnate, the gardens were restored a few years ago and are exceptionally pleasant with their fountains, artificial lake and outdoor theater.

Adjoining the **Jardín Juarez** (designed by Gustav Eiffel) is the larger **Jardín de los Héroes**, or **Alameda**, at whose eastern end is the **Palacio de Cortéz**, which the conqueror built as a summer home on the ruins of an old Indian temple. Now a museum, with a strong colonial component, it boasts a spectacularly interesting mural by Diego Rivera depicting almost 400 years of Mexican history with all its famous heroes and villains. For more than half a century it has been challenging Mexican children to identify the participants in their national saga.

Once you have visited the market it is time to cross the ravine to the east and look around the **Teopanzolco Pyramid** that lies in a park even further east – you'll need to take a taxi. The pyramid is not especially impressive, but once you've seen it and the market that's it for Cuernavaca.

However, Cuernavaca does have some excellent hotels, of which the most famous is possibly **Las Mananitas**, which lies half a dozen blocks north of the city center on Calle Ricardo Linares. If you've ever dreamed of staying in a beautiful, flower-filled garden in which fountains tinkle and peacocks strut, sleeping in a room filled with period furniture and eating first-rate food, now is the time to indulge yourself.

If Cuernavaca is somewhat disappointing, the state of Morelos, though one of the smallest in Mexico, is beautiful and full of surprises. One of these surprises involves taking a short detour from the road from Cuernavaca to Taxco to reach the ancient Indian site at Xochicalco (place of the house of flowers). Situated at the top of a hill and looking very imposing, the site predates the Aztec period and reached its peak around a thousand years ago. At that time Xochicalco was the important junction of two major trading routes.

The main structure, the remarkably well-preserved Pyramid of the Feathered Serpent, is a decoration full of writhing life.

Taxco, Mexico's famous silver-working town, is near Xochicalco, some 72 km (45 miles) south of Cuernavaca and about a third of the way between Mexico City and Acapulco. It is one of the few Mexican towns that has been declared a national monument. The Spaniards were mining metal for their cannons here from an early date. At the same

time they stumbled on the rich veins of silver in the Cerro Bermeja mountains. Taxco grew out of three mining villages on the steep slope of one of the ridges, Atachi.

It was from these mines that the European adventurer, de la Borda, shovelled his immense fortune. The entrepreneur sank part of the money into improving the town. Later, when production slackened in the mines, the town fell into a fairytale slumber from which it did not awaken until the 1930s, when a North American pioneer brought tourism to Taxco, and with it a new lease of life. William Spratling, known as "Don Guillermo," took advantage of the boom in Acapulco and established a tourist trade and silver-craft workshops in the sleepy resort. Today, the workshops employ almost the entire population of the town, which has become the silver manufacture and retail center of Mexico. Countless shops sell silverware of all qualities and all prices.

The town is protected by a preservation order. With romantic nooks and crannies, whitewashed houses, red-tile roofs and flowers everywhere, this is picture-postcard Mexico as the foreigners love it. Steep winding alleyways tempt you to explore. Cars are best parked below the town.

cannot be found elsewhere in Mexico, or, for instance, distinctively marked jewelry a cut above the usual. Many people are pleasantly surprised at how chic and stylish Mexican silver jewelry can be: as much art deco as ethnic alliance, in many cases. Silver is usually 925 sterling, with copper alloy. However, a word of warning: Alpaca, or nickel silver, contains no silver at all and is made mostly of nickel.

Unfortunately Taxco has been spoiled for many visitors by the ubiquitous traffic – hundreds of scurrying, beeping taxicabs that make strolling difficult if not actually hazardous. Narrow, cobblestone streets twist up

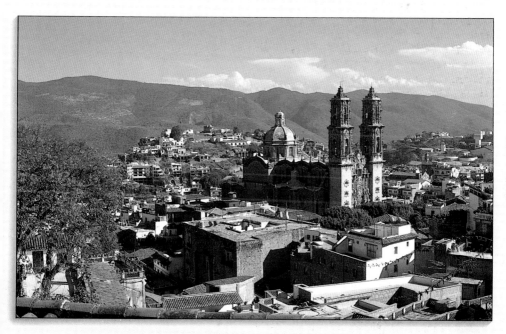

Contrary to the popular belief that mining is a thing of the past in Taxco, the silver miners are now busy once again; modern mining techniques mean that more ore is being extracted than ever before. Mexico is the world's largest producer of silver. The goods on sale in Taxco are priced pretty much the same as in Mexico City, but here competition is fierce because there are so many dealers operating in a small area. It's possible to see goods in small shops that

Left, Museo Casa Robert Brady, Cuernavaca.
Above, overview of Taxco.

and down hills, all eventually leading to the Zócalo in front of a gem of a colonial church, the **Santa Prisca** dominated by twin baroque, 40-meter (130-ft) towers. Its carved stone facade is more than matched by its gilded interior, including paintings by Miguel Cabrera, Mexico's most famous artist of colonial times. Both teem with saints and decorations. Take special notice of the organ and the excellent carvings on the wooden pulpit. Santa Prisca, completed in 1758 with colorful tiled dome and decorated steeples, was paid for by José de la Borda, the French silver miner who pulled enough silver out of the ground to become one of the richest men in Mexico. Apparently he had this church built for his son, Manuel.

The square is lined with hallowed buildings housing restaurants and silver shops. Out in the square, Indian women sell *amates* or pictures on bark. They have often painted the lively village scenes or simple patterns themselves. These enterprising souls come from the neighboring villages and speak *náhuatl*, the ancient Aztec language. You won't find these miniature works of art any cheaper anywhere else.

To the right as you leave the church, a plaque marks **Casa Borda** where the town's

Columbian designs into the jewelry. So good and so unusual were Spratling's pieces that weathly clients such as Neiman-Marcus and Bonwit Teller competed with each other to buy his output.

Many of his former student-craftsmen set up their own shops, which subsequently formed the basis of the more than 300 shops in the town itself. There are no great bargains – you'll find the prices quoted are about the same as in Mexico City. The advantage here is that you can see a tremendous variety of silverwork and also watch the artisans handcraft their exquisite products.

Spratling invested much of his well-de-

rich patron once lived, and through the adjoining arcade and downstairs is the **Silver Museum** containing a rich selection of work in the metal by Antonio Pineda, including a chess set with pieces matching the Indians against the conquistadors. In 1953, Pineda won the first of the annual contests now staged by local silversmiths.

He was the first apprentice of William Spratling, the Tulane University professor who arrived in Taxco in 1932 and virtually single-handedly created the local silver industry by hiring locals, teaching them silversmithing skills, and integrating pre-

served riches in a collection of pre-Columbian art in a large house which is now the **William Spratling Museum**. Its owner died in a car accident in 1967. Down narrow steps behind the cathedral is the street which becomes **Mercado de Artesians**. Here you will find scores of stalls selling almost everything.

On Ruiz de Alarcon (named for a local playwright who was the contemporary of Cervantes) is the **Casa de Humboldt** where the noted German explorer/scientist Baron Alexander von Humboldt (1769–1859) stayed for a single night in 1803 during his travels in Central and South America. Vast enough to have served as a convent and hospital, in recent years it was a guesthouse owned by a local architect. Now it is the **Museum of Colonial Art**, and as such it exhibits a miscellaneous collection of religious artifacts and other items. Most interesting, perhaps, are the bust and portraits of von Humboldt himself and a reproduction of a painting of a somewhat grandiose José de la Borda in a costume that must have amused even his friends.

Above the Zócalo lies the baroque **Casa Figueroa**, a colonial house which has been turned into a small museum by the Figueroas, an eccentric artist couple. The view from the

when the main church, Santa Prisca, is spectacularly floodlit.

The steep hill leading off the eastern side of Plaza Borda leads down to the shabby Plaza Bernal, at whose corner can be found the seldom-open **Museo Gráfica de la Historia Social de Taxco** which displays early photos of the town and illustrates its development as the overcrowded tourist center it has become. Residents and developers are forbidden to build in any non-local style or to change the character of the town in any way. It has understandably become a big favorite of the foreign community A Mexican comic once drew applause by saying

neighboring terrace, above the Borda fountain, opens out over the ever-lively **Zócalo**. In the afternoon, the square, the heart of Taxco, begins to echo with the sound of the *mariachis* is the nearby cafés. Those in search of a panorama from above should head for the Virgen de Guadalupe church or the Iglesia del Señor de Ojeda. There's a terrific view from the terrace of the **Hotel Rancho Taxco**, which is particularly impressive after sunset,

Left, back street of Plaza Bernal. **Above**, Santa Prisca church, Taxco (left) and (right) Taxco's shimmering industry.

he'd refused an invitation to visit Taxco because he didn't speak English.

The town proper has more than 10,000 residents and about five times that number live in scattered communities on nearby hills. Houses are of stucco-covered adobe roofed in red tile, and they have plants overflowing their balconies. Taxco, however, is well on the way to being ruined by excessive traffic. At Easter, when there are processions, penitents and a recreation of Christ's last hours, you need confirmed reservations way ahead. The rest of the time, Taxco makes for a good overnight stay on your way to Acapulco.

Puebla has always been one of Mexico's prettiest towns. Around 100 km (60 miles) east of the capital, it lies in an upland lake region at 2,160 meters (7,085 ft) above sea level, surrounded by some of the country's highest volcanoes, notably Popocatépetl, Iztaccíhuatl, Pico de Oricaba and Malinche. Surprisingly, it doesn't suffer much from pollution, despite having a population of over a million and some important industry, including the Mexican Volkswagen plant.

Founded in 1531, the town displays all the features of town planning and architecture which the Spanish adhered to so rigidly in their colonies. Here as elsewhere a network of streets was built, forming a series of rectangular blocks or *manzanas*, each about 80 meters (260 ft) wide by 160 meters (520 ft) long. One block was left empty as a central square (**Zócalo**). With its ancient trees, the square is still a favorite meeting place in the town center, especially as it is surrounded on three sides by arcades, full of numerous inviting cafés and restaurants where you can while away the time.

Grand cathedral: On the south side of the square is the city's majestic **cathedral**, built from grey basalt in the years 1588–1649. Regarded by some as the finest cathedral in the country, it is distinguished by Mexico's two tallest church towers, almost 70 meters (230 ft) high. It is a fine example of the most refined architectural style of the Spanish renaissance, the *Herreriano* – named for Juan de Herrera, the architect of the Escorial, the classic monastery and palace in New Castile, near Madrid. The style is severe and elegant, paying its respects to Roman architecture. The main altar is the work of the famous neoclassical artist, Manuel Tolsá. The interior was renovated in fine classical style during the 19th century.

On Calle 5 Oriente, beside the cathedral, the tourist office is almost next door to the **Casa de Cultura** where cultural events are held. Once a seminary, founded in 1646, it now has a sculpture garden and tiny coffee shop and serves as a community center with its open air theater.

Finding your way around the grid of streets is very simple. Only the streets forming the central axes are named. Heading west from the center is Avenida de la Reforma; running east, Avenida Maximino Avila Camacho. To the north, Calle 5 de Mayo and to the south, Calle 16 de Septiembre. All the other streets are known by numbers and points of the compass. Leading off the north–south axis are Avenidas Oriente to the east and Poniente to the west. Streets to the north take even numbers, to the south odd numbers. By contrast, the Calle 3 (5, 7 etc.) Norte and 3 (5, 7 etc.) Sur run from the Avenida de la Reforma to the north and south respectively. Calles 2 (4, 6 etc.) Norte and Sur branch off Avenida Maximino Avila Camacho.

Although this century has seen some building and renovation in the old town, the architecture is still largely characterized by the colonial-style patio houses with flat roofs, mostly three storys high. The rooms are reached via an inner courtyard (patio) around which runs a long veranda. The courtyards vary in size, but a glance through the entrance-way reveals that most are badly in need of a spring clean.

Noted for their particularly spacious court-yards are the former **Archbishop's Palace**, the religious seminary (now the Casa de la Cultura) and the **Biblioteca Palaforxiana**. This 17th-century library merits a visit, not only for its important collection of books but also for the fabulous baroque interior. The library is the oldest in America, with 50,000 volumes nestled on shelves of carved and gilded woodwork. There is a small admission charge, but you can just peek in through the open doorway.

Puebla from Talavera de la Reina in Spain and has been done since the 16th century, with designs reflecting Asian, Spanish-Arab and indigenous influences. It is kept alive to this day in several workshops.

This characteristic blue Talavera pottery can be found at **El Parián**, the central market aimed at tourists, whose stalls sell every-thing from *serapes* to sombreros. With the renewal of interest in traditional crafts, de-mand is growing for these decorative tiles and matching crockery.

Probably the most beautiful *azulejo* facade belongs to the **Casa de los Muñecos** (House of the Dolls, 2 Norte No. 1), which now

Tiled city: In spite of the rigid layout of uniformly straight streets, the townscape is far from monotonous. Innumerable churches and monasteries lend it a special character. Extensive use of Talavera tiles on Puebla's church domes and the unique facades deco-rated with *azulejos* (ceramic tiles) has given rise to its reputation as "the city of tiles."

The art of glazing ceramics in blue (*azul* in Spanish) and other colors was brought to

Left, tile picture on the side of Casa de los Muñecos. **Above**, the "Confectioner's House" in Puebla looks as if it were decorated with cream.

houses the University Museum. The indi-vidually fashioned, grotesque figures date back to the 18th century. Equally splendid is the **Casa del Alfeñique**, the Confectioner's House (4 Oriente), with its white stucco work and a particularly lovely patio. This building houses the regional museum and contains good examples of ceramics pro-duced in the state along with memorabilia from that great event in Puebla history, the battle of May 5, 1862.

Puebla's remarkable colonial architecture includes lavish churches such as the **Iglesia de la Compañía**, and mysterious convents such as **Santa Monica**, which operated secretly and unknown to the secular authorities until 1934. It is now the **Museo de Arte Religioso**. Inside the 16th-century Santo Domingo church with its tiled dome on Calle 5 de Mayo is the famous gilded **Capilla Rosary**, altar to the virgin. The ornamental gold work begins in the nave, which is lavishly embellished, but from the moment of entering the chapel visitors find themselves absolutely dazzled by the opulent gold relief work of this extravagant example of high baroque. The churchyard was opened as part of a recent renovation program, when the Calle 5 de Mayo was pedestrianised.

at the time. The market soon outgrew its site, but it was only a few years ago that both the market and the countless itinerant traders from the surrounding streets were successfully moved to new sites on the outskirts of the town. The intention is to use the market hall for cultural events in the future.

Cinco de Mayo: The surrounding streets are a warren of activity, especially 5 de Mayo which is lined with sidewalk stalls. Almost every town in Mexico has a 5 de Mayo, but Puebla is where the date first assumed its national importance, in 1862. Celebrated annually throughout the country, it was when a Mexican army, led by General Ignacio

Looking west up 6 Oriente you can see the cast-iron structure of the old **Mercado Victoria**, abandoned some years back for still-to-be-completed renovations. It was one of the last of the grand old markets built by Porfirio Díaz, who sought to transform Mexico into a carbon copy of France. The market stands on the site of the Santo Domingo monastery that occupied two whole *manzanas* within the city's boundaries. As part of the expropriation of church property (1854) these were turned into the main marketplace, which in 1912 was covered with an iron-girdered roof, the height of modernity

Zaragoza and including battalions of Indians, defeated a French army. The victory boosted Mexican morale, but could not prevent the French occupation. May 5, however, was declared a national holiday and the official title of Puebla de Zaragoza was thereafter bestowed upon the town.

Among other once-important monasteries is **Santa Rosa** (3 Norte near 14 Poniente) now housing the state's Craft Museum, and the convent of **Santa Monica**, which survived in secret after secularization in 1857 until its discovery (1934), when it was turned into a religious museum. The university developed in the 19th century from what had been the **Jesuit College**, built around several patios and a particularly fine baroque hall.

Underground river: In the past the eastern boundary of the town was marked by the Rio San Francisco, until in the 1960s the river was diverted through pipes and disappeared under the wide Boulevard Héroes del 5 de Mayo, an urgently needed relief road for the ever-increasing traffic. On this busy boulevard stands the **Teatro Principal**, which was first opened to the public in 1760 and suffered a disastrous fire in 1902. After the fire it was rebuilt to look exactly the way it had been before the blaze.

In the 19th century, factories were built in the extensive grounds of the former San Francisco monastery on the far side of the river. At that time Puebla was developing into one of the most important centers of the Mexican textile industry. Indeed, the first mechanized factory in Latin America, the Constancia Mexicana, was founded in 1835 on the Rio Atoyac to the west of the town. Machinery dating back to 1890 is still operating today in the classical-style buildings.

On Calle 2 Sur is Puebla's newest uncharacteristically high-tech attraction, the **Amparo Museum,** whose computerized catalogue and interactive videos provide further

Nearby is El Parián, a market building that dates from the beginning of the 19th century. The succession of bars, distinguished by their barrel vaulting, were used for a long time as studios until they were turned into a craft market. One section of the old Parián was turned into the **Barrio de Artista**, a complex housing several small artists' studios whose occupants are often present and exhibiting their works.

<u>**Left**</u>, a detail from the Capilla del Rosario. <u>**Above**</u>, the Cholula pyramid towers in the background behind the domes of the Capilla Real.

amplification of the art therein. Spanning several centuries, the art was the personal collection of the late Manuel Espinosa Iglesias whose colonial-era house this was. The museum allows free entry on Monday and is closed on Tuesday.

Three blocks away is the distinctive **La Compañía** church with its elaborate facade, said to be the last resting place of China Poblana, the 17th-century Asian princess whose statue surmounts a fountain at the east side of town. Her costume of frilly blouse atop an embroidered skirt has become a characteristic cliché of Mexican peasant garb.

Adjoining the church and bordering a pleasant, cobbled alley is the **University**, in a 16th-century building which formerly served as the Jesuit College.

Exotic dishes: Puebla is associated in Mexican minds with colonial grandeur, with General Zaragoza, with the start of the revolution of 1910, and also with three minor but all-important things: *camotes, mole, rompope*. Mexico has one of the richest cuisines in the world, but not all of the truly exotic dishes can be found in the restaurants usually patronized by visitors.

Camotes are sweet potatoes prepared with fruit and sugar; *rompope* is a sort of eggnog,

During the War of Independence at the start of this century, the forts of **Loreto** and **Guadalupe** were built on a hill in the northeast of the town. It was here that the Mexicans under General Ignacio Zaragoza won the decisive battle against the invading French army on May 5, 1862. This hill and the villa district of Cerro de la Paz to the west command beautiful views over the town and its environs, which include several interesting side-trips and excursions.

An attractive avenue of eucalyptus trees leads to **Cholula,** a Puebla suburb which in pre-Columbian times was the major center of a religious cult. During the conquest,

said to be the children's introduction to alcohol and *mole* is a dark sauce whose ingredients include chile peppers, spices, chocolate, nuts and bread all finely ground and then mixed with tomato sauce and chicken or turkey broth and served over cooked chicken or turkey.

Like any great dish, good *mole* requires a lot of work. It might be called the national dish, though it has a number of competitors for that honor. The sauce was said to have been invented in the kitchen of the **Santa Rosa Convent** (3 Norte near 14 Poniente), now an excellent handcraft-filled museum.

Cortéz, fearing an ambush at Cholula, set up an effective counterblow which resulted in the death of some 3,000 people. Later, a plague further reduced the population and so Cholula, once a city of great importance, became an impoverished village.

Next to the Franciscan church in the town's main square you can't miss the mosque-like **Capilla Real** with its 49 domes which was inspired by the mosque of Córdoba.

The main attraction in Cholula is the **Santuario de los Remedios,** a tiny church placed on top of what looks like a hill, but in reality is a pyramid. The stepped pyramid may be only 54 meters (177 ft) high, but it has the largest volume of any pyramid in the world. Entering along one of several archaeologists' tunnels, you can observe how the structure was built up in a number of layers. You can also view wall paintings from earlier eras.

Another of the scores of remarkable churches to be seen in this tiny place is the **Convento de San Gabriel** with its beautiful 16th-century temple and vast chapel.

Textile town: From Texmelucan (on the Puebla–Mexico motorway) the road continues to **Huejotzingo**, site of a fortress-like Franciscan monastery about 40 km (25 miles)

east of Puebla. This dates from before 1525 and features some fine Gothic vaulting. Look out for the 16th-century altarpiece. As in the neighboring convent of **Calpan**, there are *capillas pozas* – literally, inn-chapels. They were built in the corners of an atrium, a place to rest during long and tiresome religious processions. Those at Huejotzingo are among the best in Mexico. The town is also famous for woolens, sweaters and *sarapes*, or blan-

Puebla scenes: tiled kitchen in the Santa Rosa Convent where *mole* is said to have been invented (left), and the Biblioteca Palafoxiana (right).

kets. The truth is that these days the wool is mixed with synthetic fibers, but, alas, that's the blended way of the world.

To the north, the road along the foot of the Malinche leads to **Tlaxcala**, the pleasant, countrified capital of the little state of the same name. The Zócalo is pleasantly leafy and the buildings that open out onto it have recently been renovated. On a raised terrace stands the **Convento de San Francisco** (Franciscan monastery) which features a wonderful cedarwood ceiling in Mudéjar design; and, high above the town, the **Pilgrimage Church of Ocotlán**, with stucco facade and octagonal chapel (Camarin) behind the altar, a classic example of Mexican Churrigueresque.

Tlaxcala is also famous historically because the Tlaxcalans helped Cortéz conquer Mexico. Brave soldiers, they served gladly in the Spanish forces because they hated their old enemy, the Aztecs. A mural in the **Palacio de Gobierno**, painted by Desiderio Hernández Xochitiotzin, tells the story of these Indians. Other historical landmarks are the *pulque* haciendas that prospered up to the time of the revolution. Among the best are San Bartolomé del Monte, Ixtafiayuca, San Cristobal Zacacalo and San Blas.

From the Tlaxcala road, a road branches off left to San Martin Texmelucan, which leads through **Cacaxtla**, a ceremonial ground which may have flourished as long as 2,000 years ago but was abandoned for at least 1,000 years. It was excavated a few years ago. Some unusually well-preserved and very striking frescoes depict horrifically realistic and brightly colored battle scenes between jaguar warriors and their opponents in bird costume. Viewing is only allowed in the mornings until 1 pm because the frescoes must be protected from sunlight.

On the journey back to Puebla, a short detour takes you via two particularly lovely village churches. **Santa María Tonantzintla** features an overwhelming abundance of brightly painted cherubs and stucco ornamentation in rustic Indian-baroque style. The somewhat more restrained decor of **San Francisco Acatepec** shimmers with gold, against which the *azulejo* facade is all the more gloriously colorful.

The highway from Mexico City to Toluca, Mexico 15, true to Mexican taste is 67 kms (40 miles) of curves, but most drivers now prefer to save time by making the trip in about 25 minutes via the toll road. The old highway is effectively the extension of the Paseo de la Reforma and leads up to the fir forests of the Sierra de las Cruces. It is here that on weekends the masses of recreation-seeking residents of the capital gather. The rest areas are packed with *taco* and beverage stands. Northward lies Parque Nacional de Miguel Hidalgo; to the south is the Parque Nacional Desierto de los Leones, although in this "lions' desert" there are no lions. On leaving Mexico City the road goes through a surprising countryside with tall pine forests reminiscent of Germany. But once across the Paso de las Cruces mountain range (3,100 meters/10,170 ft) into the valley, you are truly in Mexico again: dry, golden fields, cacti, adobe houses.

Toluca is a typical provincial city with some Victorian-style buildings, colonial churches, a large central square, narrow streets and the usual *portales*, or arcades. They are the heart of the town, where at dusk everybody idly walks about, flirting, gossiping, window shopping. This is what makes dusk the best time of the day.

Mountain city: Mexico's highest big city, **Toluca**, (2,680 meters/8,790 ft above sea level) has for years been experiencing enormous expansion. Nissan built an automobile factory here, to add to the large chemical factory, the brewery and sundry other production plants. The population of 500,000 continues to grow, the city has good facilities, and Toluca may well benefit from the decentralization plans of politicians. It is near the capital, yet the plateau provides much space for growth and can draw on the large supply of workers who are anxious to leave the chaos of Mexico City. Since the great earthquake, many companies have shown a strong desire to leave the capital.

Left, crater lake in Nevado de Toluca.

Toluca is also the capital of the state of Mexico. The city's name comes from the *náhuatl* word Tollocan, which means "place of reeds." Under the influence of Teotihuacán, the region was settled by members of the Nahua tribe, the *Matlatzinca* (those with small nets), in the 13th century. Like many other tribes they had to submit to the control of the Aztecs – or flee from their domination. Again and again they rebeled against the violent Aztec rule, finally allying themselves with the Spaniards. In 1529, a Franciscan cloister was founded in Toluca, and it was incorporated as a city in 1667.

At the edge of the city proper, visitors are greeted by an equestrian statue of the revolutionary hero Emiliano Zapata and a monument dedicated to the Mexican flag. The **Zócalo** is officially called the **Plaza de los Mártires** (Place of Martyrs) after the hundred independence fighters who were executed here in 1812. On the plaza is the neoclassical cathedral. Many find the cathedral to be rather unattractive. Its cornerstone was laid in 1862, and as construction took many decades it only approached completion in the 1950s, being finally finished in 1978. As a result, Toluca can today boast the youngest cathedral in Mexico. A block away, on the **Plaza Garibay** beside the turn-of-the-century building that housed the market, is the attractive **Jardín Botanico y Cosmovitral**.

On the north side of the Zócalo stands the neoclassical **Palacio de Gobierno**, built in 1872. The nearby **Palacio Municipal** was designed by the same architect. A block of buildings known as the **Portales also** borders the square. It gets its name from the 120 arcades, where a significant and very attractive part of the city's life takes place. Toluca has its own food and drink specialties. The drinks, called *moscos* come in bottles with long necks and are famous because, like all street liquor, they are *muy traidores* (very treacherous). Toluca is also famous for its fruit jam, very good candy, and spicy green *chorizos*, or Spanish chili sausage, all sold in the *portales*. A few simple but good and reasonably priced restaurants can be found within the quarter.

Colorful markets: Botanical gardens have been planted near the former market hall of the Mercado 16 de Septiembre. Arching over the market is a glass mosaic, the Mexican artist Leopoldo Flores' vision of the universe. Near the bus station is the **Indian market** where Matlatzinca and Otomí Indians sell food, second-hand items, and handicrafts from stands decorated with flowers. The *mercado* is one of the largest in Mexico, and on Friday it is especially busy. It is also one of the most attractive markets in

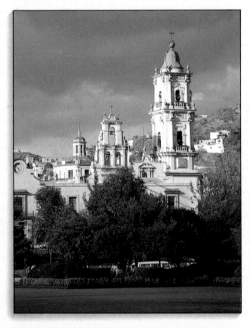

the vicinity, but if you have sampled one of the smaller markets in the south, you don't need to drive to Toluca to see this one.

In 1987 the **Centro Cultural Mexiquense** was opened on the bypass. The center houses museums for folk art, modern art, anthropology and history which are worth seeing. The adjoining state-controlled shop sells authentic folk art, but its selection is not as extensive as Casart on Paseo Tollacan.

Out of Toluca you have various options: one is to head 80 km (50 miles) west over a newly constructed road to Valle de Bravo. The highway crosses a flat valley with a snowcapped volcano to the left. The landscape changes constantly, from European-type forests to typically Mexican valleys. **Valle de Bravo** is definitely of mountain heritage at about 1,870 meters (6,135 ft) above sea level. Thatched roofs overhang the streets. There are houses with white walls and stone chimneys. It is here that residents of the capital gather on weekends to enjoy the provincial idyll, the lake and the wooded mountain scenery, as well as the very welcome pure, clear air. The lake is ideal for water sports, and golf enthusiasts enjoy the area immensely.

Ancient cultural center: An excursion to the archaeological site of **Calixtlahuaca**, 11 km (7 miles) north of Tula, is also worthwhile. The name comes from the *náhuatl* and means place with houses on the plateau. The site was once an important center of the Matlatzinca culture. It came under the influence of Teotihuacan, Xochicalco, the Toltecs and finally, in 1474, the Aztecs. Revolts from among the Matlatzinca were put down by the rulers of Tenochtitlán, and excavated structures nearby indicate Aztec influence.

Calixtlahuaca is also famous for its **Quetzalcoatl round pyramid**. It has been rebuilt at least three times and is shaped like a snail, which supposedly represents a windsock and portrays Quetzalcoatl as the wind god Ehecatl. Five minutes by foot up the slope among aloe plants is another building complex with a Tlaloc temple. Only one of four terraces remains. The *tzompantli*, a sort of cross-shaped altar adorned on one side with skull ornaments, stands opposite the Tlaloc temple.

Tenango de Arista (or Tenango del Valle) is 25 km (16 miles) south of Toluca on Mex 55. It is worth stopping in the pottery town of **Metepec** (9 km/5 miles south of Toluca) where the tall and colorful clay "trees of life" are made. On a mountain above Tenango is **Teotenango**, an archaeological site of very extensive and homogeneous construction said to date back to the 7th century. The high double walls could not prevent the Aztecs from occupying Teotenango, which must have been a Matlatzinca city. The place is still practically unknown but is worth inspecting because of its interesting museum.

South of Toluca, the 4,570-meter (14,990-ft) high volcano **Nevado de Toluca** towers over the city. Nevado means snow mountain but is an inappropriate name for the fourth-highest mountain in Mexico because there is hardly ever snow around the crater. The mountain is called Xinantécatl in *náhuatl*, which is probably the better name since Xinantécatl means unclothed man, denoting that there is no snow cover.

The trip to Nevado de Toluca is spectacular because the road leads up 4,200 meters (13,800 ft) and into the crater itself. Although the summit is only 20 km (12 miles) from the city as the crow flies, it is a 45-km

after the sun and the moon. It takes over an hour to walk around the banks of these lakes.

Where the road climbs to the crater's edge, a footpath leads south toward a saddle between the mountains. Anyone can go as far as this point, but whoever wants to get to the main summit, the **Pico del Fraile** (Monk's Summit), must now do some climbing.

The cliff may seem ominous from below but the climb needs only occasional use of hands. The path to the summit leads clockwise up the crater edges, inside and outside, over large and sometimes shaky stone masses. After two hours, you reach the main summit (4,570 meters/14,990 ft) marked with a small

(28-mile) drive. The first 27 kilometers (17 miles) through Capultitlan and San Juan are on a good paved road, but the remainder is unpaved and the traveler won't forget swallowing a huge amount of dust over the last 18 km (11 miles).

The lower slopes of the massive mountains are covered with pine forests, but only a few plants grow in the lava. The last two kilometers of the now-narrow road lead into the crater and directly to two lakes, named

Left, Toluca's modern cathedral. **Above**, fountain in the attractive Jardín Botanico y Cosmovitral.

cross. If the start was early enough – 5 o'clock from Toluca – you will have a magnificent view: of the mountains Popo and Ixta, the city of Toluca, the picturesque reservoir in the Valle de Bravo, and the polluted sky over Mexico City. To descend, the path goes clockwise around the crater's edge for about 10 minutes and then ploughs down a debris furrow to the Sun Lake.

Climbers should be careful. Although the Nevado de Toluca is *only* 4,750 meters (14,990 ft) high, one can still suffer altitude sickness. At any sign of sickness or dizziness, return to the valley as soon as possible.

INSIGHT GUIDES
Travel Tips

FOR THOSE WITH MORE THAN A PASSING INTEREST IN TIME...

Before you put your name down for a Patek Philippe watch *fig. 1*, there are a few basic things you might like to know, without knowing exactly whom to ask. In addressing such issues as accuracy, reliability and value for money, we would like to demonstrate why the watch we will make for you will be quite unlike any other watch currently produced.

"Punctuality", Louis XVIII was fond of saying, "is the politeness of kings."

We believe that in the matter of punctuality, we can rise to the occasion by making you a mechanical timepiece that will keep its rendezvous with the Gregorian calendar at the end of every century, omitting the leap-years in 2100, 2200 and 2300 and recording them in 2000 and 2400 *fig. 2*. Nevertheless, such a watch does need the occasional adjustment. Every 3333 years and 122 days you should remember to set it forward one day to the true time of the celestial clock. We suspect, however, that you are simply content to observe the politeness of kings. Be assured, therefore, that when you order your watch, we will be exploring for you the physical—if not the metaphysical—limits of precision.

Does everything have to depend on how much?

Consider, if you will, the motives of collectors who set record prices at auction to acquire a Patek Philippe. They may be paying for rarity, for looks or for micromechanical ingenuity. But we believe that behind each $500,000-plus

bid is the conviction that a Patek Philippe, even if 50 years old or older, can be expected to work perfectly for future generations.

In case your ambitions to own a Patek Philippe are somewhat discouraged by the scale of the sacrifice involved, may we hasten to point out that the watch we will make for you today will certainly be a technical improvement on the Pateks bought at auction? In keeping with our tradition of inventing new mechanical solutions for greater reliability and better time-keeping, we will bring to your watch innovations *fig. 3* inconceivable to our watchmakers who created the supreme wristwatches of 50 years ago *fig. 4*. At the same time, we will of course do our utmost to avoid placing undue strain on your financial resources.

Can it really be mine?

May we turn your thoughts to the day you take delivery of your watch? Sealed within its case is your watchmaker's tribute to the mysterious process of time. He has decorated each wheel with a chamfer carved into its hub and polished into a shining circle. Delicate ribbing flows over the plates and bridges of gold and rare alloys. Millimetric surfaces are bevelled and burnished to exactitudes measured in microns. Rubies are transformed into jewels that triumph over friction. And after many months—or even years—of work, your watchmaker stamps a small badge into the mainbridge of your watch. The Geneva Seal—the highest possible attestation of fine watchmaking *fig. 5*.

Looks that speak of inner grace *fig. 6*.

When you order your watch, you will no doubt like its outward appearance to reflect the harmony and elegance of the movement within. You may therefore find it helpful to know that we are uniquely able to cater for any special decorative needs you might like to express. For example, our engravers will delight in conjuring a subtle play of light and shadow on the gold case-back of one of our rare pocket-watches *fig. 7*. If you bring us your favourite picture, our enamellers will reproduce it in a brilliant miniature of hair-breadth detail *fig. 8*. The perfect execution of a double hobnail pattern on the bezel of a wristwatch is the pride of our casemakers and the satisfaction of our designers, while our chainsmiths will weave for you a rich brocade in gold *figs. 9 & 10*. May we also recommend the artistry of our goldsmiths and the experience of our lapidaries in the selection and setting of the finest gemstones? *figs. 11 & 12*.

How to enjoy your watch before you own it.

As you will appreciate, the very nature of our watches imposes a limit on the number we can make available. (The four Calibre 89 time-pieces we are now making will take up to nine years to complete). We cannot therefore promise instant gratification, but while you look forward to the day on which you take delivery of your Patek Philippe *fig. 13*, you will have the pleasure of reflecting that time is a universal and everlasting commodity freely available to be enjoyed by all.

Should you require information on any particular Patek Philippe watch, or even on watchmaking in general, we would be delighted to reply to your letter of enquiry. And if you send

fig. 1: The classic face of Patek Philippe.

fig. 4: Complicated wristwatches circa 1930 (left) and 1990. The golden age of watchmaking will always be with us.

fig. 9: Harmony of design is executed in a work of simplicity and perfection in a lady's Calatrava wristwatch.

fig. 6: Your pleasure in owning a Patek Philippe is the purpose of those who made it for you.

fig. 10: The chainsmith's hands impart strength and delicacy to a tracery of gold.

fig. 5: The Geneva Seal is awarded only to watches which achieve the standards of horological purity laid down in the laws of Geneva. These rules define the supreme quality of watchmaking.

fig. 7: Arabesques come to life on a gold case-back.

fig. 11: Circles in gold: symbols of perfection in the making.

fig. 2: One of the 33 complications of the Calibre 89 astronomical clock-watch is a satellite wheel that completes one revolution every 400 years.

fig. 8: An artist working six hours a day takes about four months to complete a miniature in enamel on the case of a pocket-watch.

fig. 12: The test of a master lapidary is his ability to express the splendour of precious gemstones.

fig. 3: Recognized as the most advanced mechanical regulating device to date, Patek Philippe's Gyromax balance wheel demonstrates the equivalence of simplicity and precision.

PATEK PHILIPPE
GENEVE
fig. 13: The discreet sign of those who value their time.

your card marked "book catalogue" we shall post you a catalogue of our publications. Patek Philippe, 41 rue du Rhône, 1204 Geneva, Switzerland, Tel. +41 22/310 03 66.

Reality check. Call home.

—— *AT&T USADirect® and World Connect.® The fast, easy way to call most anywhere.* ——

Take out AT&T Calling Card or your local calling card** Lift phone. Dial AT&T Access Number for country you're calling from. Connect to English-speaking operator or voice prompt. Reach the States or over 200 countries. Talk. Say goodbye. Hang up. Resume vacation.

Argentina♦ 001-800-200-1111	Guyana*†† 165
Belize♦...555	Honduras † 123
Bolivia* **0-800-1112**	**Mexico**◊◊◊ **95-800-462-4240**
Brazil...................................**000-8010**	Nicaragua.....................................174
Chile................................1-23-0-0311	**Panama ■**......................................**109**
Colombia **980-11-0010**	Paraguay (Asuncion City)† 0081-800
Costa Rica*■ **0-800-0-114-114**	**Peru**†...**171**
Ecuador * **999-119**	**Suriname**† **156**
El Salvador*■...............................**190**	Uruguay 00-0410
Guatemala* 190	**Venezuela*■** **80-011-120**

AT&T
Your True Choice

For a free wallet sized card of all AT&T Access Numbers, call: 1-800-241-5555.

Getting Acquainted

Mexico City sits on a map at 19°11'53"–20°11'09" north (a latitude similar to Port Sudan near the Red Sea or Bombay, India) and 98°11'53"–99°30'24" west (a little west of Oklahoma City in the US).

Mexico, of which Mexico City is the capital, is bordered by the US in the north and extends to Guatemala and Belize in the southeast. At 1,972,547 sq. km (761,601 sq. miles) Mexico is very nearly four times the size of France – Europe's largest country. The northern half of Mexico holds only one-fifth of its population.

The country stretches over three time zones: Northern Baja in the west shares the same time zone as California; Southern Baja, plus the states of Sonora, Nayarit and Sinaloa are on Mountain Standard Time with the rest of the country including the capital on US Central Standard Time, which is either 6 or 7 hours behind Greenwich Mean Time depending on the time of the year. Mexico does not observe Summer Daylight Time.

The centrally located valley (about 125 by 80 km/78 by 50 miles) in which Mexico City sits at 2,200m (7,200 ft), was formed by volcanic eruptions and in Aztec times was covered by lakes. The lakes were drained by the Spaniards and as a result the city is still slowly sinking into the soft former lake bed. The valley lies between two towering ranges dominated by volcanoes, five of which are higher than any in the mainland US. The tallest is Pico de Orizaba (5,754 m/ 18,850 ft) followed by Popocatépetl (5,420m/17,780ft) and Iztaccíhuatl (5,285m/17,340ft). Most of Mexico State, which occupies 21,355 sq. km (8,245 sq. miles) is above 3,000 m (10,000 ft). It has the highest population density of any of the states, largely because it completely encloses the overcrowded capital city.

When the boundaries of the Distrito Federal were first staked in 1824, it was generally thought that there was plenty of space. However, Mexico City has expanded well beyond these limits. In the west, north and east, partly independent metropolitan settlements spread well into the state of Mexico, whose capital Toluca is approximately 65 km (40 miles) away. In the south, the Distrito Federal shares its borders with the state of Morelos whose capital is Cuernavaca.

Northern Mexico has extensive desert terrain, central Mexico has pine forests and the south has tropical jungles. When all this is combined with 2,400 km (1,500 miles) of coastline and the seas of the Caribbean, it produces what specialists describe as "a unique mosaic of ecosystems" containing more plants and animals than any country except Thailand, Colombia and Brazil.

Industrial pollution has been very destructive in the past with scientists once estimating that the country lost one species of plant or animal every day. Growing eco-consciousness has resulted in almost 2 percent of the land being set aside for natural reserves. In the Lacandona rainforest in Chiapas are jaguar, eagles, toucans, macaws, monkeys as well as thousands of varieties of insects, orchids, birds, mammals and butterflies and at least 30 types of trees. Seven of the world's eight varieties of sea turtles nest on Mexican beaches, and the world's most endangered sea turtle – Kemp's Ridley – can only be found at Tamaulipas on the Gulf of Mexico.

Mexico City for most of its history has been the world's largest city. When it was the Aztec city Teotihuacán it was larger than Rome, the capital of an empire that stretched from the northern border of Texas all the way into Guatemala.

Climate

The geographical situation of Mexico City at the border of the tropical zone, its height above sea-level and its extensive air pollution all contribute to the city's weather.

As is typical for tropical zones, mid-day temperatures vary only slightly throughout the year between 19°C (68°F) in December and 25°C (78°F) in

June. Night temperatures may range from 6–13°C (43–55°F) in the same period. The big difference between day and night temperatures is caused by the city's high altitude.

The Mexican year is divided into a dry period from November to April (4–10 rainy days per month) and a rainy period from May to October (17–27 rainy days per month). During the rains the land absorbs the sun's heat, the heated air masses rise and cause thunder and lightning accompanied by heavy showers lasting only a couple of hours in the afternoon or early evening. The showers briefly overstrain the local drains and flood the streets. However, such air-cleansing showers make it a lot easier to breathe in a city which absorbs 20 percent of the total Mexican energy consumption: 20 million liters (4.4 million gallons) of petrol and 5 million liters (1 million gallons) of diesel fuel are consumed by 3 million vehicles, and 5.4 million liters of gas and 5 million liters of oil are used up by approximately 30,000 industrial and service companies.

During the winter months a phenomenon known as a thermal inversion (inversión térmica) prevents the highly polluted air masses close to the ground from rising. Lower air layers absorb polluted particles and form clouds which prevent the sun from heating up the ground air. Only the early hours of the morning (before 8am) and from about mid-afternoon on are there normally enough thermal currents to break up the city's smog blanket. Children and older people are particularly affected by this situation and are encouraged to remain indoors.

Since 80 percent of the air pollution is caused by cars and buses, the local government hoped to reduce exhaust fumes drastically by introducing the scheme of hoy no circula – day without a car. This program, originally restricted to the winter months and now extended indefinitely, decreed that cars whose registration plates end in certain digits were not allowed to drive on certain weekdays. Official sources say the scheme has reduced exhaust fumes by 10 percent. However, analysis by environmental organizations has not shown any improvement in the values of carbon monoxide, dichloride, nitrogen dioxide and ozone in the atmosphere. Since the beginning of the hoy no circula scheme, better-off families have bought an extra car to escape "no driving" days. In addition, the city government granted thousands of permits for both taxis and mini-buses (colectivos), and they cruise the city streets with or without passengers. Finding a taxi is no longer a problem (except in a downpour). Meanwhile, a new law forces all new vehicles to have a catalytic converter and certain industries to cut back on production.

The People

The city area has increased to approximately 1,483 sq. km (572 sq. miles), home to approximately 20 million people – one quarter of the total population of Mexico.

Although the national increase in population was reduced in the 1980s from 3 percent to 2.5 percent, the annual increase in Mexico City of 5 percent, i.e. one million people per year, half of them poor workers from rural areas, still causes major problems.

The average population density of 350 inhabitants per square km (906 per square mile) is comparable to the large urban or industrial centers in Europe. However, this average value tells nothing of the old city center and areas of extreme poverty. It is said that the old city center houses approximately 20,000 people per sq. km (51,800 per sq. mile).

In general, Mexico City shows a clear social decline from west to east within its city boundaries. The well-kept quarters of the wealthy capitalinos in the rolling hills of the capital's west and the south of the city are characterized by very few houses and a low population density. The barrios on the other hand, partly planned and partly growing uncontrollably, house the lower social classes (more than 50 percent of all inhabitants). The north and east are marked by colonias populares and so-called ciudades perdidas, i.e. the regions with the large settlements of squatters.

The Economy

Mexico City is the pivot of Mexico's economy – in private and public sectors. The service industry (banks, insurance companies, commercial enterprises, tourist companies, etc.) tends to concentrate in the center, factories in the industrial parks to the north.

Seventy percent of all Mexican banking activities are carried out in Mexico City, and more than 50 percent of the total industrial output is manufactured here by 35 percent of the country's industry. The decentralization movement stopped the construction of manufacturing plants in the DF after 1975 and in the Estado de México after 1980.

The economy grew rapidly between 1958 and 1970 with an average growth of 6.8 percent a year but heavy government spending. In 1970–76 under President Luís Echeverría Alvarez and again in 1976–82 under President José López Portillo there was a drop in the GNP and the government borrowed heavily to subsidize industry with the aim of modernizing the economy. However, a world recession plus a steep drop in oil prices brought more financial problems and heavy indebtedness. In the 1980s barely visible economic growth and heavy inflation added to the country's woes.

When President Carlos Salinas de Gortari signed up Mexico for NAFTA in 1994 it was intended to help the country's long-term economic plans, but the chief beneficiaries so far have been the big multinational companies. The middle classes are complaining bitterly, and although massive devaluation of the peso means Mexico is an incredible bargain for tourists, it has effectively undercut poorer people's incomes by as much as 50 percent.

"NAFTA will create a framework for orderly commerce" an official optimistically opined before its inception. Theoretically it was intended to lower production costs and attract a flood of foreign investment, but this clearly is going to take time and meanwhile many of Mexico's inefficient and outdated companies face fierce competition from north of the border.

New government schemes offer hope for an industrial boom and new jobs. And the influx of people from the country could diminish if the 10-point plan of the Salinas government succeeds. It seeks a revival of agriculture (which employs over 40 percent of the working population), the extension of agricultural areas, improved storage and marketing systems, and the building up of a processing industry.

The lower budget deficit and the "stability contracts" agreed between government and industry in 1987 over prices, wages and exchange rates stemmed inflation considerably: 1987 – 159 percent, 1988 – 52 percent, 1989 – just under 20 percent. However, the living standards of the population have not improved at the same rate. This is why the large masses of the lower classes – especially in Mexico City – are very suspicious when it comes to the abolition of fixed prices under which their personal standards of living would again deteriorate.

Government

Mexico City is the capital of a federal republic and the home of a president who serves a non-renewable six-year term, as do the 64 senators (two from each state and the federal district). There is also a Chamber of Deputies whose 400 members each serve for three years. Since the Partido Revolucionario Institucional (PRI) was formed in 1929 it has won every presidential election. The other main political parties are the Partido Accion Nacional (PAN), which has proved to be the PRI's strongest opponent in recent elections, and the Partido Popular Socialista (PPS).

In Mexico City, the offices of the municipal administration, government and ministries were originally situated in the quarter around the central Zócalo. After the 1985 earthquake there was a much debated decentralization campaign to move several government offices to the provinces. Except for the Department of Federal Bridges and Highways, which moved to Cuernavaca, the project never got off the ground.

Coat of Arms

On July 4, 1523, in Valladolid, Spain, the emperor Charles V, awarded the City of Mexico, then capital of the colonial overseas empire of Nueva España (New Spain), the following coat of arms. Out of the center of a blue background (a symbol for the Lago de Texcoco which surrounded the old city) rises a golden tower surrounded by – but not connected with – three stone bridges. The two bridges on either side of the tower carry a lion standing on his hind legs, his front paws resting on the tower. This symbolised the victory of the Christian rulers over the Aztecs (the Spanish kings also had lions in their coat of arms). The ten cactus leaves (with green thorns) on the frame of the coat of arms symbolize the vegetation and rural features of the Mexican highlands.

The Federal District (Mexico DF) is run by a *regente* hand-picked by the country's president although there is currently a proposal under consideration to have the *regente* picked by direct election.

Planning the Trip

What to Bring

Clothing

The city climate allows for spring and fall clothes with a sweater or light coat for early morning and the evening throughout the year. Business circles, however, insist on formal wear. Churches should not be visited in shorts or with bare shoulders. Elegant restaurants and hotels prefer more formal wear, but a necktie is not always required.

Always carry an umbrella or raincoat if you are planning any excursions in the late afternoon during the rainy season. A warm sweater is recommended for the cool winter evenings.

Electricity

The power supply is 110 volts, and US plugs fit sockets. For other plugs, use an adaptor as for the US.

Photography

Everywhere you look in Mexico City there's a picture. However, be tactful if you take photos of people and ask permission. Some Indians may be shy or even aggressive when a camera is pointed their way. Museums and archaeological sites normally demand a fee to take photographs. Films in Mexico are manufactured by Kodak and are much more expensive at kiosks than in supermarkets where the prices compare with those in Europe. UV or skylight filters are recommended due to the strong sun and intense ultra-violet light.

Beware thieves interested in your equipment: camera bags betray the tourist. Take care on public transport or when waiting for a bus or a taxi.

Maps

The most detailed map of Mexico City is the *Guía Rojia* which is available as a book or foldable map everywhere, sometimes even at street stalls. The *Mapa Turístico de Carreteras* (free of charge) has a street map on the back. It is available from the Mexican Tourist Authority overseas or in Mexico from the tourist information centers: Guía Rojia, Gob José Moran 32, tel. 271 8699; INEGI Insurgentes, Metro Plaza 23, tel. 514 6134.

Entry Regulations

Europeans and North Americans need a passport valid for at least 6 months and a Tourist Card issued by Mexican consulates or airlines. Tourist Cards (free and valid for up to 6 months) are also available at the border and in all aircraft landing in Mexico.

Children must be registered in a parent's passport or have their own passport/children's pass. Any adolescents under 18 traveling on their own need a written agreement signed by their parents or legal representative. Accompanied by one parent, they still need the written and officially legalized agreement of the other parent.

On arrival, the Tourist Card is stamped. It has to be submitted again on departure. The only place where it can be replaced if lost or extended by a further 90 days is: Oficinas de Gobernación, Calle Albañiles 19; Metro: San Lázaro, Mexico City. Get written confirmation from your embassy first if you have lost your card. An extension will only be granted if you can show a transit or return ticket and – if necessary – prove you have enough money to last your stay.

Customs

The following personal items can be imported free of customs duties: 1 still camera, 1 film or video camera with 12 films or cassettes, 1 pair of binoculars, 1 portable musical instrument, 1 tape recorder, 1 portable typewriter, one set of used sports and camping equipment for each traveler, 20 books or magazines. Adults over 18 may also import the following: 400 cigarettes or 50 cigars or 250 gms tobacco, 3 liters of wine or spirits, an adequate amount of perfume, medicine for personal use and presents valued up to US$300 (no spirits or tobacco). Most goods and services in Mexico are subject to 15 percent VAT. Retail prices are always tax inclusive (*IVA incluido*). You can save yourself the surprise and hassle of a higher bill in hotels and restaurants by asking in advance whether the meals or services include VAT.

Health

Travel insurance policies that include repatriation are recommended since many health insurance policies only cover limited costs for medical treatment or drugs (ask before you set out).

Travelers dependent on special drugs should carry an adequate supply. It is also recommended that you take medicines for gastric illnesses, migraines or colds. Some Mexican medicines (e.g. Acanol) are quite effective in curing "Montezuma's Revenge," a gastric disease which can have various causes. For preventive measures, avoid drinking tap water or consuming ice cubes or ice cream from street vendors. *Agua purificada*, filtered water, replaces tap water in many hotels. If not, you can always buy mineral water (e.g. Tehuacán).

Be careful when choosing raw fruit or vegetables (including salads) in your restaurant. Ice-cold drinks or extremely spicy dishes may also cause severe stomach upsets.

Do not plan exhausting outings for the first few days. Your body needs time to get acclimatized to the time difference and the altitude.

Medical services are always paid for in cash. Some countries have reciprocal health agreements that allow for reimbursement at home. Check with your embassy before you go.

Currency

Mexico's currency is the peso and its symbol is $, exactly like the American dollar. Look out for price tags on goods. You may find an additional M or MN (*moneda nacional*).

Bills are in circulation in denominations of $10, 20, 50, 100, 200, and 500. Coins are available in values of 10 centavos, 20 and 50, and $1, 2, 5, 10 and 20.

All banks and bureaux de change (*casas de cambio*) as well as larger hotels, restaurants and shops will change US$ cash and US$ travelers' checks. European currencies will probably cause inconvenience.

Banking hours for currency exchange are 9am–1pm (sometimes 1.30pm) even if the bank is open in the afternoon. The exception is the bank at the airport which changes money around the clock.

Credit Cards

Visa, Eurocard (Mastercard/Mastercharge/Access), and American Express are well known. Hotels and more expensive shops will also accept Diners Card. Certain banks will also pay cash on credit cards. There are no restrictions on the import and export of Mexican or foreign currencies.

Public Holidays

1 January – *Año Nuevo* (New Year's).
5 February – *Día de la Constitución* (Constitution Day).
21 March – *Aniversario* – birthday of the former president Benito Juárez.
Maundy Thursday to Easter Sunday
1 May – *Día del Trabajo* (Labor Day).
5 May – *Día de la Batalla de Puebla* (Day of the Battle of Puebla).
1 September – National Holiday.
16 September – *Día de la Independencia* (Independence Day).
12 October – *Día de la Raza* (Day of the Race). Anniversary of Columbus discovering America.
1–2 November – *Todos los Santos* (All Saints') and *Día de los Muertos* (All Souls' Day).
20 November – *Día de la Revolución*. The anniversary of Madero's call to start the revolution.
12 December – *Fiesta de Nuestra Señora de Guadalupe* (Festival of the Virgin of Guadalupe).
25 December – *Navidad* (the Spanish name for Christmas Day).
31 December – New Year's Eve.

Religious Festivals

Religious festivals falling on weekdays may be postponed to the weekend.

Getting There
By Air

As many as 400 flights to Mexico City leave from main cities throughout the US in a single week. Miami is the major gateway. Mexicana and Aéromexico are the two principal national carriers.

Numerous European airlines (Lufthansa, KLM, British Airways etc.) fly directly to Mexico City several times a week. Often a cheaper alternative from Europe is to fly with an American airline (United, American Airlines, etc.) which travels to Mexico, normally via an intermediate airport in the US for which European travelers will need an American visa, since transfer passengers do not remain in the transit area. British travelers do not need an American visa, provided their passport is valid. Average flight time from Europe is 12–16 hours, non-stop flights take approximately 11 hours.

AIRLINE OFFICES

Mexicana and Aéromexico have reservation counters at the airport: Mexicana near C, Aéromexico near A.
Aeromar, Leibniz 34, tel. 627 0207.
Aero California, Paseo de la Reforma 332, tel. 207 1392.
Aeromexico, Paseo de la Reforma 445, tel. 228 9910. Further offices all around town. At the airport near A.
Air Canada, Andrés Bello 45, 18th Floor, tel. 281 4581.
Air France, Paseo de la Reforma 404, tel. 627 6000.
Alaska Airlines, Hamburgo 213, tel. 533 1746.
America West, Chiapas 207, tel. 584 1251.
American Airlines, Paseo de la Reforma 314, tel. 203 9444.
British Airways, Paseo de la Reforma 10, tel. 628 0500.
Continental, Andrés Bello 45, tel. 280 3434.
Delta, Paseo de la Reforma 381, tel. 202 1608.
Iberia, Paseo de la Reforma 24, tel. 703 0709.
KLM, Paseo de las Palmas 735–7th floor, Lomas de Chapultepec, tel. 202 3936, 202 4444.

Lufthansa, Paseo de las Palmas 239, tel. 202 3535.
Mexicana (Compañía Mexicana de Aviación), Av. Xola 535, Col. del Valle, tel. 660 4433. Other offices all around town. At the airport near C.
Taesa, Paseo de la Reforma 30, tel. 227 0700.
United, Hamburgo 213, tel. 627 0222.

By Rail

All railway lines from the north and south of Mexico arrive at the main station of Mexico City, the **Estación Central Buenavista**, Calle Insurgentes Norte/Mosqueta.

Special Facilities
Disabled

The following organizations can offer information to the disabled in advance of a visit. **Partners of the Americas**, 1424 K St NW, Washington DC 20005, tel. (800) 322-7844 04 or (202) 628-3300. The **Information Center for Individuals with Disabilities**, 27 Wormwood St, Boston MA 02210, tel. (617) 727-5540 has a list of suitable tour operators and travel agents.

Women Alone

Mexico isn't a bad place for women traveling alone. The national attitude remains irredeemably macho, but despite appearances to the contrary women are generally respected in what now seems an old fashioned way. Women travelers may get whistled at or approached, but they will rarely encounter anything worse or face situations that cannot be handled by any alert, determined woman.

Students

Students might find it useful before arrival to join the **Council on International Educational Exchange**, 205 East 42nd St, NYC 10017, tel. (212) 661-1414, to get a widely-recognized international student card. CIEE also publishes *Work, Study, Travel Abroad: The Whole World Handbook* with jobs and educational programs. Members of AYHA (PO Box 37613, Washington DC 29913) should request a list of Mexican hostels. If you want to live with a Mexican family, write to Experiment in International Living, POB 676, Brattleboro, VT 05302, USA.

On Departure

There is a **departure tax** to be paid in cash for international departures.

Mexican Embassies Abroad

London: 8 Halkin Street, London SW1, tel. (0171) 235 6393.
Los Angeles: 125 Paseo de la Plaza, tel. (213) 624-3261.
New York: 8 East 41st Street, tel. (212) 689-0456.

Practical Tips

Emergencies

Security and Crime

A traveler in Mexico City may very easily become the victim of street crime. The crush in overcrowded buses or the Metro and the queues at bus stops are classic danger sites. Robbery with violence is relatively rare, but you should not tempt fate by walking through deserted streets at night or taking late Metro rides. Contact your embassy as well as the police if you are victim of a crime. They will help find an English-speaking lawyer.

Earthquakes

Make sure you read the notes on emergency exits displayed in lifts and staircases in many hotels. The doorframe can protect you in cases of extreme emergency.

Lost Tourist Card

Go first to your embassy to obtain *Constancia de la Embajada* or *Carta de Salva Conducto*. Next go to *Migración* at Insurgentes roundabout. You will need proof of funds (credit card, substantial travelers' checks, plane ticket out of Mexico within the next week).

You may extend your Tourist Card for 30 days, three times, after which you must leave the country and re-enter.

Emergency Numbers

Police (*Policia*): 08; also inner city, tel. 672 0606; Ciudad Satélite, tel. 562 0708; Naucalpan, tel. 560 3868; Tlalnepantla, tel. 565 0758.
Red Cross (*Cruz Roja*): tel. 557 5757.
Fire Brigade (*Bomberos*): inner city, tel. 768 3700; Naucalpan, tel. 560 3868; Tlalnepantla, tel. 565 3638.
Breakdown Services (*Angeles Verdes – Green Angels*): tel. 250 8221.
LOCATEL (*service for tracing missing persons*): tel. 658 1111.

Useful Addresses

American Express (Reforma 234, tel. 598 7966); **Thomas Cook** (Campos Eliseos 345); **Western Union** (Banca Promex, Insurgentes Sur 22, tel. 703 0301, also at Reforma 199).
Lost/stolen cards or travelers' checks: **Amexco** 326 2666, **Mastercard** 227 2727, **Visa** 605 9115.
Laundromat: Lavanderia Edison, Edison 91, Monday to Friday 10am–7pm, Saturday 11am–6pm.

Health

General Advice

Vaccinations are not obligatory unless you arrive from yellow-fever areas. For lengthy stays, however, it may be advisable to have an immune globulin (IG) shot to guard against **hepatitis**. Symptoms include loss of appetite, lack of energy and nausea, and it can be cured only by complete rest for 10 days to two weeks. In lowland areas there is risk of **malaria** which can be avoided by using mosquito repellent, sleeping under netting, etc. Symptoms include bed sweats, headaches, fever, chills, loss of appetite and energy.

When **diarrhea** strikes avoid milk, spicy and greasy foods. Drink fluids and eat crackers, toast, hot tortillas, bananas, and rice. As you begin to feel better, potatoes and roast chicken can be taken. Pepto Bismol is best in tablet form. *La Turista* is marked by nausea, fever and is best left to run its course rather than using antibiotics. Rest, take manzanilla tea and fruit juice with honey.

Typhoid: The vaccination is not always 100 percent effective but recommended for those traveling to rural areas for lengthy stays.

Altitude sickness is sometimes acquired by new arrivals, and is characterized by light-headedness, slight headache, insomnia, shortage of breath. Avoid alcohol and over-eating.

Where to get Treatment

A "first class" pharmacy, supervised by a doctor and well equipped, can be recognized by its green cross symbol. "Second class" pharmacies only store basic medicaments.
El Fenix is a chain of pharmacies found at Av. Fco. Madero 39, corner of Motolinía; Isabel La Católica 15; Iturbide 6, corner of Plaza Hidalgo and elsewhere. There are *farmacias* in the department store chain **Sanborns**, e.g. Paseo de la Reforma 45 and 333, and in many supermarkets. Your hotel or embassy/consulate can help you find an English-speaking doctor.
Dentists: Antonio Arqamirez Garcia (Edison 92, between Ponciano Arriaga and José Mariaglesias, tel. 546 8372) and Charles Voigt (Miguel Angel de Quevedo 121, tel. 661 3036).
English-language hospital: ABC Hospital, Sur 136, corner Observatorio, tel. 277 5000 or in emergency 515 8359.
Vaccinations: Dr Angel Brioso (Benjamin Hill 14, tel. 515 4899).
International Red Cross: (Luis Vibes 200, tel. 395 1111).
Medical laboratory for any lab work: Laboratorio Chopo (Dr E. Gonzales, Martinez 109, open 24 hours).
Gynecologist: Roberto Almanza at ABC Hospital (Sur 136), Tuesday, Wednesday, and Friday 1.20–5.20pm, tel. 277 5000.
Ophthalmologist: Eduardo Ortiz and Raul Santos (Aristoteles 98, tel. 531 8162).
Homeopathic pharmacy: Representaciones Homeopaticas Internacionales (Insurgentes Sur 11-F, tel. 591 0833).

Business Hours

Banks: Monday to Friday 9am–1pm (sometimes 5pm).
Offices: Open to the public Monday to Friday 9am–2pm.
Shops: Monday to Saturday 10am–6 or 8pm. Only a few small shops (usually one-person operations) close for lunch (2–4pm). Large centers like Perisur or Plaza Satélite are open late and sometimes on Sundays.

Museums, monasteries, archaeological sites: Tuesday to Saturday 9 or 10am–5 or 6pm. Sunday until 4pm. Smaller museums may close for one or two hours at lunchtime. Archaeological sites also open on Monday.

Tipping

Restaurant bills almost never include service charges. The total should therefore be generously increased by 10–12 percent. Hotel employees and porters expect approximately US$1–2 per person. Taxi drivers do not normally receive a tip.

It may be difficult for a traveler to know when a small financial "extra," or what is locally known as *la mordida* ("the bite"), will help to obtain a special service, etc. If in doubt, restrain yourself. The government is trying hard to stop corruption.

Religious Services

Despite widespread attempts beginning in the 19th century to restrict the power and property of the Catholic Church, nine out of ten Mexicans profess to be Catholics with less than 5 percent claiming to be Protestant. Religious services of all denominations are held regularly and are listed in the local papers.

Media
Print

Mexico City is the largest publishing city in Latin America. In the early hours of the evening, newspaper vendors make an unusual scene in the area of the streets Bucareli and Morelos, riding their bicycles with adventurously high newspaper stacks on the front and back. The most important daily papers are *Excelsior*, *El Financiero*, *Reforma*, *El Economista*, and *La Jornada*. *La Prensa* is the most widely read national tabloid. The English-language daily The *News* contains largely wire service reports; almost as good is the (free) *Mexico Daily Bulletin* usually to be found in tourist places. Major American magazines such as *Time* and *Newsweek* are available in all larger towns and cities of Mexico.

Every Friday, the weekly magazine *Tiempo Libre* (in Spanish) publishes information about cultural and tourist events in the city. The title, issued by the same company which publishes the daily newspaper *Uno más Uno*, is available from all newsagents.

Radio and TV

There is no English-language radio broadcasting in Mexico City. The American stations CBS and NBC broadcast their music, advertising, and sports programs on VHF and medium wave. The Mexican stations only broadcast in Spanish. English-language television programs from the US are via cablevision or parabolic antennas.

Mexican TV is dominated by soap operas (*telenovelas*) whose numerous drama packed episodes unite the whole family in front of the television every evening. Even though the national broadcasting stations are trying very hard to convey some culture via the screen, they are always outrun by their private competitors (e.g. Televisa) with 24-hour sports programs from the US, shows and music broadcasts, exciting movies, series à la Roseanne and ER interrupted by advertising.

Postal Services

Main post office: Calle Tacuba, corner of Lázaro Cárdenas (opposite the Palacio Bellas Artes), open Monday to Friday 9am–6pm, Saturday 9am–1pm. **Aeropost** at the airport is open 8am–8pm every day of the year and accepts packages up to 2kg. Mail sent from here usually embarks a little faster than from other Mexican post offices.

Since the airmail postage for postcards is almost the same as for a letter (up to 20 g), you should put a postcard in an envelope and post it at the nearest post office (safer than a post box). The reception service at the major hotels is normally reliable. It takes between one and three weeks for a letter to reach Europe.

Airmail packages and parcels: Calle Aldama 218, Col. Guerrero (Metro Revolución), parcel counter closes 2pm; packages, 6pm.

Surface mail: Aduana Postal, Ceylan 468, in the north of the city. Take a taxi from La Raza Metro station. Monday to Friday 9am–1pm.

You can receive letters *poste restante* (*lista de correos*) at any post office in Mexico. They will be kept for 10–14 days.

It is difficult to send packages and parcels to Europe – there are special wrapping regulations and several forms to fill in. However, this does not apply to books, brochures, etc. They can be sent from any post office (subject to normal weight restrictions). Surface mail (by ship) normally takes three months or longer. Airmail is extremely expensive and takes about one month. Some shops offer a courier service. For sending important and urgent documents, most people rely on the more costly but far more efficient courier services: **DHL International** (Reforma 76, tel. 227 0299); **Federal Express** (Reforma 308, tel. 228 9904, open until 8pm weekdays, until 1.30 Saturday); **United Parcel Service** (Campos Eliseos 345, tel. 228 7900).

Telephones

Normal telephone boxes can only be used for local calls. However, they only cost $1 or may even be free of charge. Long-distance and international calls are cheaper from the new *Ladamatico* telephone boxes. Credit card telephones have now also been installed. Make your long-distance calls via an operator from the cheap *Casetas de Larga Distancia* (special telephone boxes marked with a blue telephone symbol, also in shops), or go to the telegraph office.

The luxury tax charged on international calls (one unit lasts 3 minutes) makes your phone call home very expensive. Reverse-charge (collect) calls to some countries in Europe are difficult, if not impossible, although reverse-charge calls to the UK provide no problem. Collect calls to the US should be equally trouble-free. Bear in mind that hotels usually charge a hefty fee for placing reverse-charge calls, even when dialed directly.

Sanborn's sells **phone cards** and invariably is a quieter place than the street from which to make phone calls.

Discount rates: Within Mexico, 50 percent less after 8pm and all day Sunday; to US and Canada, 33 percent less after 7pm weekdays, all day Saturday, and until 5pm Sunday. Calls to Europe and Africa, 33 percent less after 6pm weekdays and all weekend; to Asia and Oceania, 33 percent less after 5pm weekdays and all weekend.

Useful Telephone Numbers

01 directory enquiries for Mexico
02 national long distance
03 exact time
04 direct enquiries for Mexico City
07 information about long-distance charges
08 emergency
09 international operator
91 prefix for direct long-distance calls within Mexico
95 prefix for direct calls to the US or Canada
98 prefix for direct calls to Europe

Telegraph Offices

Telegraph offices (*Oficinas de telégrafos*) are very often separated from normal post offices.

International **telegrams** can be sent from Balderas 14–18, corner of Colón, Metro Hidalgo (near Alameda Park), open 8am–11pm. You can also make international telephone calls here.

Tourist Offices

Secretaría de Turismo, Av Pres. Masaryk 172, corner Hegel, tel. 250 0151 or 250 0589. Information about Mexico and free maps. Information line: tel. 525 9380.

Lodge your complaints by telephone at 250 0123, 8am–8pm. The same number gives out tourist information.

Further tourist information offices are at the airport, coach stations, the main station, and in the Zona Rosa, Amberes 54, tel. 525 9380–85.

Information leaflets and maps from Cámara Nacional de Comercio (Chamber of Commerce), Paseo de la Reforma 42, tel. 705 0424.

Embassies

Australian: Jaime Balmes 11-b, piso 10, tel. 395 9988.
Canadian: Schiller 529, tel. 724 7900.
UK: Rio Lerma 71, tel. 207 2089, 207 2288.
US: Paseo de la Reforma 305, tel. 211 0042.

Getting Around

On Arrival

After you go through passport control in Benito Juárez (Mexico City's international airport), you can change money at several counters. The airport has five areas: (A) national arrivals, (B) national departures, (C) airline counters and temporary exhibitions, (D) international departures, (E) international arrivals.

Once in the arrival hall you will be approached by gypsy taxi drivers. Be careful who you trust: there is an official taxi service into the city (see below) that is safe and reliable. There is a large hotel, the Continental Plaza Aeropuerto opposite the airport, connected by overhead walkway.

The airport building houses a post and telex office (near C), a bank (open from 4am), car hire companies (near E) as well as a representative of the Mexican hotel association **Asociación Mexicana de Hoteles y Moteles** (open from 10am) where people will help you make a reservation in one of the city hotels or to get a collective taxi to the hotel. The lost luggage department (*equipaje/objetos perdidos*) is on the first floor. You can store bags (expensively) in lockers to the right of the Aeromexicana counters.

Airport to City

A taxi is the quickest way into the city center, which is approximately 13 km (8 miles) away. You simply buy a ticket (different prices for different zones) at the taxi counter in the arrival hall and later hand it over to your driver. The price is reasonable – about 32 pesos.

By Train

From the main railway station of Mexico City, the **Estación Central Buenavista**, Calle Insurgentes Norte/ Mosqueta, the Metro stations Guerrero (line 3) and Revolución (line 2) are within easy reach. Take the Metro if

you have no luggage, otherwise take a taxi. For train information, tel. 547 1084 or 547 1097. First class tickets (guaranteeing a seat) can be purchased up to two months ahead.

In the City

No matter what means of transport you use in Mexico City, your first impression will be dominated by frightening and chaotic traffic. When the traffic is not stationary, it flows with incredible speed and apparent anarchy. However, if you obey certain rules you should be fairly safe. Pedestrians should take the high curbs into account when attempting to cross the street and go out of their way to walk to the next set of traffic lights rather than risk an accident with a speeding car. Passing through a line of stationary cars is equally dangerous and should be avoided. The *hoy no circula* scheme has not markedly improved the traffic situation, but it is now much easier to find a taxi cruising the streets or an uncrowded bus or minibus traveling the city's main arteries.

If you decide to use public transport in Mexico City, get yourself an *abono*, a ticket valid for 15 days on the Metro and the buses on *Ruta 100*. It is available at Metro ticket counters.

Metro

Most Mexicans use the Metro. It carries 4 million passengers a day on eight lines, which are constantly being extended. A small exhibition at the Zócalo station displays the plans. The network is displayed on large posters and on Metro maps, available at ticket counters in the main stations. Each station is shown by its name and a symbol, the lines are characterized by different colors and the terminal name indicates the direction of the train.

The Metro is open Monday to Friday 6am–midnight, on Saturday until 1am and on Sunday 7am–midnight. Avoid the rush hour (6–9.30am and 4–9pm). During these hours, some compartments are reserved for women and children. At other times the Metro is quick, reliable, and very cheap. Beware of pickpockets.

Lines 1, 2, and 3 run until half past midnight; Lines 4–9 run until 1.30 am, except Sunday. Buy 5 tickets for 2 pesos or 10 for 4 pesos. If you have an *abono* (see *Domestic Travel*) you must use the blue Metro entrances.

You are not allowed to carry large pieces of luggage in the Metro.

By Coach

Private coach companies connect Mexico City with the rest of the country. Long overland distances are served by modern Pullman coaches. Shorter journeys can be made in simpler buses.

The bus is one of the most popular means of transport in Mexico, so it is not surprising that Mexico City has four

coach stations for long distance travel, named after the four directions the coaches come from and go to.

Connections to Central and Northern Mexico (e.g. Guadalajara) – Terminal Central de **Autobuses del Norte** (TAN), Av. Cien Metros 4907, tel. 567 5858; Metro from Revolución to Autobuses del Norte (line 5) takes 20 minutes; town buses into the center, information stand.

Connections to the South of Mexico (e.g. Cuernavaca, Taxco, Acapulco): Terminal Central de **Autobuses del Sur** (TAS), Calzada Tasqueña 1320, at the corner of Tlalpan 2205, tel. 549 0257;

Metro from Revolución to Tasqueña (line 2) takes 40 minutes; town buses into the center. Make sure of early reservations for journeys to the south.

Connections to the East of Mexico (e.g. Puebla, Veracruz, Oaxaca, Yucatán): Terminal Central de **Autobuses del Oriente** (TAPO), Calzada Ignacio Zaragoza 200; Metro from Revolución to San Lázaro (line 1) takes 20 minutes; information from 10am.

Connections to the West of Mexico (e.g. Toluca, Morelia): Terminal Central de **Autobuses del Poniente** (TAP), Av. Sur 122, at the corner of Av. Rio Tacubaya, tel. 271 0038 or 762 5977;

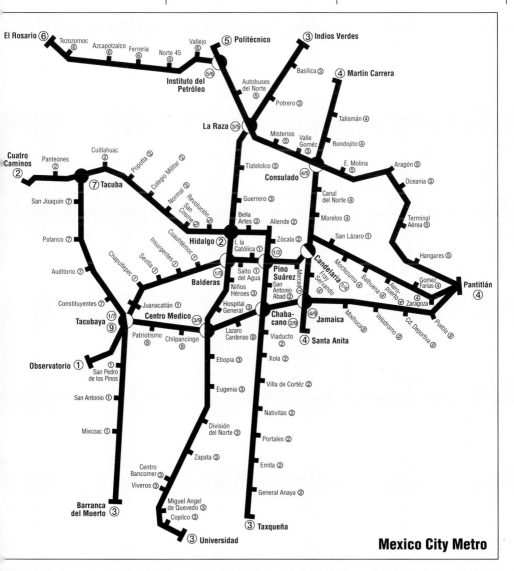

Mexico City Metro

257

Metro from Revolución to Observatorio (line 1) takes 30 minutes; town buses into the center.

There are taxis at all coach stations waiting to take you into the city center. As with travel from the airport, make sure you buy your ticket at the taxi counter in the hall and hand it to the driver once you are inside the taxi.

Taxi rates go up 20 percent after 10pm. A taxi from the airport to downtown is inexpensive, to Terminal del Sur cheaper, to others even less.

Bus Companies

There are dozens of bus companies, too many for a complete listing. Below are some of the main ones, with a few of their destinations. Enquiries must almost certainly be made in Spanish.
ADO (Campeche, Cancun, Merida, Oaxaca, Palenque, Puebla, Veracruz, Villahermosa), tel. 542 7192 or 586 6688.
Autobuses Pullman de Morelos (Cuernavaca), tel. 549 3405.
Cristobal Colón (Oaxaca, San Cristobal de las Casas, Tapachula), tel. 549 0257 or 542 7263.
Estrella Blanca (Chihuaha, Durango, Guadalajara, Guanajuato, Laredo, Monterey, Puerto Vallarta, Tampico, Taxco), tel. 587 5219.
Estrella de Oro (Acapulco, Cuernavaca, Taxco, Zihuatenejo), tel. 549 8520.
Estrella Roja (Cholula, Puebla), tel. 689 8000.
ETN (Guanajuato, Leon, Manzanillo, Morelia, Puerto Vallarta, San Luis Potosi, Toluca), tel. 567 3773 or 273 0251.
Flecha Amarilla (Guadalajara, Morelia, Patzcuaro, San Miguel de Allende), tel. 587 5200.
Flecha Roja (Acapulco, Huatulco, Puerto Escondido, Queretaro, Toluca, Zihuatenejo), tel. 689 6309.
Transportes del Norte (Aguascalientes, Matamoros, Nuevo Laredo), tel. 587 5399.
Tres Estrellas de Oro (Hermosillo, Los Mochis, Mazatlan, Mexicali, Nogales, Tepic, Tijuana), tel. 729 729 or 271 0578.

Buses

The number of bus routes is so confusing that it is much easier to concentrate on a few bus connections.

The most popular route for visitors goes from the Zócalo, via Calle 5 de Mayo, along Avenida Juárez and Paseo de la Reforma to the National Auditorium in Chapultepec Park. Another route goes from Indios Verdes (in the north) via Avenida Insurgentes to San Angel and the university (in the south).

The area around Chapultepec Metro, by the entrance to Chapultepec Park, serves as the depot for many city bus routes. Peribuses travel along the *anillo periférico*, or loop.

Taxis

The airport has a fleet of taxis that charge a flat fee (around $10) to most hotels. A regular taxi will cost about two-thirds of that or less. English-speaking drivers in big and expensive saloon–taxis with the logo *turismo* wait in front of hotels for tourists. They are recommended for sightseeing tours, but it is absolutely necessary to agree on the fare before you set out.

You can wave for the cheaper cabs (often yellow or green Volkswagens) but you should take care that the fare-meter is switched on, if it works. Agree on the price in advance if the meter is broken. Drivers, often newly arrived from rural regions, will sometimes not know where they are going. It is helpful to have the address written out on a piece of paper. The *sitio*-taxis are more expensive but can be called by phone from their taxi rank (*sitio*).

Cheap *colectivos* or *peseros* (vans) travel along the city's major arteries. The driver indicates with his fingers how many places he still has available. There are fixed stops along the routes.

Car Rental

You can hire a car with your national driving license, but an international license is recommended. The driver must be at least 25 and present a credit card when taking out a contract.

Small national car hire companies are often cheap, but international brands may have inexpensive offers for longer hire periods and may let you hire the car in advance from home. Many car hire companies distribute their brochures in the city hotels or run small offices there.

The hire price does not include 15 percent VAT. A return fee is charged if the car is not returned to the same office. Passenger and comprehensive car insurance is recommended. Stolen spare parts must in all cases be replaced (or paid for) by the hiring party.

Check the main functions of the car and the spare tire before you set out, and also ask for a list of repair garages for your particular make and model. Also check the gas tank. It isn't customary in Mexico for rental car agencies to fill the tank.

Car rental prices at the airport are (by US standards) exceptionally high.
Avis, at the airport, tel. 762 0099; Dr Velasco 146, tel. 578 1044; Reforma 308, tel. 207 3939; Av. M. Avila Camacho 1830, tel. 572 1611. Reservations, tel. 566 6800.
Budget, at the airport, tel. 784 22 89; Atenas 40, tel. 566 8815.
Dollar, Reforma 157B, tel. 592 8312.
Hertz, Londres 87–3, tel. 566 0099; 511 5686; Insurgentes Sur 725, tel. 543 1324; Campos Eliseos 204, tel. 255 2266.
National (InterRent in Europe), Marsella 48, tel. 533 0375; at the airport, tel. 784 2241; agents in the hotels Camino Real and Krystal.

Driving

Driving a car is not exactly a pleasure in the chaos of Mexico City's streets. For the duration of your stay, you should leave your own car in a parking space at the hotel or in one of the numerous guarded car parks (*Estacionamiento* or simply *E*). Often these are temporarily set up in empty lots in the city. Here, you may also have your car washed. You normally have to hand over your keys since the cars are parked by the guards and moved from time to time.

If you intend to use your own car, you should learn the meaning of traffic signs and find out on which days you are not allowed to use your own or any hired car, depending on the last digit of your registration number (the scheme *hoy no circula* is described in the "Climate" section of "Getting Acquainted"). Driving your car on forbidden days may cost you a high fine.

Orientation

A chessboard network of main thoroughfares (*ejes viales*) makes it fairly easy to navigate. They are numbered from the crossroads of *eje central* (Av. Lázaro Cárdenas) and Av. Juárez/Fco. Madero towards the north (*norte*), east (*oriente*), south (*sur*) and west (*poniente*). The motorway *Circuito Interior* surrounds the center and the *Anillo Periférico* is the ring road in the western and southern suburbs.

Speed Limits

In urban areas the speed limit is 40 kph (25 mph), on dual carriageways 80 kph (50 mph), and on motorways 100 kph (60 mph).

On most motorways you have to pay a toll charge (toll = *cuota*; toll counter = *caseta de cobro*).

Beware of *topes* or *vibradores*, artificial road bumps forcing you to reduce your speed in urban areas. They are not always signposted!

Breakdown Services

Ángeles Verdes (Green Angels) of the *Departamento de Información e Auxilio Turístico* (tel. 250 4817 or 250 3221) and the yellow cars of the service technicians from the Mexican Automobile Club (AMA) will help you on motorways and dual carriageways. A *vulcanizadora* repairs your flat tires. New tires are extremely expensive.

Sightseeing Tours

Organized tours are offered in all hotels. Most companies collect their customers from the hotel. Individual tours are best organized with a taxi. Ask your hotel receptionist for the appropriate fare for the number of hours you want and agree it in advance with the driver.

Excursions

Cuernavaca

Information office: Av. Morelos Sur 802, tel. 14 39 20. Coach stations 1st class: *Estrella de Oro*, Av. Morelos 900 (south of the city), tel. 549 8520; and *Pullman de Morelos*, Abasolo, corner Nezahualcoyotl, tel. 549 3505. Coach station 2nd class: *Flecha Roja*, Av. Morelos 255, tel. 689 6309.

Cholula

Quaint colonial town with an enormous pyramid (free admission Sunday and holidays). Estrella Roja (tel. 689 8000) buses every 15 minutes from TAPO terminal or take an express bus from

same terminal to Puebla and then a *pesero* for the last five miles.

Popocatéptl

This volcano, visible from the capital on a clear day, offers great views from its slopes. A day trip lets you reach the snowline. Overnighters can stay in the Albergue Vicente Guerrero hostel at Tlamacas at the end of the road to the volcano. Take refreshments. Buses from TAPO to Amecameca or *pesero* from San Lázaro metro station. Then *pesero* to Tlamacas.

Teotihuacán

Pyramids and ancient temples spread over a vast area. Arrive as soon after the 8am opening as possible to avoid scorching sun and afternoon showers. Take refreshments. Hide cameras. Metro to Indios Verdes station then *Pyramides* bus from platform J. The town of San Juan de Teotihuacán is 2 km (1 mile) from the site.

Tepotzotlán

A village with mythical, legendary associations marks the entrance to El Tepozteco National Park with its much-climbed cliffs. *Autobuses de Morelos* runs a half-hourly service from Central Terminal del Sur, and there are regular buses from Cuernavaca.

Tula

Enormous stone warriors (*Atlantes*) atop a small pyramid date from the 10th century Toltec civilization. Buses from the Terminal del Norte about every half hour take 90 minutes to Tula from which it's necessary to hire a taxi. Make sure you arrange for the taxi driver to pick you up later.

Where to Stay

Hotels

Arriving in Mexico City without a hotel reservation is unproblematic. The information stands at the airport, the station and the national coach stations will help you get a room.

International hotel chains, such as Best Western, Holiday Inn, Inter-Continental, Nikko and Sheraton, accept reservations from Europe. According to their equipment and services, hotels are characterized by one to five stars. First class luxury hotels are allowed to display GT (Gran Turismo) after their name.

The hotel prices below are for accommodation only, sometimes called EP (European Plan). More comprehensive services are called MAP (Modified American Plan – half board) and AP (American Plan – full board).

The start of the peak season varies from mid–November to the beginning of December. Peak season ends at the end of May. Peak prices are usually 20–30 per cent more.

Mexico City's luxury hotels are concentrated around Zona Rosa and Chapultepec. Mid-range hotels can be found along the Paseo de la Reforma and around the Alameda Park. Simpler hotels are in the old city around the Zócalo and north of the Plaza de la República toward the station.

Prices for a double room in all categories are as follows:

$$$ = luxury (GT) US$150–200
$$ = four-star US$75–150
$ = three-star US$50–75
one and two-star under US$50

Zona Rosa and Chapultepec

Four Seasons, Paseo de la Reforma 500, tel. 286 6020, fax 286 5588. Between Chapultepec and the Zona Rosa. Central courtyard, rooftop pool, health club, top class restaurant. **$$$**
Century, Liverpool 152, tel. 227 7272, fax 525 7475. Highrise anchoring the southern side of the Zona

Rosa. Classy restaurant, bar with panoramic views, cafeteria. **$$$**

Marquis Reforma, Reforma 465, tel. 211 0577, fax 211 5561. High-class accommodations in distinctive building. Health club, sauna. **$$$**

Hotel Nikko Mexico, Campos Eliseos 204, in the heart of Polanco near Chapultepec, tel. 280 1111, fax 203 0655. Pool, sauna, tennis courts, and restaurants. **$$$**

Hotel Camino Real, Mariano Escobedo 700, tel. 203 2121, fax 250 6897. Huge, modern complex with many restaurants, pool and dramatic whirlpool, just across from Chapultepec Park. **$$$**

Westin Galeria Plaza, Hamburgo 195, tel. 211 0014, fax 207 5687. In Zona Rosa. Three restaurants and a rooftop pool. **$$$**

Maria Christina, Rio Lerma 31, tel. 546 9880, fax 566 9194. Mansion-style building. Restaurant and bar. **$$**

Imperial, Reforma 64, tel. 705 4911, fax 703 3122. A historic hostelry with restaurant and piano bar. **$$**

Hotel Fiesta Palace, Reforma 80, tel. 566 7777. Large, efficient hotel with business center near Columbus glorieta. **$$**

Calinda Geneve, Londres 130, tel. 211 0071, fax 208 7422. Colonial, traditional, comfortable. **$$**

Hotel Aristos, Reforma 276, tel. 211 0112, fax 514 8005. Pool, sauna, coffee shop. **$$**

Doral, Sullivan 9, tel. 592 2866; fax: 592 2762. Just off Insurgentes. Restaurant, bar with live music. **$**

Downtown

Howard Johnson Gran Hotel, 16 Septiembre 82, tel. 512 9275, fax 512 2085. Just off the Zócalo in the splendid old shell of an ornate former department store complete with gilded elevators and awesome ceiling. **$$$**

Hotel Sevilla Palace, Reforma 105, near Cristobal Colón statue, tel. 566 8877, fax 703 1521. Pool, sauna, restaurants. **$$$**

Hotel Majestic, Av. Madero 73, tel. 521 8600, fax 512 6262. On the Zócalo with a terrace restaurant offering a terrific overview. **$$**

Hotel de Cortes, Av. Hidalgo 85, behind the Alameda, tel. 518 2182, fax 512 1863. Former 18th-century hospice mixing colonial charm with modern comfort. Patio restaurant. **$$**

Ritz Best Western, Av. Madero 30, tel. 518 1340, fax 518 3466. Very central near Torre Latinamericano. **$$**

Hotel Bamer, Av. Juárez 52, tel. 521 9060, fax 510 1793. Very central, very reasonable. Restaurant. **$**

Hotel Leon, Brasil 5, tel. 512 9031. One block from the Zócalo. Noisy but clean. **$**

Hotel Rioja, Cinco de Mayo 45, tel. 521 9031. Rock-bottom cheap. No services but good value for money. **$**

Casa de los Amigos, Ignacio Mariscal 132, tel. 705 0646, fax 705 0771. Friendly Quaker-run guesthouse near Revolution Monument. Low-budget hideaway ideal for students, writers, academics. **$**

Hotel Texas, Ignacio Mariscal 129, tel. 705 5782. Across the street and only slightly higher rates. **$**

Hotel Galicia, Calle Honduras 11, just beyond Plaza Garibaldi, tel. 529 7791. Interesting location in musical area – adjoins Guadalajara night club. **$**

Along Insurgentes Sur

Hotel Roosevelt, Insurgentes Sur 287, tel. 208 6813. Low-key, budget-priced place about a mile from the Zona Rosa. **$**

At the Airport

Continental Plaza Aeropuerto, Blvd Puerto Aereo 502, tel. 230 0505. All the advantages and disadvantages of being at the airport. **$$**

Ramada Inn Aeropuerto, tel. 785 8522.

Youth Hostels

To get accommodation in Mexican hostels you need an international youth hostel card. An international student's card would also be useful. The youth hostels are run by several different organizations which will send you written information on request:

Asociación Mexicana de Albergues de la Juventud (AMAJ): Madero 6, Of. 314, México 1, DF.

Consejo Nacional de Recursos para la Atención de la Juventud (CREA): Oxtocopulco 40, Colonia Oxtocopulco, App. Postal 04310, México, DF.

Youth Hostel CREA: Insurgentes Sur, corner of Camino Sta. Teresa, Deleg. Tlalpan, south of the university, in the former Olympic village, tel. 573 7740 or 655 1416.

The **Mexican Students' Associa tion** (SETEJ) runs a guest house south of the Zona Rosa, Calle Cozumel 57 (Metro Sevilla), tel. 514 9240 or 514 4210. You need a student card, available from the SETEJ office in Hamburgo 273 (Zona Rosa, also Metro Sevilla) tel. 514 4213 or 511 6691.

Camping

Camping sites are rare in Mexico, but there is a caravan park 42 km (26 miles) northwest of the city at the entrance to the colonial village of Tepotzotlán.

Out of Town
Cuernavaca

Camino Real Sumiya, Fracc. Sumiya Japanese-style former estate of millionaire Barbara Hutton, tel. 209 199. **$$$**

Las Mañanitas, Ricardo Linares 107 tel. 141 466, fax 183 672. Also excellent garden restaurant. **$$$**

Papagayo, Motolinia 13, tel. 141 711. **$$**

Posada Jacaranda, Av. Cuauhtémoc 805, tel. 157 777, fax 157 888. **$$**

Villa Internacionale, Carlos Cuauglia 406, tel. 250 985. **$$**

Shopping: Arts and crafts and souvenir enthusiasts will find a real treasure trove at the market, *mercado principal* and the shopping arcades Las Plazas Pasaje Florencia, Los Arcos, and Pasaje Catedral. Particularly beautiful pieces (also furniture) can be found at BIO-ART, Blvd Díaz Ordaz, tel. 141 458

Puebla

Many hotels are near the Zócalo.

Aristos, Av. Reforma, corner of 7 Sur tel. 32 09 64. **$$$**

Colonial, 4 Sur 105, tel. 46 4199, fax 46 0818. **$$**

El Mesón del Angel, Hermanos Serdán 807, tel. 24 30 00, fax 487 935. **$$**

Mision Park Plaza Puebla, 5 Poniente 2522, tel. 489 600, fax 489 733. **$$**

Lastra, Calzada de los Fuertes 2633 tel. 35 15 01; reservations in Mexico City, tel. 592 8496. **$$**

Posada San Pedro, 2 Oriente 202, tel. 46 50 77, fax 465 736. **$$$**

Many good restaurants can be found at or near the central Zócalo.

Information office: Puebla Tourist Office, Avenida 5 Oriente Number 3 (near the cathedral), tel. 461 285. The o

fice also organizes sightseeing tours.
Coach station: CAPU (*Central de Autobuses Puebla*), Blvd Norte (at the junction to Tlaxcala). Taxi service into the city center; get your tickets in the departure hall. Numerous connections from Mexico City, TAPO.

Shopping: Typical souvenirs from Puebla are *talavera* ceramics or onyx. Small shops in the **Mercado El Parian**, Calle 8 Norte, and the **Barrio del Arista** (also with workshops). **Creart**, Av. 2 Oriente 202/204, tel. 468 974, and Av. 7 Oriente, corner of Calle 16 de Septiembre, tel. 420 459, offers a good choice of arts and crafts.

Cholula

Although Cholula is only 8km (5 miles) from Puebla, some visitors prefer to stay the night in this colonial town after visiting the pyramid. There are pretty churches to visit at nearby Tonantzintla and Acatepec, both of which are accessible on the local bus routes.

Villas Arqueologicas, 2 Poniente 501, Cholula (near the ruins), tel. 471 966. **$$$**
Hotel Calli Quetzacoatl on the Zócalo, tel. 471 555. **$**
Hotel Reforma, Hidalgo and 4 Sur, tel. 470 149.
From the capital, TAPO buses leave several times per hour for Cholula, but most tourists take an express bus to Puebla, then a *pesero* from 4 Pte and 11 Nte. In Cholula, *peseros* for Puebla leave from 6 Pte and 3 Nte.

Taxco

Monte Taxco, Fracc. Lomas de Taxco, tel. 213 00. Above the city and easily reached by cable car. Fantastic view and restaurant recommended. **$$$**
De La Borda, Cerro del Pedregal 2. **$$$**
Posada de La Misión, Av. John F. Kennedy 32, tel. 2 40 63. **$$**
Posada de los Castillos, Jan Ruiz de Alarcon 7, tel. 2 34 71. **$**
Santa Prisca, Cena Obscuras 1, tel. 200 80. **$$**
Very stylish dinners can be had in the **Hacienda del Solar**, in the southern outskirts of the city. Also recommended are **Cielito Lindo** and **La Taberna**, both near the Zócalo. **Information office**: at the town entrance from Cuernavaca and Casa Borda, Plazuela Bernal.

Coach station 1st class (*Estrella de Oro*): Av. Presidente John F. Kennedy (in the southwest of the city); several connections daily from Mexico City, TAS. Coach station 2nd class (*Flecha Roja*): Av. John F. Kennedy, between the streets Hidalgo and Veracruz.

Shopping: silver in all variations and prices. The best shops are directly near the Zócalo. Prices are sometimes higher than in Mexico City. Look out for the 925 stamp, a guarantee of high silver content.

Toluca

Plaza las Fuentes, Carr. Mex-Tolucas km. 57.7, tel. 160 010, fax 16 4798. **$$$**
Alameda, Ezequiel Ordonez 104, tel. 14 3377. **$**
Motel del Rey Inn, at the town entrance from Mexico City, tel. 12 12 22, fax 122 567. **$$**
By the motel is the **Real de Oro**, a first class restaurant with international cuisine. Another good restaurant, **Cabana Suiza**, is nearby. Recommended restaurants in the city center are **La Jaula** and **Nautilus**.
Information office: Palacio de Gobierno, Lerdo de Tejada Poniente 300, and Lerdo de Tejada Poniente 101, Edif. Plaza Toluca.
Coach station: outside the city center, on the southern ring road Paseo Tollocan. Numerous connections from Mexico City.
Shopping: Toluca is well known for its Friday market (near the coach station) selling almost everything from fruit and vegetables to pots and pans, pottery and Indian textiles. Some of the fixed stands stay open throughout the week, but the main market day is still Friday. **Casart**, Paseo Tollocan 700 Oriente, is a government shop for arts and crafts from the State of Mexico; large choice of good quality products.

Eating Out

Capitalinos enjoy eating foreign food from time to time, so the Zona Rosa houses a good selection of European and even Asian restaurants. The grand hotels also serve an international menu. There are plenty of alternatives if you do not want to indulge in Mexican cuisine right away.

However, once you have experienced good Mexican food, you are likely to stick to *guacamole, pollo con mole poblano* or *tortillas* in abundance. A juicy steak and *frijoles* in a simple restaurant with a 1950s Formica decor is as enjoyable as dining extensively in one of the romantic *hacienda* restaurants. Try the different regional specialties, particularly fish *à la veracruzana* or pork *à la yucatán*.

In many of the bigger restaurants, there is music with the meals at weekends and reservations are necessary.

Mexicans are hardly ever late for meal times, which are the same as in Spain. Lunch is 2–5pm; dinner is from 8.30pm and may last two hours or more. Many restaurants are closed on Sunday or public holidays. Check opening times before setting out.

Where to Eat

Below is a small selection of recommended restaurants and cafés that sometimes serve food during the day. We have listed a few of the many excellent Mexican and international restaurants in the hotels.

$$$ = expensive
$$ = average
$ = cheap

Zona Rosa and Reforma

Anderson's, Paseo de la Reforma 382, tel. 208 2150. Good Mexican and international cuisine with lots of choice. Popular with young Mexicans, casual atmosphere. **$$**
Antigua Fonda Santa Anita, Londres 38, tel. 514 4728. The owners have

been cooking traditional Mexican food for over 40 years. **$$**

Bellinghausen, Londres 95, tel. 207 6149. Specializes in fish and steak dishes. The quiet patio is full of businessmen at lunchtime. **$$$**

El Parador de José Luis, Niza 17, tel. 533 1840. Excellent Spanish cuisine, good daytime menu. Crowded at lunchtime but quieter in the evening. **$$**

Focolare, Hamburgo 87, tel. 207 8257. Excellent Mexican and international dishes. Piano music at lunchtime, *marimbas* in the evening. Interesting folklore performances. Sunday brunch. Cantina bar **El Trompo** at the entrance to the restaurant. **$$$**

Fonda el Refugio, Liverpool 166, tel. 207 2732. Traditional Mexican restaurant with very pleasant atmosphere. Reservation recommended. **$$**

La Marinera, Liverpool 183, tel. 511 2466. Fantastic fish and seafood *à la Mexicana*. Popular with Mexicans. **$$**

Las Fuentes, Rio Panuco 127, corner of Rio Tiber near the Angel on Reforma. A vegetarian place with new and interesting dishes. **$**

Las Piranas, Mercado Hidalgo, near Obrera metro station. A market stall offering fruit plates piled high with fresh, juicy combinations. **$**

Loredo (A/B), Hamburgo 32, tel. 566 3636. Classic *Mexican* cuisine, particularly their *sabana*. Popular with business people. **$$**

Mesón del Perro Andaluz, Copenhague 26, tel. 533 5306. Spanish cuisine. Very popular with young Mexicans and well known in artists' circles; also a street café. **$$**

New York Daily Bagel, Revolución 1321 San Angel, south of Barranca del Muerto metro station. Bagels to eat in or to go. **$**

Yug, Varsovia 3, tel. 574 4475. Good vegetarian menu. You have to queue but it is well worth it. **$**

Chapultepec – Colonia Polanco

Fonda Casa Paco, J. Velazquez de Leon 125, near the offices of the telephone company, tel. 546 4060. Fine Mexican cuisine served in a cozy remodeled Mexican home. Reservations necessary after 9pm. **$$**

Fonda de Santa Clara, Homero 1910, tel. 557 0565. Traditional Puebla cuisine served in colonial-style surroundings. Reservations necessary. **$$$**

Lago Chapultepec, at the large lake near the west of Chapultepec Park, tel. 515 9585. *Haute cuisine* in an extravagant building. Very formal, reservation necessary. **$$$**

La Fonda del Recuerdo, Bahía de las Palmas 39, Col. Anzures, near Hotel Presidente, tel. 260 7339. Serves excellent Veracruzian cuisine. Live music daily. Open from 1pm. Reservations are essential. **$$**

La Hacienda de los Morales, Vázquez de Mella 525, Col. del Bosque, tel. 281 4554. Mexican and international cuisine in beautiful 17th-century *hacienda* with covered patio. Very elegant, ties must be worn after 6pm. Reservation necessary. **$$$**

Old City

Bar Opera, 5 de Mayo, corner of Filomeno Mata. Recommended for a drink and a snack in quiet and historic surroundings. Pancho Villa once took the bar by storm. **$**

Danubio, Uruguay 3. Simple Mexican menu, particularly fish dishes. **$**

El Vegetariano, Filomeno Mata 13, tel. 521 1895; and Madero 56, tel. 521 6880. Cheap vegetarian meals, open Monday to Saturday 8am–8pm. **$**

Hosteria de Sto Domingo, Belizario Dominguez 72, at the Pl. Sto. Domingo, tel. 526 5276. Probably the oldest restaurant in Mexico City, it has served local dishes since 1860. **$$**

Las Cazuelas, Rep. de Colombia 69, tel. 702 1140. Traditional Mexican restaurant, crowded at lunchtime. **$$**

Lincoln Grill, Revillagigedo 24, near Alameda Park, tel. 510 3317. Stylish old Spanish restaurant. **$$**

Prendes, Av. 16 de Septiembre 10, tel. 521 1878. One of the oldest restaurants in the city (founded 1892) whose famous guests, from Pancho Villa and other revolutionaries to Walt Disney, are pictured in murals. Reservation necessary at lunchtime. **$$**

Sanborns, Av. Fco. Madero 17, Casa de Azulejos, tel. 521 6058. From small breakfast to extensive lunch, the service is fast and efficient. Attractive tiled patio serves as a dining hall. **$$**

There are several new upscale Mexican restaurants in the downtown area, including Los Girasoles, next door to the National Art Museum on Tacuba, La Circunstancia, at Honduras 17, and Cicero Centenario, República de Cuba 79. All are expensive, but they have excellent ambiance and food. The capital's tiny Chinatown is one block south of the Alameda.

Elsewhere

Antigua Fonda Santa Anita, Insurgentes Sur 1038, tel. 559 8061 or 539 8140. Sister restaurant to the long-established business in Zona Rosa; traditional Mexican food. **$$**

Antigua Hacienda de Tlalpan, Calzada de Tlalpan 4619, south of the Anillo Periférico, tel. 573 9933 or 573 9959. Exquisite Mexican and international dishes, elegant atmosphere in a restored 18th-century *hacienda*, beautiful gardens, music performances in the evenings. Open from 1pm. **$$$**

Circulo del Sureste, Lucerna 12, tel. 535 2704. The best restaurant in the DF for Yucatacan food, e.g. *cochinita pibil* or *papatzules*. Casual atmosphere, overcrowded at lunchtime. **$**

Hosteria del Trovador, at the main square in Coyoacán. Friendly Mexican restaurant, very crowded at lunchtime, many white-collar workers and business people. **$**

Hosteria Sta Catarina, Jardín Sta. Catarina 10, tel. 554 0513. Good, lowcost Mexican food in pleasant atmosphere. **$**

Loredo San Angel, Av. Revolución 1511, tel. 548 6717. Classic Mexican cuisine. **$**

San Angel Inn, Palmas 50, corner of Altavista, San Angel, tel. 616 1402. Exquisite Mexican and international food; upscale atmosphere in an 18th-century *hacienda*. Live music. A tie is obligatory and an early reservation is recommended. **$$$**

Lynis's. A fast-food chain (with service for Mexican and international dishes. Subsidiaries: Newton 7, Col. Polanco Gutenberg 231, Col. Nueva Anzures Paseo de la Reforma 423; Insurgentes Sur 866, Col. del Valle.

Potzolcalli. Simple and clean restaurants with a large menu of Mexican food. Popular with Mexican families. Subsidiaries in the city center: Xola 32; Molière 325. Further subsidiaries on the outskirts.

Sanborn's. Well-organized restaurants in department stores of the same name. Mexican and international food; cheap daytime menu.

Many coffee houses with some kind of music or entertainment have opened recently in the Colonia Condesa.

Bellas Artes. A quaint café tucked away inside the palace. Canned classical music but sometimes a live pianist. Tuesday to Sunday, 10.30am–6pm.

Cafebreria El Pendulo, Nuevo Leon 115, Condesa, tel. 286 9493. Quiet café with music in a large bookstore.

Café la Blanca, 5 de Mayo 40, city center, tel. 510 0399. Traditional coffee house which serves Mexican breakfast but also plain dishes.

Café la Habana, Morelos 62 at Bucareli. Slow service and relatively high prices, but this is a popular hangout for famous Mexican poets, writers and journalists.

Café Tacuba, Tacuba 28, city center, tel. 518 4950. Traditional Mexican café-restaurant (established 1912), most famous for its *enchiladas*. Very crowded at lunchtime.

Café Tacuba, Newton 88, Col. Polanco, tel. 250 2633. Offspring of the restaurant with the same name in the old city center.

Café Viena, Cacahuamilpa 8, Col. Hipódromo Condesa, tel. 528 6029. The right place if you crave cakes.

El Moro, San Juan de Letran 42, city center. The best of the *churrerias* for hot chocolate, coffee and *churros* any time of the day or night.

Franz Meyer Museum, Av. Hidalgo 45. Soft music and a gentle fountain serenade visitors to this café in the museum's inner courtyard. Tuesday to Sunday 10am–5pm.

Konditori, Genova 61, Zona Rosa, tel. 208 1887. Open daily 7am–midnight, deliciously fresh puff pastry, cakes, and small dishes.

Konditori, Euler, corner of Masaryk, tel. 250 1032. As above.

Restaurant Focolare, Hamburgo 87, tel. 207 8257. Flamboyant folklore shows in the evenings.

Attractions

There are numerous celebrations throughout the year in the suburbs of the capital, many of which retain all the rural characteristics of former villages – in the north, Gustavo A. Madero and Azcapotzalco; in the west, Alvaro Obregón and Cuajimalpa (de Morelos); in the south, Tlalpan; in the southeast, Xochimilco and Milpa Alta; in the east, Iztapalapa and Tláhuac. The central districts are called Cuauhtémoc (old city), Benito Juárez and Coyoacán (adjacent to the south).

1 January. *Año Nuevo* (New Year's Day). Fireworks on New Year's Eve everywhere in the city, parades and fiestas in the streets on New Year's Day.

Early January. Festival week in Chalma, a place of pilgrimage approximately 100 km (63 miles) to the south of Mexico City toward Cuernavaca.

6 January. *Fiesta de los Reyes* (Epiphany). People exchange presents.

17 January. *Santa Prisca.* Animals are blessed in the churches. On the 18th and the following weekend, blessings of animals and fiesta in Taxco.

2 February. *Candelaria* (Candlemas). Fireworks and dances.

5 February. *Día de la Constitución* (Constitution Day). In remembrance of the constitution, created in 1917.

Carnival. Parades and celebrations throughout the city. Xochimilco celebrates two weeks later.

Sunday after 9 March. Celebration of Gregory the Great (*Gregorio Magno*) in San Gregorio Atlapulco in Xochimilco. Interesting folk dances.

19 March. Festival of St Joseph in Tláhuac, Iztapalapa, and Tlalpan.

21 March. *Aniversario* (birthday) of the former president Benito Juárez. Schools and nurseries celebrate a spring festival.

25 April. Festival of St Mark in Milpa Alta and Azcapotzalco. Folk festival with dances and fireworks.

Maundy Thursday to Easter Sunday. People traditionally head for the beach or visit their relatives during the *Semana Santa* (Easter week), so public transport is overcrowded. Passion plays in Iztapalapa, candle processions in Taxco.

1 May. *Día del Trabajo* (Labor Day).

3 May. Festival of the Holy Cross. Workers erect crosses decorated with ribbons at their building sites. They erect altars in Milpa Alta, Cuajimalpa, and Xochimilco where dances and firework displays are also held.

5 May. *Día de la Batalla de Puebla* (Day of the Battle of Puebla). In remembrance of the victory over the French army in 1862.

May/June. Corpus Christi. Processions in the church communities. Little donkeys made of maize leaves are given to children. Parents take their children dressed as Indians to the cathedral or the Basílica de Guadalupe.

24 June. Midsummer Day. Folk festival with markets and dances in Milpa Alta, Tláhuac, Coyoacán, and Iztapalapa.

16 July. Festival of the Virgen del Carmen in Cuauhtémoc, Cuajimalpa, and Alvaro Obregón. Festival and dances around the monastery del Carmen in San Angel.

25 July. Festival of St James (*Santiago*) in the quarters of Azcapotzalco, Cuajimalpa, Cuauhtémoc, and Gustavo A. Madero. Folk dances and dance evenings with music.

Sunday after 25 July. (*Santiago*) Large festival on the Plaza de las Tres Culturas, from 10am dances and market. Fun fair and dance performances in Xochimilco (in the afternoon).

13 August. Holiday in remembrance of the Battle of Tenochtitlán. Wreath-laying at the Cuauhtémoc memorial on Paseo de la Reforma. Indian dances on Plaza de las Tres Culturas.

15 August. Assumption Day. Dances of "Moors and Christians," Indians, shepherds and cowboys in Milpa Alta. Fireworks and dance performances in many parts of the city.

Folk festival in Huamantla (near Puebla) with multi–colored flower and sand carpets in the streets.

28 August. Religious festival in Chalma (see January).

1 September. National Holiday. The President reports on the nation's situation (traditional since 1824).

8 September. Nativity of the Virgin. Dances and fireworks in Alvaro

Obregón, Benito Juárez, Iztapalapa, and Xochimilco.

Festival of the Virgien de los Remedios in Cholula. Dances and fiesta in Tepoztlán.

13 September. Day of *Niños Héroes*, the young heroes. In 1847, cadets defended the military academy (today the Castillo de Chapultepec) against American troops.

16 September. *Día de la Independencia* (Independence Day). On the eve of this day the bell over the entrance to the Palacio Nacional (at the Zócalo) rings out, and at 11pm the president repeats the *Grito de Dolores*, Father Hidalgo's call to the nation against the patronizing Spanish leaders (1810). On 16 September military parade from the Zócalo to the park of Chapultepec.

29 September. Festival of the Archangel Michael. Festivities in the quarters of Gustavo A. Madero, Iztapalapa, Tláhuac and Tlalpan. Folk festival with fireworks and dances in Chalma (the place of pilgrimages).

4 October. Festival of St Francis. Festivals in many communities.

12 October. *Día de la Raza* (Day of the Race). The anniversary of the day Columbus discovered America. National holiday in many Latin American countries. Mexico celebrates the merging of the Indian and European races to form the Mexican people.

1–2 November. *Todos los Santos* (All Saints') and *Día de los Muertos* (All Souls' Day). On the night of 1–2 November, people take flowers, food, drink and candles to the cemeteries to celebrate with the deceased. Particularly impressive in Mixquic, a suburb in the east of the city.

20 November. *Día de la Revolución*. A parade marking the day Madero gave the call to start the revolution.

22 November. Festival of St Cecilia, the patron saint of musicians. Festival on the Plaza Garibaldi, in Tláhuac and Xochimilco.

30 November. Festival of St Andrew in Azcapotzalco and Xochimilco as well as Texcoco (in the east of the city).

8 December. Festival of the Immaculate Conception. Religious celebrations in many communities.

12 December. *Fiesta de Nuestra Señora de Guadalupe*. Long pilgrimages to the Basilica of the Virgin of Guadalupe in Mexico City. Solemn masses, dance performances on the forecourt of the basilica. Processions all over the country.

16–24 December. Time of the *posadas*, celebrations at home in remembrance of Mary and Joseph searching for shelter in Bethlehem. People traditionally serve *ponche* (punch), a cold drink made of various fruits and spirits, and hang *piñatas* (colored papier-mâché figures usually in the shape of stars or animals and filled with candies and fruit) from a heavy cord. Someone, usually the host, pulls on the cord to make the *piñata* jump up and down, and blindfolded guests take turns swinging at it wildly with a stick, trying to break it open. When it breaks, everyone dives for contents.

25 December. *Navidad* (the Spanish name for Christmas Day).

31 December. Fireworks on New Year's Eve everywhere in the city. Parades and fiestas in the streets on New Year's Day.

Entertainment

Mexico City, the cultural Mecca of the country, offers a wide spectrum of evening entertainment even to the non–Spanish speaker. The weekly magazine *Tiempo Libre* (which appears on Fridays and is available at newsagents) publishes comprehensive information about cultural events (including pop music). It lists events, locations, telephone numbers for reservations, and the nearest Metro station.

Advance tickets for theater performances, concerts, sport and other events are available from **Boletrónico**, either by telephone (tel. 325 9000) or through ticket offices at some theatres and several record shops.

Below are the contact details and nearest Metro of Mexico City's most important music and concert halls, cultural centers and theaters as well as discos and pubs with live music.

The **Ballet Folklórico**. The most famous night show, and has been for years. The dance group, swirling across the stage to traditional music in frilly and brightly colored costumes, gives a memorable display of the variety of Mexican music and dance. Performances: Palacio de Bellas Artes, *see* following listing, tel. 512 3633,

Sunday 9.30am, Wednesday 9pm.

The **Teatro de la Ciudad**, Donceles 36, tel. 510 2197, also has excellent folklore performances on Tuesday at 8.30pm, Sunday at 9.30am.

Anfiteatro Simón Bolivar, Justo Sierra 16, Centro, former Colegio de San Ildefonso, Metro: Zócalo.

Auditorio Alejo Peralta, Unidad Cultural López Mateos, Zacatenco (north), tel. 586 2847, Metro: Lindavista.

Auditorio Nacional, Paseo de la Reforma, corner of Campo Marte, Chapultepec, tel. 520 9060, Metro: Auditorio.

Biblioteca Pública de México, Plaza de la Ciudadela 4, Centro, Metro: Balderas.

Casa de Cultura del Periodista, Eje Central Lázaro Cárdenas 912, Col. 2a del Periodista.

Casa de la Cultura Jesús Reyes Heroles, Francisco Sosa 202, Col. Coyoacán, tel. 658 5223, Metro: Viveros.

Casa del Lago, Bosque de Chapultepec, tel. 553 6318, Metro: Chapultepec.

Centro Cultural Universitario, Ciudad Universitario, Insurgentes Sur 3000, tel. 622 7137, Metro: Universidad. Several halls for cultural events.

Centro Cultural/Foro Coyoacánese, Allende 36, Col. Coyoacán, tel. 554 6030.

Centro Nacional de las Artes, Avenida Rio Churubusco and Calzada de Tlalpan, tel. 689 4757.

El Desvan de las Quimeras, hall in the Fritz restaurant, Dr Rio de la Loza 221, Col. Doctores, tel. 709 2305.

El Hijo del Cuervo, Jardín Centenario 17, Col. Coyoacán, tel. 659 8869.

El Juglar, Manuel M. Ponce 233, Col. Guadalupe Inn, San Angel, tel. 660 7900.

Foro de la Libreria Luís Buñuel, Insurgentes Sur 32, tel. 592 8204.

Foro Gandhi (Libreria), Miguel Angel de Quevedo 134, Col. Chimalistac/ Coyoacán, tel. 550 2524, Metro: M.A. de Quevedo.

Museo Universitario del Chopo, Enrique González Martínez 10, Col. Sta. María la Ribera, tel. 535 2186, Metro: Revolución.

Palacio de Bellas Artes, Av. Juárez, at the Alameda Park, Metro: Bellas Artes, tel. 512 2593.

Palacio de Mineria, Tacuba 4, Centro, tel. 510 1668, Metro: Bellas Artes.

Polyforum Cultural Siqueiros, Insurgentes Sur, corner of Filadelfia (Hotel de México), tel. 536 4520.
Premier, Av. San Jerónimo 190, Pedregal de San Angel, tel. 616 2020.
Sala Carlos Chavez, in the Centro Cultural Universitario, see above.
Sala Manuel M. Ponce, in the Palacio de Bellas Artes, see above, tel. 512 2593.
Sala Miguel Covarrubias, in the Centro Cultural Universitario, see above, tel. 655 6511, ext. 7071.
Sala Nezahualcoyotl, in the Centro Cultural Universitario, see above, tel. 622 7110.
Sala Ollin Yoliztli, Periférico Sur 5141, Tlalpan, tel. 655 3311.
Teatro de la Ciudad, Donceles 36, Centro, tel. 510 2942, Metro: Allende.
Teatro de la Ciudadela, Tresguerras 91, Centro, tel. 710 2942, Metro: Balderas.

Central Cinemas

Consult *La Jornada* or *Tiempo Libre* for current listings.
Arcadia Plus (Balderas 39), **Metropolitan Plus** (Independencia and Balderas), **Palacio Chino** (Bucareli and Iturbide), all near Juárez Metro station.
Elektra Plus (Rio Guadalquivir 106), **Insurgentes Plus** (Insurgentes and Genova), **Gem. Plaza del Angel** (Londres 161), **Latino Plus** (Reforma 296), all near Insurgentes Metro.
Mariscala Plus (Lázaro Cárdenas 23), **Olimpia** (Av 16 de Septiembre 11), **Savoy Plus** (Av. 16 de Septiembre 6), **Variedades Plus** (Juarez 58) all near Bellas Artes Metro.

Theaters

Benito Juárez, Villalongín 15, Col. Cuauhtémoc, tel. 546 0820, ext. 48, Metro: Insurgentes.
Hidalgo, Av. Hidalgo 23, Centro, tel. 521 5859, Metro: Bellas Artes.
Insurgentes, Insurgentes Sur 1587, Col. San José Insurgentes, tel. 660 2304.
Juan Ruiz de Alarcon, Centro Cultural Universitario, Cd. Universitario, Insurgentes Sur 3000, tel. 655 1344, Metro: Universidad.
Julio Prieto, Xola, corner of Nicolás San Juan, Col. del Valle, tel. 639 9816, Metro: Etiopía or Xola.
Reforma, Paseo de la Reforma, corner of Burdeos, tel. 211 3622, Metro: Chapultepec.

San Rafael, Virgínia Fábregas 40, Col. San Rafael, tel. 592 2142.
San Jerónimo, Periférico Sur, corner of San Jerónimo, Unidad Habitacional del IMSS, tel. 595 2117.
Tepeyac, Calzada de Guadalupe, corner of Victoria, tel. 517 6560.
Teatro Polyforum, Insurgentes Sur, corner of Filadelfia, tel. 536 4520.
Teatro Hidalgo, Hidalgo 23, tel. 521 5859.
Claustro de Sor Juana, Izazaga 92, tel. 709 5566.
Teatro El Galeon, Reforma and Campo Marte, behind the Auditorium, tel. 280 8771.
Foro Nueva Dramaturgia, Laurel 33, tel. 541 4858.

Discos

Cero Cero, in the hotel Camino Real, Leibnitz 100, tel. 203 2121. Elegant and expensive. Open 9pm–4am. Reservation recommended at weekends.
Dynasty, in the Hotel Nikko, Campos Eliseos 204, Col. Polanco, tel. 280 1111. Hypermodern disco. Open 8pm–4am.
Lady 'O, in the Royal Pedregal hotel in the southern part of the city, tel. 726 9036. Open 10pm–2am.
Lipstick, in the Hotel Aristos, Paseo de la Reforma 276, tel. 211 0112. Mixed clientèle, casual. Open Wednesday to Sunday after 9pm.

Music and Nightclubs

Some of the music clubs below have a restaurant and provide folkloric music. Others are casual, bar-like pubs with small groups playing everything from hard rock to Caribbean reggae. Most of the grand hotels have very elegant nightclubs. The *cantinas*, similar to pubs, are normally only for men. Some of them, however, now admit women.
Antillano's, Francisco Pimentel 74, San Rafael, tel. 592 0439. Mainly Afro–Caribbean music (salsa, etc.) in a relaxed atmosphere. Open after 9pm.
Cafebreria El Pendulo, Nuevo Leon 115, tel. 286 9493. A combination café/bookshop with live music.
Cantina la Guadalupana, Calle Higuera 14, Metro: Coyoacán, tel. 554 6542.
Cantina la Valenciana, Av. Brazil 29, tel. 747 2404.
Disco Bar 9, Londres 156, Zona Rosa, tel. 514 4387. Gay club.
El Corral de la Moreria, Londres 161, Zona Rosa, tel. 525 1762. Nightclub

with dinner service, Spanish music, flamenco show. Open after 10pm, show begins at midnight.
El Patio, Atenas 9, Zona Rosa, tel. 535 3904. Traditional, elegant nightclub, dinner service, dance (two orchestras). Open 9pm–4am.
Gatsby's Musical Bar, in the hotel Presidente Inter-Continental, tel. 250 7700. Elegant nightclub, performances by international stars. Reservation recommended. Open 7pm–3am.
Hosteria del Bohemio, former Convento San Hípolito, Av. Hidalgo, west of Alameda Park. Relax in the beautiful patio. Lively music pub, young people. Open 5pm–10pm.
La Bodega, Popocatépetl 25, Col. Hipódromo Condesa, tel. 525 2473. Bohemian restaurant, pleasant for eating out. Mixed, unconventional crowd.
La Escena, Ameyalco, corner of Insurgentes Sur, Col. del Valle, tel. 687 7893. Bar with club atmosphere, music and show performances in turns. Open 7pm–3am.
La Mancha, in the hotel Aristos, Paseo de la Reforma 276, tel. 211 0112. Stylish hotel bar. Popular with Mexicans, *mariachi* music.
La Planta de Luz, Rio Magdalena and Avenida Revolución (Plaza Loreto), tel. 616 4761. Good for political satire.
Las Sillas, in the Hotel Crowne Plaza, Paseo de la Reforma 80, tel. 705 1515. The "bar of the funny chairs" (*sillas*), entertaining live music and shows. Closed on Sunday.
L'Baron, Insurgentes Sur 1231. One of the city's gay clubs.
L'Fameux, Hamburgo 41, Zona Rosa. Gay club with many transvestites.
New Orleans, Av. Revolución 1980, San Angel, tel. 550 1908. New Orleans by name and by nature. *The* classic jazz bar in Mexico City.
Pena de Gabriel del Rio, Pasaje Balderas 33. Latin-American music.
Pena el Condor Pasa, Calle Rafael Checa 1, tel. 548 2050. Latin-American music.
Pena el Payador, Rio Amazonas 36, north of the Zona Rosa. Latin-American music, popular with young set.
Popstock, Insurgentes 2380. Younger crowd looking for mostly American dance music.
Rockotitlan, Insurgentes Sur 952-202, Col. Nápoles, tel. 584 4730. Sophisticated rock music program, interesting atmosphere.

Rock Stock Bar, Paseo de la Reforma, corner of Niza, Zona Rosa, tel. 533 0906. Rock groups always changing.

Plaza Santa Cecilia, Callejon de la Amargura 30 (Plaza Garibaldi), tel. 526 1804. Restaurant/bar with lively *mariachi* music and folklore performances. Open 9pm–3am.

Tenampa (Salon), Plaza Garibaldi 12, tel. 526 6176. *The* classic *cantina* (also for women) at the Plaza Garibaldi. Non-stop *mariachi* music.

Un Lugar de la Mancha, on Prado Norte, Lomas de Chapultepec.

Yesterday's, in the Hotel Aristos, tel. 211 0112. Disco and live music on alternating days, pleasant atmosphere. Open after 8pm.

Salsa

Salsa Clubs with live bands, usually from Colombia, play at **La Maraka** (Eugenia and Mitla) and **Mocambo** (Puebla and Oaxaca, near Insurgentes Metro station). No cover or admission fee before 10pm on Thursday; $50 cover charge at other times. **Salon Riviera** is a large club at Division del Norte 1157, cover $30; Rockstock (Niza and Reforma) offers Latin style rock and roll, women free, men $120.

Jazz

New Orleans (Av. Revolución 1980, corner San Angel) Tuesday to Sunday. Open 9pm; no cover charge for diners. Two downtown bars with rooftop patios on Filomena Mata near Lázaro Cárdenas are **El Bar Mata** and **El Bar Rocco**. Open Tuesday to Sunday and usually crowded with young people.

Also downtown is the famous bar **L'Opera** (Cinco de Mayo 10) with its equally famous bullethole in the ceiling, made when a drunken Pancho Villa visited on horseback.

Culture Plus

Museums

Alvar y Carmen T. de Carrillo Gil (Museo de Arte), Av. Revolución 1608, San Angel, tel. 550 3983. Tuesday to Sunday 10am–7pm. Modern and contemporary paintings.

Anahuacalli/Diego Rivera (Museo), Calle del Museo 150, Coyoacán, tel. 677 2873. Tuesday to Sunday 10am–2pm, 3–6pm. Unconventional building designed by Rivera. Contains his collection of pre–Spanish and folk art and

his own works. Celebrations in remembrance of Rivera during the first week of November.

Antiguo Colegio de San Ildefonso, Justo Sierra 16, Centro Histórico. Tuesday to Sunday 11am–6pm. Restored masterpiece of colonial architecture housing the collection of Mexico's National Autonomous University.

Antropología (Museo Nacional de), Paseo de la Reforma, corner of Gandhi, Bosque de Chapultepec, tel. 553 6381. Tuesday to Friday 9am–7pm; Saturday, Sunday, and bank holidays 10am–6pm. Essential. Two floors of the best and most comprehensive display of Mexico's Indian culture from pre–Spanish to modern times.

Arte (Museo Nacional de), Tacuba 8, tel. 512 3234. Tuesday to Sunday 10am–6pm. Comprehensive collection of arts and crafts from pre–Spanish to modern times.

Arte Contemporaneo (Centro Cultural), Campos Eliseos, corner of Jorge Eliot, Col. Polanco, tel. 282 0355. Tuesday to Sunday 10am–6pm. Departments for contemporary arts, the history of photography (largest collection in South America) and pre–Spanish art. Also cultural center with a library, theater, cinema, etc.

Arte Moderno (Museo de), Paseo de la Reforma, corner of Gandhi, tel. 553 6313. Tuesday to Sunday 10am–6pm. Permanent exhibition of modern Mexican painters such as Orozco, Tamayo, Frida Kahlo, Cuevas, Coronel and Toledo. Numerous cultural events, temporary exhibitions.

Artes e Industrias Populares (Museo Nacional de), Av. Juárez 44, tel. 552 6679. Tuesday to Sunday 10am–2pm and 3–6pm. Exhibition of Mexican arts and crafts from all over the country. Some of the objects in the exhibition are for sale.

Caricature (Museum of), Antiguo Colegio de Cristo, Donceles 99, tel. 795 1187. Depicts Mexican colonial architecture.

Carmen (Museo Regional del), Av. Revolución 4–6/Avenida de la Paz, San Angel, tel. 548 5312. Open daily 10am–5pm. Former Carmelite monastery (17th century), collection of religious paintings from the 17th and 18th centuries, e.g. Villalpando and Correa. The basement houses mummies conserved by a special combination of humidity and soil.

Casa del Risco (Museo de la), Plaza de San Jacinto 15, San Angel. Open Tuesday to Friday 10am–3pm, Saturday and Sunday 10am–2pm. Typical mansion of an aristocratic family in the 18th century, collection of European paintings from the 14th to the 18th centuries, Mexican paintings from colonial times, luxurious rooms on the upper floor. Cultural center.

Castillo de Chapultepec, see Historia (Museo Nacional de).

Cera de la Ciudad de Mexico (Museo de), Londres 6. Open Monday to Friday 11am–7pm, Saturday and Sunday 10am–7pm. Interesting waxworks in an equally interesting art nouveau city palace (by the same architect who designed the Revolution Memorial).

Charreria (Museo de la), Isabel la Católica 108, tel. 521 0665. Open Monday to Friday 9am–6pm, Saturday 9am–1pm. Convent church of the late 16th century, interesting collection of clothes from the *charros* and other artifacts used at the *charrería* (Mexican rodeo). On special display is Pancho Villa's saddle and revolver.

Ciudad de Mexico (Museo de la), Pino Suárez 30, tel. 542 0487. Open Tuesday to Sunday 9.30am–7.30pm. Former city palace of the Earl of Santiago Calimaya (18th century). The documentation of the city's development since pre–Spanish times is well worth seeing.

Cuicuilco (Museo Arqueológico de), Insurgentes Sur (south of the junction with the Periférico Sur). Open Tuesday to Sunday 10am–5pm. Small museum next to the circular pyramid explaining the role of the most important ceremonial center in the highlands and the social order at the time of its building 4,000 years ago. Pretty figurines.

Culturas (Museo Nacional de las), Calle Moneda 13, tel. 512 7452. Open Tuesday to Friday 9.30am–6pm, Saturday and Sunday 9.30am–4pm. In the northwestern corner of the National Palace, ethnographical collection about many tribes of the world. The hall has a mural by Rufino Tamayo.

Culturas Populares (Museo Nacional de), Hidalgo 289, Coyoacán, tel. 554 8357. Monday and Thursday 10am–4pm; Wednesday, Friday, and Saturday 10am–8pm; Sunday 11am–5pm. Museum in the style of a colonial house, temporary exhibitions on different aspects of Mexico's culture.

Diego Rivera (Museo Estudio), Calle Diego Rivera, corner of Altavista, Col. San Angel Inn, tel. 550 1189. Restored residence and studio of the painter Diego Rivera.

Dolores Olmedo (Museo), Avenida Mexico 5843, Ex-Hacienda La Noria, Xochimilco. Open Tuesday to Sunday, 10am–6pm. Friend and patron of Diego Rivera, Dolores Olmedo donated part of her home and grounds for a museum housing her vast collection of works by Rivera and Frida Kahlo as well as an impressive collection or archeological artifacts.

Franz Mayer (Museo), Av. Hidalgo 45, north of the Alameda Park, tel. 518 2265. Open Tuesday to Sunday 10am–5pm. Former hospital (16th century), excellent museum for applied arts in colonial times, fantastic paintings, furniture, textiles as well as arts and crafts from Mexico and Spain.

Frida Kahlo (Museo), Londres 247, Coyoacán, tel. 554 5999. Open Tuesday to Sunday 10am–6pm. Former residence and studio of the artist couple Kahlo–Rivera, very stylish and at the same time unconventional interior. Death mask of Frida Kahlo, the urn with her ashes and some clothes in her bedroom.

Historia (Museo Nacional de), Castillo de Chapultepec, Bosque de Chapultepec, tel. 553 6202. Open Tuesday to Sunday 9am–5pm. In the west wing of the castle of the viceroys (18th and 19th centuries). Ground floor holds exhibition of Mexico's history (from the conquest to the revolution in 1910). The first floor documents Mexico's social and economic development from 1759 to 1917. Also valuable art and murals by great artists (Orozco, Siqueiros, and others).

Intervenciones (Museo Nacional de las), 20 de Agosto, corner of Xicotencatl, Coyoacán, tel. 604 0699. Former Churubusco monastery; history of the period from the War of Independence until the revolution in 1914, when Mexico had to defend herself against the interventions (*intervenciones*) of foreign powers. Also religious art from colonial times.

Leon Trotsky (Museo), Viena 45, Coyoacán, tel. 658 8732. Open Tuesday to Friday 10am–2pm and 3–5.30pm, Saturday and Sunday 10.30am–4pm. Former residence of Leon Trotsky and his wife. It was here

the Russian revolutionary was murdered by a Spanish communist on April 20, 1940. The garden has a monument with urns holding the couple's ashes.

Mexican Medicine (Museum of the History of), Brasil 33. Documents, instruments, books, paintings.

Palacio de Bellas Artes (Museo del), Av. Juárez, corner of Lázaro Cárdenas, tel. 510 1388. Open Tuesday to Sunday 10.30am–6.30pm. Works of the most famous Mexican muralists in the entrance hall and upper floors. Collection of Mexican paintings from the 19th century and etchings by José Guadalupe Posada.

Papalote Children's Museum, Chapultepec Park, tel. 237 1772. Open Monday through Sunday from 9am–1pm and 2–6pm. Hands on exhibits for children and their guests.

Pinacoteca Virreinal de San Diego, Dr Mora 7, at the Alameda Park. Open Tuesday to Sunday 9am–5pm. Some rooms and the church of the former convent of San Diego (17th century) house one of the most valuable collections of paintings from the time of the viceroys (16th–18th centuries), mainly religious motifs. The Pinacoteca also includes part of the entrance hall of the old hotel Del Prado.

Polyforum Cultural Siqueiros, Insurgentes Sur, corner of Filadelfia, tel. 536 4524. Open Monday to Sunday 10am–9pm. There is also a *son et lumière* show. Exhibitions of Mexican folk art and works of Siqueiros' school are in the Foro de las Artesanías. Contemporary art is in the Foro Nacional. In the Foro Universal is Siqueiros' huge masterpiece *The Way of Mankind*, a 2,400-sq. m (26,000-sq. ft) picture with collages.

Revolución (Museo Nacional de la), Plaza de la República, below the Revolution Memorial, tel. 566 1902. Tuesday to Friday 10am–5pm, Saturday and Sunday 9am–5pm. Impressive display of the history of the revolution.

Rufino Tamayo (Museo), Paseo de la Reforma, corner of Gandhi, Bosque de Chapultepec, tel. 286 5889. Open Tuesday to Sunday 10am–6pm. Extraordinary collection of modern art, including several works by Tamayo.

San Carlos (Museo de), Puente de Alvarado 50, west of the Alameda Park, tel. 566 8522. Wednesday to Monday 10am–6pm. Former palace of

the Earl of Buenavista designed by the famous Spanish architect Manuel Tolsá. Works by the most famous European painters of the 16th–19th centuries. Also contemporary paintings.

Templo Mayor (Zona Arqueológica del), Seminario 8, at the Zócalo, tel. 542 1717. Tuesday to Sunday 9am–5pm. Excellent presentation of pre-Spanish finds, including the stone of the moon goddess Coyolxauhqui at the border of the archaeological site of the Templo Mayor.

Murals

Here is where you can find the most famous murals in Mexico City.

THE OLD CITY

Palacio Nacional, Plaza de la Constitución. In the stairwell is Diego Rivera's most famous mural, *La Historia de México*. In the gallery on the first floor is a picture sequence about the ancient tribes of the country and their way of life, also by Rivera.

Suprema Corte de Justicia, Plaza de la Constitución, Pino Suárez, corner of Corregidora. In the stairwell is the very expressive cycle of paintings by J.C. Orozco, *Justice* and *The National Weal*. At the library entrance is *War and Peace* by George Biddle.

Museo de la Ciudad de México, Pino Suárez 30. *Vision of the Defeated* by Francisco Moreno Capdevilla. The upper floor was Joaquin Clausell's studio with the unconventional patterns he made on the wall by wiping his brush.

Iglesia del Hospital de Jesús Nazareno, Pino Suárez, corner of Av. Rep. de El Salvador. On the ceiling and the choir wall is J.C. Orozco's apocalyptic and cruelly portrayed version of the *Spanish Conquest*.

Anfiteatro Simón Bolívar, Calle Justo Sierra 16. In the hall, *The Genesis*, Rivera's first masterpiece. Also Leal's *Festival of the Lord of Chalma*.

Escuela Nacional Preparatoria, San Ildefonso 33. Famous cycle of socio-critical paintings by J.C. Orozco in the great hall, e.g. *La Trinchera* (The Trench), *La Huelga* (The Strike), *El Juicio Final* (The Last Judgement). Also *Allegory of the Virgin of Guadalupe* by F. Revueltas, *The Elements* and *The Worker's Funeral* by D.A. Siqueiros, and The *Massacre of Templo Mayor* by Jean Charlot.

Secretaría de Educación Pública, between Rep. de Argentina, Luis González Obregón and Rep. de Venezuela. In two patios is a sequence of 235 paintings by Rivera (more than 1,600 sq. meters/17,200 sq. ft) about Mexican life. In the second court are paintings by Jean Charlot and Amado de la Cueva. In the library is *Red Riding Hood* by Carlos Merida.

Antigua Aduana, Plaza de Santo Domingo. In the stairwell is *Patrician and Patricide* by David A. Siqueiros.

Antigua Camara de Senadores, Xicoténcatl 9. In the stairwell is a sequence of paintings about Mexico's history by Jorge González Camarena.

Palacio de Bellas Artes, Eje Central Lázaro Cárdenas, corner of Av. Juárez. On several floors, in the great hall and in the corridors are works by the great muralists J.C. Orozco, David Alfaro Siqueiros, Rivera, J.G. Camarena, M. Rodríguez Lozano and Rufino Tamayo.

Casa de los Azulejos, Fco. Madero. In the stairwell of the patio-restaurant is the huge *Omniscience* by J.C. Orozco.

Pinacoteca Virreinal de San Diego, Dr Mora 7, at the Alameda Park. A building specially designed for Diego Rivera's *Sunday Afternoon Reverie in the Alameda*, which was moved here when the Hotel del Prado was demolished after the 1985 earthquake.

PASEO DE LA REFORMA

Sindicato de Electristas (Electricity Company), Antonio Caso 45. In the stairwell is the extremely critical *Picture of Bourgeoisie* by David Alfaro Siqueiros.

Instituto Mexicano del Seguro Social (Mexican Institute for Social Security), Paseo de la Reforma 476. A concrete wall became a work of art: *Mexico* by Jorge González Camarena.

Secretaría de Salubridad y Asistencia, Paseo de la Reforma, corner of Lieja, just before Chapultepec Park. Several paintings by Rivera showing the different cycles of life.

Comisión Federal de Electricidad (National Electricity Commission), Rio Rodano 14. Here, Jesús Guerrero Galvan painted his interesting *Allegory of Electricity*.

Castillo de Chapultepec, Bosque de Chapultepec. A representative cross-section of murals. *The History of Mexican Independence* by Juan O'Gorman; *Juárez, the Church and the Imperialists* by J.C. Orozco (in the room *Refor-*

ma e Imperio); *The Conquista Crush Indian and Spanish Culture* (in the room *Conquista*) and *Venustiano Caranza* (in the room *La Constitución*), both by J.G. Camarena; *From the Porfiriat to the Revolution* by D.A. Siqueiros (in the room *Revolución*). Also *The Revolutionary Leaders* by Eduardo Solares, *The Landscape* by Gerardo Murillo (Dr Atl), and *The Return of Benito Juárez to Mexico on 15 April 1857* by A.G. Orozco.

Museo Nacional de Antropología, Paseo de la Reforma, corner of Gandhi. Murals complement the exhibits, e.g. The *World of the Tzeltales and Tzotziles* by Leonora Carrington or *The Fantastic World of the Yucatán Peninsula* by Rafael Coronel are both in the Maya room. *The Expression of Culture in Mesoamerica* by José Chavez Morado is in the Mesoamerica room. Also works by Arturo Covarrubias, A.G. Bustos, Matias Goeritz, Iker Laurrauri, Leopoldo Mendez and others.

Hotel Camino Real, Mariano Escobedo 700. *Man confronted with the Infinite* by Rufino Tamayo is in one of the entrance halls. Life is seen as a street where human beings hide behind illusion and hope.

Lerma–Bassin, in the new, western part of the Chapultepec Park. Imaginative underwater relief by Diego Rivera in the large pool.

AVENIDA INSURGENTES

Polyforum Cultural Siqueiros, Insurgentes Sur, corner of Filadelfia, next to the Hotel de México. The 12 outer walls display historical scenes, painted by 30 artists according to Siqueiros' design. Inside the building, *The Way of Mankind*, Siqueiros' huge masterpiece. Next to the Polyforum you can find another huge work by Siqueiros, showing the artist himself together with several other muralists such as Gerardo Murillo (Dr Atl), J.C. Orozco, and Rivera.

Teatro Insurgentes, Av. de los Insurgentes Sur 1587. A huge mosaic in mural style according to Diego Rivera's design. The actor Cantínflas is at the center of a group of artists.

Ciudad Universitaria, Insurgentes Sur. One of the most impressive mosaic façades in the style of a mural can be found in the library. It was created according to the design of Juan O'Gorman and covers the following

subjects: the cosmologies of Ptolemy and Copernicus (south), Mexico's history before the Spanish conquest (north), and the New Age (west) as well as a future vision of the country (east). In the rectorate, Siqueiros designed a relief mural, *People for the University – the University for the People*.

The designs for the glass mosaics at the facade of the lecture hall for natural sciences (*Conquering Energy*) and at the plaza of the same faculty were created by José Chávez Morado. *Life, Death and the Four Elements* – a gigantic mosaic created by Francisco Eppens, is in the medical faculty.

Estadio Olimpico, Insurgentes Sur, opposite the Ciudad Universitaria. The glass mosaic showing an allegory of sport was designed by Diego Rivera.

IN THE NORTH

Instituto Politechnico Nacional, Prolongación Carpio/Lauro Aguirre. Mural by David Alfaro Siqueiros: *Man – Master of Technology, not its Slave*.

Books

Mexico City is the major publishing center of Latin America, so there are many book shops. Larger book shops often serve as cultural meeting points, and readings by authors are usually listed in the weekly magazine *Tiempo Libre*. Literature on Mexico can also be found in many museums.

BOOKSHOPS

Deutsche Buchhandlung, Benjamin Hill 193, Col. Condesa.

American Bookstore, SA, Madero 25, tel. 512 0306.

Librería Britanica, Serapio Rendón 125, tel. 705 0595. Including a small selection of used paperbacks

Librería Hamburgo, Insurgentes Sur 58, tel. 514 5086.

Librería (Foro) Gandhi, Miguel Angel de Quevedo 134, Col. Chimalistac/Coyoacán, tel. 548 1990. Monday to Friday 10am–11pm, weekends 10am–10pm. The largest bookshop in Mexico and a cultural meeting place.

Librería (Foro) Luís Buñuel, Insurgentes Sur 32, tel. 592 8204. Cultural meeting point.

El Juglar, Calle Manuel M. Ponce 233, Col. Guadalupe Inn, tel. 660 7900. Beautiful rooms in an old villa with literary café. A cultural meeting point.

Parnaso de Coyoacán, Av. F. Curillo

Puerto 6, Coyoacán, tel. 658 5718. Also open on Sunday. In the style of a university bookshop. Wide range of books. Readings are given.

Libros, Libros, Libros, Monte Arrarat 220, tel. 540 4778. Wide selection of books and magazines in English.

Sanborn's. Book departments in all subsidiaries of the chain.

SECOND-HAND BOOKS

The easiest place to find cheap, used books in English is on Calle Donceles (between República de Cuba and Tacuba) in the downtown area. Look for Librería de Viejo, Mundo Feliz, El Mercado de Libros and Librería El Gran Remate all in the same block.

Librería Britanica, Serapio Rendón 125, tel. 705 0595, has a small selection of used paperbacks.

LIBRARIES

British Council, Antonio Caso 127, tel. 535 5146. Magazines, newspapers, books. Open 9am–7pm, Saturday until 1.30pm.

Instituto Francés de America Latina (IFAL) Rio Nazas 43, tel. 566 0777. Library in French.

Instituto Goethe, Calle Tonala 43, tel. 533 6889. Library in German.

American Society of Mexico, Rio Panuco 15, tel. 592 1800.

Shopping

It does not matter whether you are interested in buying arts and crafts (*artesanías*), jewelry or elegant clothes, you will find everything in the Zona Rosa. **Sanborn's** department stores also offer a comprehensive choice of high quality goods.

The choice of exotic spices and chilis at the old **Mercado de la Merced** is great. The *mercado* covers a complete quarter, with small greengrocers and spice shops reaching from the southeast of the Zócalo to the Merced market hall (Metro: Merced).

Many galleries selling modern Mexican art or folk art (such as naive paintings or *papel amate*) are also in the Zona Rosa. However, quality and famous names mean a high price.

Arts & Crafts

Arts, crafts and folk art (*arte popular*) are best bought and sold at one of the larger markets (where haggling is possible) or in special shops.

You should stick to specialized silver or jewelry shops if you want to buy items made of silver. Many can be found in the Calle Amberes in the Zona Rosa, amongst them the well-known **Tane** and **Los Castillo**, a subsidiary of Taxco's most famous silversmith.

Specialist Shops

FONART (Fondo Nacional para el Fomento de las Artesanías), a government organization promoting arts and crafts. Subsidiaries selling goods: Av. Patriotismo 691 (headquarters); Avenida Juárez 89, near the Alameda Park; Londres 136, Zona Rosa; Av. Insurgentes Sur 1630, Col. del Valle; Av. de la Paz 37, San Angel; Av. Manuel E. Izaguirre 10, Cd. Satélite.

Artesanias Finas Indios Verdes, Insurgentes Norte, corner of Acueducto 13. A department store for arts and crafts and souvenirs, also silver, leatherware and clothes.

Feder's, Av. de la Presa 1, behind the Indios Verdes monument, also at the Bazaar del SEabado. Blown glass in a variety of colors and designs, from glasses and Christmas ornaments to chandeliers and tables.

Galeria Reforma, Reforma Norte, corner of Gonzáles Bocanegra (at the second roundabout north of the junction of Av. Juárez). Excellent choice of arts and crafts of all kinds; also jewelry, leatherware and textiles.

La Carreta, Insurgentes Sur 2105, near Sanborn's, San Angel. A kind of market with many stalls and small shops where artists sell their works.

Museum Shop, Centro Cultural/Arte Contemporaneo, Campos Eliseos and J. Eliot, next to the Inter-Continental hotel. An outstanding but costly selection of Mexico's finest crafts.

Museo Nacional de Artes e Industrias Populares, Av. Juárez 44, close to the Alameda Park. A wide choice of high quality arts and crafts.

Markets

Some markets specialize in arts and crafts (and kitschy souvenirs), in others you have to look out for artesanía amongst the daily necessities.

Chopo, beside Buenavista railway station. Underground music market on Saturday with alternative music and paraphernalia not found in conventional stores.

La Ciudadela, Mercado Central de Artesanías, Av. Balderas, Metro: Balderas or Juárez; open Monday to Saturday 9am–6pm, Sunday 9am–2pm. Inexpensive items from jewelry to hammocks from all over the country. The large store of Jaime Morett Manjarrez has a wide selection.

Green Door, Calle Cedro 8, near San Cosmo Metro. Sells at wholesale prices; will ship goods abroad; accepts credit cards.

Mercado San Juan, C. Ayuntamiento, corner of Dolores, Metro: Salto del Agua or walk from the Alameda Park. Weekdays 9.30am–6pm. Huge building with small shops, arts and crafts and kitsch at appropriate prices.

Mercado de Curiosidades, Calle Dolores, near Salto del Agua Metro. Has a reasonable selection, but bargaining is mandatory.

Insurgentes Market on Calle Londres near Florencia, in the Zona Rosa. Silver and ceramics at good prices.

El Bazar del Sábado, Plaza San Jacinto, San Angel. Every Saturday. Bric-a-brac and arts and crafts (good quality) with an outdoor art show, live music and a pleasant courtyard café.

La Lagunilla, Calle Allende/Rayón. Sunday. A typical flea market with second-hand clothes, junk, and rubbish as well as arts and crafts.

Food Markets

La Merced, beside Merced Metro station. Largest market in the Americas with food halls, clothing, leather goods, and restaurant clothes.

Jamaica Market near Jamaica Metro station. Fruits, vegetables live birds and animals.

Aurrera, four blocks north of Ignacio Mariscal on Insurgentes. This is a US-style grocery/department store.

San Cosme, street market on Puente de Alvarado leads to food market.

Where Goods Come From

The following are areas of Mexico which specialize in particular products.

Ceramics and pottery from Tonalá (near Guadalajara, Jalisco). *Loza bruñida*, unglazed highly polished fine ceramics, often decorated with plants or animals. Gray, brown, and white.

Green-glazed ceramics from Patam-ban and other Taraska villages in the state of Michoacán.

Black and shiny ceramics from San Bartólo Coyotepec (Oaxaca).

Animal figures from Santa María Atzompa (Oaxaca). Made of clay and used for growing cress.

Clay figures from Tlaquepaque (near Guadalajara, Jalisco). Nativity figures.

Conifers mainly from Metepec (near Toluca, Est. de México) and Acatlán de Osorio (Puebla).

Talavera ceramics from Puebla. Glazed, multicolored ceramics of Span-ish origin (e.g. crockery and tiles).

Lacquerwork. Many items made in Mexico are decorated with elaborate lacquerwork. From Pátzcuaro (Michoacán) gold-leaf decorations. From Urápan (Michoacán) inlaid work. From Olinalá (Guerrero) pumpkin ves-sels, boxes in scratch technique (multicolored) and jaguar masks. From Chiapa de Corzo (south of San Cristóbal, Chiapas) black pumpkin ves-sels with painted flower decorations.

Embroidered blouses from San Pablito Pahuatlán and Cuetzalan (Puebla) as well as Oaxaca and Chiapas.

Fabrics and **belts** are woven in Oaxaca and Chiapas.

Carpets are woven from wool in Mitla (Oaxaca).

Scarves (*rebozos*) are finely woven in black and gray in the villages of the Estado de México and Oaxaca.

Dresses and **blouses** in modern de-signs with traditional embroidery come from the states of Jalisco and Michoacán as well as other places.

Glassware is handmade mainly in the region of Guadalajara.

Onyx chess and domino sets, bowls or vases come mainly from Puebla.

Hand-made paper (*Papel amate*). The paper is produced in San Pablito (in the north of Puebla) and then painted in various villages such as Xalítla, Toliman and San Agustín de las Flores in the state of Guerrero.

Wickerwork and **basketwork**. Ham-mocks, sisal bags, and mats are made in Yucatán. Reed mats and baskets are made in Michoacán. Palm wicker-work comes from the state of Puebla. Finely woven hats come from the Gulf Coast, Campeche.

Woodwork. Animal figures are carved from ironwood by the Seri Indians from Bahía de Kino (Sonora).

Furniture in the colonial style is made in Cuernavaca (Morelos) and Micho-acán. Mahogany and cedar wood furni-ture (also chests and other small pieces of furniture) comes from Yucatán, Tabasco and Campeche.

Guitars are often made in Paracho (Michoacán).

Silverwork (jewelry, bowls, vases, cut-lery) comes mainly from Taxco.

Copper art masterpieces are found in Santa Clara del Cobre (Michoacán).

Coral jewelry comes from the Gulf and Caribbean coast.

Gold jewelry created after designs found in pre-Spanish tombs (e.g. imita-tion of jewelry from Mte Albán) is made in Oaxaca.

Sports

Sport in Mexico

Soccer is the most popular sport in Mexico. Children kick their footballs in courtyards and parks; the profession-als play in the Ciudad Deportiva (Insurgentes Sur), in the Estadio Azteca (Aztec stadium, near the junc-tion of the Periférico Sur with the Calzada Tlalpan) or in the Estadio Olím-pico, a short walk along Tintgoretto from San Antonio Metro. Matches are every Thursday evening at 9pm, Satur-day at 5pm and Sunday at midday.

Jai-alai: A *frontón* (*jai-alai* hall) is sit-ated near the Revolution Memorial. Games take place Tuesday through Saturday at 7pm, Sunday at 5pm. Coat and tie is required except on Sunday.

Hiking. Exercise without pollution comes with a brisk walk up one of the nearby mountains. From Viveros Metro station take a *pesero* to San Francisco and then another to the mountain.

Horse racing. There is thoroughbred horse racing in the Hipódromo de las Américas in the southwest of the city on Wednesday and Sunday 2.30–9pm; Thursday, Friday and Saturday 2.30pm–midnight. Betting is an inte-gral part of the races. There is a pretty restaurant in the Derby Club – for res-ervations, tel. 557 4100.

Charreadas. Organized by *charro* clubs, mainly on Sunday, e.g. in the Rancho Grande de la Villa, Insurgentes Norte (north of the Metro station Indios Verdes); Lienzo del Charro, at the Periférico, west of San Angel; Charros del Pedregal, Camino a Sta. Teresa 305, Tlalpan, tel. 655 9353; and Lienzo Rancho del Charro, Av. de la Constituyentes 500. Information: Asociación Nacional de Charros, AC, tel. 277 8706.

Tennis. A few hotels have adjacent ten-nis courts. The Club Reyes near the Chapultepec Park is open to non-members. Reservations are recom-mended, tel. 277 2690.

Golf is played in the Club Campestre (est. 1906) in Mexico City (Churu-busco). This club and the Club de Golf de México (in Tlalpan), the Club de Golf Chapultepec and the clubs Bellavista, Hacienda and Valle Escondido (to the west of the city in the Estado de México), are open to visitors accompa-nied by a club member. Several luxury hotels can arrange playing privileges for their guests at private clubs. On presentation of a membership card and payment of a green fee you can play in the following clubs: Chiluca, Bosques del Lago (also in the west) and Coral Golf Resorts (in the east, towards Puebla). Enquire before set-ting out. Playing conditions may change from season to season.

Bullfighting is a hotly debated issue all over the world, but it has many fans who on Sunday between October and May attend the Plaza México, the larg-est arena in Latin America, with 50,000 seats. It is at Calle Augusto Rodin 241, about 10 minutes' walk from Metro San Antonio.

Language

Many Mexicans speak some English, but it is good to have basic Spanish phrases at your disposal. In remote areas, it is essential. In general, Mexicans are delighted with the foreigner who tries to speak the language, and they'll be patient – if amused. Pronunciation is not difficult if you only want to make yourself understood. If you want to sound a bit more authentic, practice before you go.

The Sounds

a as in father
e as in bed
i as in police
o as in hole
u as in rude
Consonants approximate those in English, the main exceptions being:
c is hard before **a**, **o**, or **u** (as in English), and soft before **e** or **i**, when it sounds like **s** (as opposed to the Castilian pronunciation of **th** as in think). Thus, *censo* (census) sounds like *senso*.
g is hard before **a**, **o**, or **u** (as in English), but whenever the English **g** sounds like **j** (before **e** or **i**) the Spanish **g** sounds like a guttural **h**. **G** before **ua** is often soft or silent, so that agua sounds more like *awa*, and Guadalajara like *Wadalajara*.
h is silent.
j sounds like the English **h**.
ll sounds like y.
ñ sounds like ny, as in the Spanish word *señor*.
q is followed by **u** as in English, but the combination sounds like **k** instead of like **kw**. *¿Qué quiere Usted?* is pronounced: *Keh kee-ehr-eh oostehd?*
r is often rolled.
x between vowels sounds like a guttural **h**, e.g. in *México* or *Oaxaca*.
y alone means *and*, and is pronounced **ee**.

ch is a separate letter in the Spanish alphabet. Alphabetically, words beginning with **ch** are listed after words beginning with **c**.

Numbers

1 – *uno*	11 – *once*
2 – *dos*	12 – *doce*
3 – *tres*	13 – *trece*
4 – *cuatro*	14 – *catorce*
5 – *cinco*	15 – *quince*
6 – *seis*	16 – *dieciseis*
7 – *siete*	17 – *diecisiete*
8 – *ocho*	18 – *dieciocho*
9 – *nueve*	19 – *diecinueve*
10 – *diez*	20 – *veinte*

21 – *veintiuno*	60 – *sesenta*
25 – *veinticinco*	70 – *setenta*
30 – *treinta*	80 – *ochenta*
40 – *cuarenta*	90 – *noventa*
50 – *cincuenta*	

100 – *cien*
101 – *ciento uno*
200 – *doscientos*
300 – *trescientos*
400 – *cuatrocientos*
500 – *quinientos*
600 – *seiscientos*
700 – *setecientos*
800 – *ochocientos*
900 – *novecientos*

1,000 – *mil*
2,000 – *dos mil*
10,000 – *diez mil*
100,000 – *cien mil*
1,000,000 – *un millón*

Phrases
Courtesy

Please – *Por favor*
Thank you – *Gracias*
You're welcome – *De nada* (literally, *for nothing*)
I'm sorry – *Lo siento, Perdón, Perdóneme; Discúlpeme.*
Yes – *Sí*
No – *No*

Can you speak English? – *¿Habla (Usted) inglés?*
Do you understand me?– *¿Me comprende? ¿Me entiende?*
Just a moment please – *Un momento, por favor*

Good morning – *Buenos días*
Good night, Good evening – *Buenas noches*
Goodbye – *Adiós*

Getting Around
Where is...? – *¿Dónde está...?*

the exit – *la salida*
the entrance – *la entrada*
the subway – *el metro*
the taxi – *el taxi*

the airport – *el aeropuerto*
the duty-free shop – *el duty free*
the train station *la estación del ferrocarril*
the express bus station – *la central de autobuses*

the police station – *la delegación de policía*
the embassy – *la embajada*
the consulate – *el consulado*

the post office – *el correo, la oficina de correos*
the telegraph office – *la oficina de telégrafos*
the public telephone – *el teléfono público*
the bank – *el banco*

a hotel – *un hotel*
an inn – *una posada*
a restaurant – *un restaurant*
a café, coffee shop – *un café, una fonda, un merendero*

the restroom – *el sanitario*
the (private) bathroom – *el baño*
public bathhouses – *los baños públicos*

the ticket office – *la oficina de boletos*
the dry cleaners – *la tintorería*
the department store – *la tienda, los almacenes*
the market, marketplace – *el mercado*
the souvenir shop – *la tienda de curiosidades*

airplane – *avión*
the ferry boat – *el transbordador*
train – *tren*
bus – *autobus*
bus stop – *parada*
reserved seat – *asiento reservado*
first class – *primera clase*
second class – *segunda clase*

Please call a taxi for me – *Pídame un taxi, por favor*

I'm going to... – *Me voy a...*

How many kilometers is it from here to...? – *¿Cuántos kilómetros hay de aquí a...?*

How long does it take to go there? – *¿Cuánto se tarda en llegar?*

What will you charge to take me to...? – *¿Cuánto me cobra para llevarme a...?*

Please stop here – *Pare aquí, por favor*

Please go straight – *Vaya derecho, por favor.*

How much is a ticket to...? – *¿Cuánto cuesta un boleto a...?*

I want a ticket to... – *Quiero un boleto a...*

Where does this bus go? – *¿Adónde va este autobús?*

Down! (to yell at a bus driver when you want to get off) – *¡Bajan!*

What is this place called? – *¿Cómo se llama este lugar?*

Shopping

This is good – *(Esto) Está bueno*

This is bad – *(Esto) Está malo*

What is the price? – *¿Cuánto cuesta?*

It's too expensive – *Está muy caro.*

Can you give me a discount? – *¿Me puede dar un descuento?*

Do you have....? – *¿Tiene usted....?*

Please show me another – *Muéstreme otro (otra) por favor*

I will buy this – *Voy a comprar esto*

Asking for Food & Drink

Please bring me... – *Tráigame por favor...*

a beer – *una cerveza*

cold water – *agua fría*

a soft drink – *un refresco*

mineral water (with/without fizz) – *agua mineral (con/sin gas)*

fruit juice blended with water/milk – *licuado de agua/de leche*

refreshing drink, lemonade – *refresco*

fermented agave juice, the national drink of Mexico – *pulque*

camomile tea – *té de manzanilla*

black tea – *té negro*

hot water – *agua caliente*

regular coffee – *café americano*

coffee with hot milk – *café con leche*

coffee with cream/with a drop of milk – *café /con crema/con un poquito de leche*

coffee brewed together with cinnamon and sugar – *café de olla*

strong, black coffee – *café negro/solo*

a menu – *un menú*

the daily special – *la comida corrida; el especial del día*

bread rolls – *bolillos*

butter – *mantequilla*

salt – *sal*

May I have more beer? – *¿Me puede dar más cerveza, por favor?*

May I have the bill? – *¿Me da la cuenta, por favor?*

To get the attention of a waiter – *¡Oiga!, ¡Señor!, ¡Joven!* (Literally, young man!)

Reading a Menu

desayuno – breakfast

comida – lunch

comida corrida – dish of the day

merienda – tea break

cena – supper

aguacate – avocado

aguas naturales – fruit or flower water made with tamarind, melon, lime, guava, or hibiscus

albóndigas – meat balls

antojitos – snacks (usually tortilla-based)

arroz – rice

arroz con leche – rice pudding with cinnamon

atole – maize meal drink

atún – tuna

azúcar – sugar

barbacoa – meat cooked in a barbecue pit

bistec – beef cutlet

bolillos – bread rolls

cabrito – goat

café americano – regular coffee

café con leche – coffee with hot milk

café /con crema/con un poquito de leche – coffee with cream/with a drop of milk

café de olla – coffee brewed together with cinnamon and sugar

café negro/solo – strong, black coffee

calabacita – courgettes/zucchini

calabaza – pumpkin

calamares – octopus

caldo – clear meat, fish, or chicken broth

caldo tlalpeño – chicken soup with rice and vegetables

camarones – prawns

carne (de res) – meat (beef)

carne asada – grilled meat

carnitas – small pieces of pork fried in lard or dripping

cebolla – onion

cerdo – pork

cerveza (clara/oscura) – (light/dark) beer

ceviche – raw pieces of fish, marinaded with lime juice, coriander, tomato, chilli and onions

chicharrón – pork crackling

chilaquiles – strips of tortillas in a spicy tomato sauce

chiles en nogada – stuffed chillis in a cheese-nut sauce garnished with pomegranate pips

chiles rellenos – green chillis filled with meat, fish or cheese

chirimoya – sugar pear

chocolate – hot chocolate

chuleta – pork chop

cilantro – fresh coriander

cochinita pibil – spicey pork dish from the Yucatán

conejo – rabbit

consomé – clear meat broth

cordero – lamb

elote – corn on the cob

enchiladas (suizas) – tortillas, rolled up with meat or chicken and simmered in a spicey tomato sauce

ensalada – salad

ensalada de nopales – salad of steamed cactus leaves

epazote – a strong-flavored herb

flan – caramel pudding

flor de calabaza – squash flowers served as a vegetable

fresa – strawberry

frijoles (refritos) – cooked dried beans (mashed and fried)

gorditas – small filled *tortillas* deep fried or fried in a lot of oil

guacamole – avocado puree with sliced onions, chillis and red tomatoes (called *jitomate*)

guajolote – turkey

guayaba – guava

gusanos de maguey – agave worms crisply fried (an Aztec speciality)

helado – ice cream
higos – figs
hongos – mushrooms
huachinango – red snapper
huevos – eggs
huevos á la mexicana – scrambled eggs with tomatoes and finely chopped chillis
huevos estrellados – fried eggs
huevos rancheros – fried eggs on tortillas with frijoles and a spicey tomato sauce
huevos revueltos – scrambled eggs
huevos tibios – boiled eggs

jamaica – hibiscus
jamón – ham
jícama – tuber, containing starch
jitomate – red tomato
jugo – juice

langostas – crayfish or lobster
lechuga – lettuce
licuado de agua/de leche – fruit juice blended with water or milk
limón – lime

mantequilla – butter
margarita – tequila with lemon juice
mariscos – seafood
melocotón – peach
merluza – hake
mezcal – crystal-clear agave schnapps
mojarra – seafish
mole poblano – slightly thick and dark sauce which gets its sweet–hot taste from a mixture of chillis and chocolate

naranja – orange
nopal – leaves of the fig cactus, served as a salad or vegetable

ostiones – oysters
pampano – seafish
pan – bread
pan dulce – yeast pastry
pan tostado – toast
papas – potatoes
pepino – cucumber
pescado – fish (when served as a dish)
pez espada – swordfish
pimienta – pepper
piña – pineapple
pipián – thick mild sauce made with pumpkin seeds and chilli
pitaya – cactus fruit
plátano – banana
pollo – chicken

postre – dessert/pudding
puchero – stew dish
pulque – fermented agave juice, the national drink of Mexico

queso – cheese
quesadilla – a baked tortilla filled with cheese
refresco – refreshing drink, lemonade
romeritos – rosemary, usually served with mole

sabana – sheet of beef
sal – salt
salsa verde/roja/mexicana – cold spicy sauce (green/red/Mexican), served with meat, fish, etc.
sandia – watermelon
sopa de arroz – dry rice with vegetables (e.g. as an intermediate course)

tacos – filled tortillas rolled up and fried
tamales – spicey maize semolina puree wrapped up in maize or banana leaves and boiled
té de manzanilla – camomile tea
té negro – black tea
tequila (con sangrita) – agave schnapps (with a tiny glass of spicy tomato juice)
ternera – veal
tocino – bacon
toronja – grapefruit
tortas – oval or round bread rolls, filled with cheese or meat, salads and chillis
tortilla – flat maize bread
tortilla de huevos – omelette
tostadas – crisply fried tortillas, covered in lettuce, frijoles, cheese and meat
tuna – fruit of the fig cactus (nopal)

venado – venison
verduras – vegetables
zanahoria – carrots

Accommodations

Where is an inexpensive hotel? – ¿Dónde hay un hotel económico?
Do you have an air conditioned room? – ¿Tiene un cuarto con aire acondicionado?
Do you have a room with bath? – ¿Tiene un cuarto con baño?

Where is the dining room? – ¿Dónde está el comedor?
Can you cash a travelers' check? –

¿Se puede cambiar un cheque de viajero?

the key – la llave
the manager – el gerente
the owner – el propietario, el dueño (male), la dueña (female)
the credit card – la tarjeta de crédito
tax – impuesto
the letter – la carta
the postcard – la tarjeta postal
the envelope – el sobre
a stamp – una estampilla

Driving

Where is...? – ¿Dónde está...?

a gas station? – una gasolinera?
a repair garage? – un taller mecánico?
an auto parts store?– una refaccionaria para coches?

Fill it up, please – Lleno, por favor
Please check the oil – Vea el aceite, por favor

Please fill up... – Favor de llenar...
the radiator el radiador
the battery – la batería

I need... – Necesito...
a jack – un gato
a towtruck – una grúa
a mechanic – un mecánico
a tune-up – una afinación
a tire – una llanta
a fuse like this one – un fusible como éste

The... is broken – El/la.... está roto/a
The... are broken – Los/las.... están rotos/as

Further Reading

General

Travel

Mexico Travel Book. American Automobile Association, 1995. A few lines about almost every place along with hotel and restaurant listings.
Sanborn's Mexico Travelog. Travelog and General Printing, P.O. Box 310, McAllen, Texas. A series of guidebooks by Insight Guides contributor Mike Nelson written specifically for drivers with mile-by-mile directions to every road in

Mexico. Has specific itineraries, maps, hotel, restaurant and RV parks.

Travelers' Guide to Mexico. Mexican Secretariat of Tourism, 1995, 20th edition. Updated yearly and found in every room of the bigger hotels. For sale at the hotel newsstands. Well-written, large-format paperback guide containing everything about Mexico from history to shopping and traveling.

History

Bernal Díaz del Castillo: *Conquest of New Spain*. Penguin, 1969.

Bernal: *The Vanished Civilizations of Middle America*. Thames & Hudson, 1980.

Brenner, Anita, and George R. Leighton. *The Wind that Swept Mexico*. University of Texas Press, 1971. Brief account of the revolution with excellent historical photographs.

Caso, Alfonso. *The People of the Sun*. University of Oklahoma Press, 1978. Authoritative source on the Aztecs.

Paz, Octavio. *Pre-Columbian Literatures of Mexico*. University of Oklahoma Press, 1986.

Raat (ed.): *From Independence to Revolution, Mexico 1810–1910*. University of Nebraska Press, 1982.

Reed, John. *Insurgent Mexico*. International Publishing, 1969. Exciting account of the 1910 revolution by the reporter famous for his coverage of the Russian Revolution.

Guzmán, Martín Luis. *Memoirs of Pancho Villa*. University of Texas Press, 1965. Based on the author's personal experiences with Pancho Villa and other revolutionary leaders.

De Sahagun, Bernardino. *General History of the Things of New Spain*. University of Utah Press, 12 volumes. A gold mine of information about the Aztecs and neighboring peoples written by an early Spanish missionary.

Singletary, Otis. *The Mexican War*. University of Chicago Press, 1960.

Smith, Peter. *The Eagle and the Serpent*. Based on the author's personal experiences with Pancho Villa and other revolutionary leaders.

Turner, John Kenneth. *Barbarous Mexico*. University of Texas Press, 1969, first published 1908. Turner's reporting of misery and death among the slaves working Mexico's tobacco and henequen plantations led many Americans to question Porfirio Díaz's reputation as a benevolent dictator.

Womack, John. *Zapata and the Mexi-* can Revolution. Knopf, 1968. Readable and well-researched.

Politics & Society

Calderón de la Barca, Fanny. *Life in Mexico: The Letters of Fanny Calderón de la Barca, with New Material from the Author's Private Journals*. Edited by H.T. and M.H. Fisher, Doubleday, 1966, first published 1913. The author was a Scotswoman living in Spain whose husband became Spain's first ambassador to independent Mexico. She was intelligent, curious, loved to travel, and spoke Spanish fluently.

Esquivel, Laura. *Like Water for Chocolate* (*Como Agua para Chocolate*). First published 1989; English version by Doubleday, 1992. Bestselling novel about family life in turn-of-the-century Mexico. The film won eleven awards.

Paz, Octavio. *The Labyrinth of Solitude*. Grove, 1962. By Mexico's famous novelist. Not an easy read, but essential reading for those who want to go beyond a superficial understanding of the psychology and culture of contemporary Mexicans.

Lewis, Oscar. *Five Families*, Basic Books, 1959. *The Children of Sanchez*, Random House, 1961. *Pedro Martinez*, Random House, 1964. *A Death in the Sanchez Family*, Random House, 1969. Lewis spent years interviewing members of Mexico's "culture of poverty."

Riding, Alan. *Inside the Volcano*. Hodder & Stoughton, 1989.

Art, Culture & Cuisine

Anderson, Lawrence. *The Art of the Silversmith in Mexico, 1519–1936*. Hacker Art Books, 1974.

Edward, Emily, and Bravo Alvarez. *Painted Walls of Mexico*. University of Texas Press, 1966. Mexican murals from pre-Columbian times.

Baird, Joseph. *The Churches of Mexico*. University of California Press, 1962. An excellent reference on Mexican colonial art, almost all of which is in churches.

Charlot. *Mexican Mural Renaissance, 1920–1925*. Hacker Art Books, 1980.

Covarrubias, Miguel. *Indian Art of Mexico and Central America*. Knop, 1957.

Detroit Institute of Arts. *Diego Rivera – A Retrospective*. W.W. Norton, 1986.

Fuentes, Carlos. *Where the Air Is Clear*. Farrar, Straus & Giroux, 1971. Considered by some to be the best novel of modern Mexico.

Harvey, Marian. *Mexican Crafts and Craftspeople*. Philadelphia Art Alliance Press, 1988.

Herrera, Hayden. *Frida*. Bloomsbury Publications, 1989.

Justino, Fernández. *Guide to Mexican Art*. University of Chicago Press, 1969. An excellent introduction, rather dry but certainly informative.

Penaloza, Martínez Porfirio. *Popular Arts of Mexico*. Editorial Panorama, 1981. A compact and inexpensive book by one of the outstanding authorities on Mexican art.

Paz, Octavio. *Convergences*. Bloomsbury Publications, 1987.

Ramírez Vázquez, Pedro, and others. *The National Museum of Anthropology, Mexico: Art, Architecture, Archeology, Anthropology*. Abrams, 1968. The story of the creation of the remarkable National Museum, written by the men responsible.

Ross, Patricia Fent. *Made in Mexico: The Story of a Country's Arts and Crafts*. Knopf, 1960. A classic work on the history of Mexico's popular arts, written by an American who lived for many years in Mexico.

Sayer, Chloe. *Crafts of Mexico*. Doubleday, 1977. Step-by-step instructions for making traditional Mexican craft items. Excellent photographs.

Toor, Frances. *A Treasury of Mexican Folkways*. Crown, 1947. Covers folk art, fiestas, music and dance. A classic in its field.

Rochford. *Murals of Diego Rivera*. Journeyman Press, 1987.

Schmeckebier. *Modern Mexican Art*. Greenwood Press.

Verti, Sebastián. *Mexican Traditions*. Editorial Diana, 1993. One of Mexico's strongest cultural advocates writes on religious celebrations; regional festivities, dances and traditions; history and legend; the origins of *mariachi* and the *charrería*; and Mexican culinary legacy including traditional recipes.

Zamora. *Frida Kahlo – The Brush of Anguish*. Art Data, 1990.

Literature

Fuentes, Carlos. *Costancia and Other Stories for Virgins*. Deutsch, 1990.

Correas de Zapata, Celia (ed.). *The Magic and the Real*. Arte Publico, 1990. Short stories by Latin-American women writers.

Nicholson, Irene (ed.). *Mexican and*

Cenrtal American Mythology. Newnes Books, 1983.

Campos (ed). *Mexican Folk Tales*. University of Arizona Press, 1977.

Foreign Fiction about Mexico

Ferlinghetti, Lawrence. *The Mexican Night: Travel Journal*. New Directions, 1970.

Greene, Graham. *The Power and the Glory*. Viking, 1962. Considered Greene's finest novel by many critics. Set in Tabasco during the persecution of the Catholic clergy.

Kerouac, Jack. *Mexico City Blues*. Grove, 1959.

Kesey, Ken. *Kesey's Garage Sale*. Viking, 1973.

Lawrence, D.H. *The Plumed Serpent*. Knopf, 1951. Lawrence argues for the adoption of a new state religion based on the ancient worship of Quetzalcoatl. With all its flaws, one of the very best novels ever written about Mexico.

Lowry, Malcolm. *Under the Volcano*. Lippincott, 1965. Deceptively simple story of a British Consul who drinks himself to death in 1938, the crisis year when Cárdenas nationalized the oil industry, leading to the cutting of Mexican–British diplomatic relations.

MacLeish, Archibald. *Conquistador*. Houghton Mifflin, 1932.

Morris, Wright. *Love Among the Cannibals*, Harcourt, Brace, 1957. *One Day*, Atheneum, 1965.

Porter, Katherine Anne. *The Collected Stories*, Harcourt, Brace, 1965. *The Collected Essays*, Delacorte, 1970. In contrast to fellow Catholics Graham Greene and Evelyn Waugh, Porter understood the oppressive role the Church played in Mexican history.

Steinbeck, John. *The Forgotten Village*, Viking, 1941. *The Pearl*, Viking, 1947.

Traven, B. *The General from the Jungle*, Robert Hale, 1945. *The Rebellion of the Hanged*, Knopf, 1952. *March to Caobaland*, Robert Hale, 1961. *The Bridge in the Jungle*, Hill & Wang, 1967. *The Treasure of the Sierra Madre*, Hill & Wang, 1967. *The Carreta*, Hill & Wang, 1970. No other author has written so much and so well about Mexico as the mysterious B. Traven (his identity is still a matter of some controversy). Most of Traven's books are set in southern Mexico, and his knowledge of that area is astounding.

Waugh, Evelyn. *Mexico: An Object Lesson*. Little, Brown, 1939. Also published as *Robbery Under Law*.

Williams, Carlos. *The Autobiography of Carlos Williams*. New Directions, 1951.

Williams, Tennessee. *The Night of the Iguana*. New Directions, 1962.

Other Insight Guides

Nearly *200 Insight Guides* and more than 100 *Insight Pocket Guides* cover every major travel destination in the world. Other titles which highlight destinations in Mexico are:

The companion guide to the present book, *Insight Guide: Mexico* provides in-depth coverage of the entire country, complete with authoritative features and stunning photography.

Insight Pocket Guide: Mexico City is designed for the visitor with limited time to spare and includes a selection of carefully timed itineraries and personal recommendations.

Two other guides for short-stay travelers are *Insight Pocket Guide: Baja* and *Insight Pocket Guide: Yucatan*. Mexican experts seek out and explore the best beaches, the best bargains and the best places to stay.

Art/Photo Credits

Archivo Casasola 53, 54
Archivo General de la Nación 84, 85
Christa Cowrie 1, 9, 16/17, 18, 22,
36L, 49, 60, 63, 64, 66, 69, 71,
72/73, 74/75, 76/77, 78, 79, 80,
83, 86/87, 88, 91, 94, 95, 96/97,
99, 102/103, 104, 106, 107, 116,
117, 125, 126, 127L&R, 128, 129,
132/133, 134, 137, 139, 141, 142,
144/145, 146L&R, 149, 151, 152,
153, 154/155, 158, 159, 163, 172,
173, 176, 177L&R, 179, 182/183,
184, 188, 189, 190, 192/193, 194,
196, 202, 203, 208/209, 226/227,
228, 232, 233
Wolfgang Fritz 58/59, 82, 169, 187
Gabriele Gockel 235
Erdmann Gormsen 10/11, 35, 70, 81,
198/199, 241
Till Gottbrath 24, 217, 223, 224, 225,
229, 231, 244, 246
Andreas Gross 29, 30, 31, 166, 168,
170, 171, 207, 220, 223
Hans Haufe 90
Wolfgang Koch 230
Kal Müller 27, 93
**Armando Salas Portugal, Artes de
México** 38
Jutta Schütz Archive 14/15, 25, 26,
36R, 37, 40/41, 44L&R, 46, 47, 48,
50, 51, 55, 56, 57, 105, 138, 147,
150R, 167L&R, 191, 216, 221, 237L,
238, 239, 240
Hans-Horst Skupy 62, 186, 195, 186,
200, 219
**Jorge Vertíz, Artes de
México** 32, 39L&R, 42, 45
Marcus Wilson Smith 2, 12/13, 61,
65, 98, 108/109, 110/111, 112/113,
123, 130, 131, 135, 136, 140, 143,
150L, 156, 157, 160, 161, 162,
164/165, 174/175, 180R, 181,
196R, 197, 204, 205, 206, 210/211,
212/213, 214, 234, 236, 237R, 242,
243, 247, 248
Werner Zuschratter 100/101,
118/119

Maps Berndtson & Berndtson

Visual Consultant V. Barl

276

Index